THE ULTIMATE PLAYER'S GUIDE TO LEGO® DIMENSIONS™
[UNOFFICIAL GUIDE]

James Floyd Kelly

The Ultimate Player's Guide to LEGO® Dimensions™ [Unofficial Guide]

Copyright © 2017 by Pearson Education, Inc.

ISBN-13: 978-0-7897-5742-5
ISBN-10: 0-7897-5742-7

Library of Congress Control Number: 2015959186

1 16

Trademarks and Copyrights

Editor-in-Chief
Greg Wiegand

Senior Acquisitions Editor
Laura Norman

Development Editor
Ginny Bess Munroe

Managing Editor
Sandra Schroeder

Senior Project Editor
Tonya Simpson

Copy Editor
Kitty Wilson

Indexer
Brad Herriman

Proofreader
Charlotte Kughen

Technical Editor
Melissa Ford

Publishing Coordinator
Cindy Teeters

Cover Designer
Chuti Prasertsith

Compositor
Mary Sudul

Warning and Disclaimer

Every effort has been made to make this book as complete and as accurate as possible, but no warranty or fitness is implied. The information provided is on an "as is" basis. The author and the publisher shall have neither liability nor responsibility to any person or entity with respect to any loss or damages arising from the information contained in this book.

Special Sales

For information about buying this title in bulk quantities, or for special sales opportunities (which may include electronic versions; custom cover designs; and content particular to your business, training goals, marketing focus, or branding interests), please contact our corporate sales department at corpsales@pearsoned.com or (800) 382-3419.

For government sales inquiries, please contact governmentsales@pearsoned.com.

For questions about sales outside the U.S., please contact intlcs@pearson.com.

Contents at a Glance

Table of Contents

About the Author

James Floyd Kelly has degrees in both industrial engineering and English. He is an avid maker, tinkerer, and teacher. He excels at taking complex technology and finding a way to demystify it for nontechnical readers. Jim has written more than 25 books on a variety of technical subjects, including open source software, LEGO robotics, 3D printing, and game programming. He lives in Georgia with his wife and children.

Dedication

For Ashley, who didn't shake her head too obviously when I explained that I would be writing a video game book. For my two boys, who got to share in the adventures as we played the game, and for Rick Kughen, editor-extraordinaire and great friend.

Acknowledgments

This book took an incredible amount of time and energy to write—lots of playing a level, and then RE-playing that level and then RE-RE-playing... you get the idea. Writing a book for a video game is very challenging, and I can only imagine the work involved by the great folks who helped make the book you're holding a reality. Flip back a few pages and take a look at all those names listed: each and every one of them is invaluable to an author trying to get a book written and done. Thank you, each and every one, for helping me to get this book to all the LEGO Dimensions fans out there.

A very special thank you, however, goes to Rick Kughen. Rick has championed many of my books over the years, taking them from the most basic idea (that would often consist of a few sentences I'd email to him) to the final printed book. It's been fun writing for Rick, and I can think of no better book to dedicate to him than a book about a fun game.

I'd also like to thank the team at TT Games for all their hard work in creating a game that appeals to both kids and adults. There's something in this game for every age, and that's quite hard to find these days.

We Want to Hear from You!

As the reader of this book, *you* are our most important critic and commentator. We value your opinion and want to know what we're doing right, what we could do better, what areas you'd like to see us publish in, and any other words of wisdom you're willing to pass our way.

We welcome your comments. You can email or write to let us know what you did or didn't like about this book—as well as what we can do to make our books better.

Please note that we cannot help you with technical problems related to the topic of this book.

When you write, please be sure to include this book's title and author as well as your name and email address. We will carefully review your comments and share them with the author and editors who worked on the book.

Email: feedback@quepublishing.com

Mail: Que Publishing
           ATTN: Reader Feedback
           800 East 96th Street
           Indianapolis, IN 46240 USA

Reader Services

Register your copy of *The Ultimate Player's Guide to LEGO Dimensions* at quepublishing.com for convenient access to downloads, updates, and corrections as they become available. To start the registration process, go to quepublishing.com/register and log in or create an account*. Enter the product ISBN, 9780789757425, and click Submit. When the process is complete, you will find any available bonus content under Registered Products.

*Be sure to check the box that you would like to hear from us to receive exclusive discounts on future editions of this product.

Introduction

Welcome to the *Ultimate Player's Guide to LEGO® Dimensions*™! This book is all about helping you master the game and all its secrets, and you're going to be amazed at just how many secrets there are in this game. *LEGO Dimensions* is unlike any other LEGO videogame. *LEGO Dimensions* mashes up 44 characters from 14 different LEGO universes, allowing you to assemble them as a team to work together to defeat bad guys, uncover secrets, and ultimately save the LEGO universes that are at risk from a really BIG BAD GUY. Which LEGO universes and characters will you have access to? Good question, and here they are:

- **The DC Comics™ Universe**—Aquaman, Bane, Batman, Cyborg, Harley Quinn, Joker, Superman, Wonder Woman
- **The Lord of the Rings™ Universe**—Gandalf, Gimli, Gollum, Legolas
- **The LEGO® Movie Universe**—Bad Cop, Benny, Emmet, Unikitty, Wyldstyle
- **The Simpsons™ Universe**—Bart Simpson, Homer Simpson, Krusty
- **The Ninjago™ Universe**—Cole, Jay, Kai, Lloyd, Nya, Sensei Wu, Zane
- **The Chima™ Universe**—Cragger, Eris, Laval
- **The Back to the Future™ Universe**—Doc Brown, Marty McFly
- **The Scooby-Doo™ Universe**—Scooby-Doo, Shaggy
- **The Ghostbusters™ Universe**—Peter Venkman, Slimer, Stay Puft
- **The Doctor Who™ Universe**—Cyberman, The Doctor
- **The Jurassic World™ Universe**—ACU Trooper, Owen
- **The Portal™ 2 Universe**—Chell
- **The Midway Arcade™ Universe**—Gamer Kid
- **The Wizard of Oz™ Universe**—Wicked Witch

Here are just a few of the unique features, many you've probably already discovered for yourself:

- The character you play is determined by an actual LEGO minifig placed on the Toy Pad, a special device that is included with the basic game. Every character has unique skills and abilities, and because you can have up to seven characters on the Toy Pad at once, you can mix and match the characters to try for the largest range of skills to solve puzzles and defeat bad guys.
- *LEGO Dimensions* pulls together characters from many different LEGO themes; you can find *Scooby-Doo* working alongside good guys *Batman* and *Gandalf* as well as bad guys *Joker* and the *Wicked Witch of the West*.
- There are two game modes for you to explore: a Story Mode that you play through to save the LEGO Universe and a World Mode, where you get to explore the various individual worlds of the LEGO minifigs you own.
- Many characters come with their own special vehicles (so you have a physical minifig of the character and the physical vehicle that you build from real LEGO parts) that have their own powers and can be upgraded with additional special abilities. You can tear

down and rebuild these vehicles because you own the actual physical pieces used to build each vehicle minifig.

LEGO Dimensions is called a *toy-to-life game*; this simply means that playing the game requires an actual toy. In this case, each LEGO minifig (and the various vehicles that are also available) can act as a true LEGO toy. You can build it, attach it to your other LEGO creations, and even upgrade the minifig with parts from your existing LEGO brick collection.

But you can also treat the *LEGO Dimensions* minifigs as keys to open new worlds. When you place the Wonder Woman minifig on the Dimensions Toy Pad, Wonder Woman appears onscreen, and you can control her actions and use her to defeat bad guys and solve puzzles. The toy comes to life!

How many toys are there? There are 44 characters and more than a dozen vehicles. The basic Dimensions game starts you out with three characters: *Batman*, *Wyldstyle*, and *Gandalf*. It also starts you with one vehicle, the Batmobile. You can purchase additional characters in packs, with each pack offering either a single minifig or two minifigs, and some of these packs come with a bonus vehicle or special item that can be used in the game. (You'll learn all about how to browse the various characters and vehicles that are available in Chapter 1, "Gameplay and Story Mode," and Appendix A, "Character Abilities," contains a complete list of each character's abilities.)

As mentioned previously, you can play *LEGO Dimensions* in two ways:

- **Story Mode**—You can work through the Story Mode, using *Batman*, *Gandalf*, and *Wyldstyle* to defeat the evil *Lord Vortech*, who is attempting to merge all the LEGO worlds into a single world that he can control. While those three characters are required for Story Mode, you can bring in additional characters to provide additional abilities and skills that can be helpful in finishing Story Mode's 14 different levels. You can have up to seven characters onscreen at once.

- **World Mode**—You can also open 14 different worlds in World Mode if you possess the right LEGO minifigs. For example, *Batman* gives you access to the DC Comics world, *Gandalf* opens up *The Lord of the Rings* world, and *Wyldstyle* opens up *The LEGO Movie* world. You can open a world only if you own a character from that world, so purchasing the Peter Venkman pack (which comes with the Ecto-1 vehicle and a Ghost Trap) opens up the *Ghostbusters* world for you to explore.

Inside both Story Mode and World Mode are characters to meet, puzzles to solve, villains to defeat, races to finish, quests to solve, and rewards to collect.

There's a *lot* to do, isn't there? It might feel a bit overwhelming the first time you play through a Story Mode level or jump into a world, but this book is here to help. This is what you'll find in the pages ahead:

- A complete walkthrough to help you solve all 14 levels of Story Mode. You'll also get tips and tricks to defeat bad guys and solve puzzles as well as some hints about the various secrets hidden in the game. (I don't reveal every secret, though, because I don't want to steal all your fun!)

- A summary of the different worlds you can explore, including complete listings of all quests found in each world and the various upgrades/repairs (and their costs) that you can perform to unlock additional secrets.
- A list of all the characters you can play and their respective skills/abilities.
- An explanation of vehicles and how to go about upgrading them for additional powers and abilities.
- Dozens and dozens of tips on locating hidden treasures, finding valuable studs, and completing quests and puzzles.

So, jump right in and read Chapter 1 to get an overview of how the game works, its controls, and other special features that will be helpful to you as you explore *LEGO Dimensions*. Then, when you're ready, you can jump to Chapter 2, "The Adventure Begins," which covers the first level of Story Mode or jump to Chapter 17, "Adventure Worlds Overview," and learn how World Mode works. Whichever you choose, have fun and enjoy every minute of *LEGO Dimensions* and all the surprises that await you.

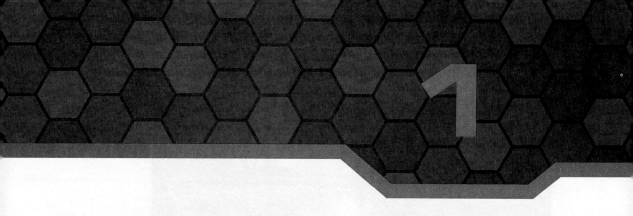

Gameplay and Story Mode

Chapter Summary

- Navigate the main menu
- Understand the controls
- Use Vorton and the in-game Toy Pad
- Get to know the gateway options
- Play keystone puzzles
- Figure out where to start

You are probably extremely anxious to get playing, but if you can be patient and get through this chapter, you'll be armed with some tips and advice on making the most of the Dimensions game. If you just can't wait and want to start playing now, at least read the very first section to learn how to start up with the Story Mode immediately. If you're more patient that that, you can read the whole chapter to gain some insight into other areas of the game, such as the controller, various menus, puzzles you're going to encounter, and more.

Navigating the Main Menu

To install LEGO Dimensions, you need to follow the instructions specific to your game console. Once the game is installed and you start it up, you see the main menu, shown in Figure 1.1.

If you want to start playing immediately, select the New Game option on the right side of the screen. After selecting New Game, you can pick one of four different slots to save your game's progress. Make note of which slot you use, especially if others will be playing Dimensions and saving their own progress. Make certain other players choose a different slot so they do not make any changes that could affect your game.

FIGURE 1.1   The main menu is where LEGO Dimensions starts.

NOTE

How to Select a Menu Option

LEGO Dimensions runs on many different game platforms, and your controller may be different than the one used for the screenshots in this book. An Xbox One controller was used for all the figures in this book, and selecting New Game requires using that controller's left joystick (LJ) to select the New Game option and then pressing the A button. You can jump to the Controller section later in this chapter for details on other controller types. And throughout the book, if you see a button referenced in parenthesis, such as (A) or (LJ), it means to push that button to perform the described action. A combination (LJ and B) means you'll need to use both the left joystick and the B button.

In addition to New Game, the main menu includes the following options:

- **Help**—This launches a small selection of topics onscreen that you can select with your controller's joystick.
- **Select Profile**—If you are using a game console that has Internet access and uses player profiles for tracking stats and scores, you can select this option and then choose which player profile to use.
- **News**—This option displays any new information from the LEGO Dimensions developers, including news about new minifig releases and new features to the game.
- **Load Game**—Once you've selected a slot (from the available four slots), this is the option you choose to load your saved game. Your score, stud count, and any worlds or levels visited are saved to your slot.

■ **Options**—Select this option to turn music on or off, control the volume of sound effects, turn on and off subtitles, show the game controls, view the game credits, and configure the maximum height and width of the viewable game area.

Understanding the Controls

As mentioned previously, all the figures taken for this book were done on the Xbox One version of LEGO Dimensions. If you select Options from the main menu and then select Controls, you see the game controls, as shown in Figure 1.2, including a description of the function of each button.

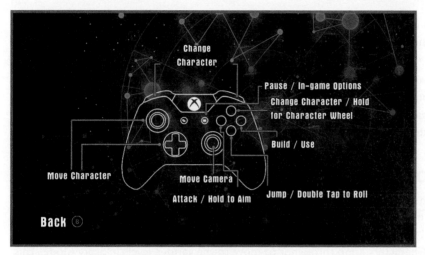

FIGURE 1.2   The controller descriptions for an Xbox One controller.

Because LEGO Dimensions also runs on other platforms, including Nintendo Wii, PlayStation 3 and 4, and Xbox 360, you may find that one or more of the buttons on your controllers do not match perfectly to the ones in Figure 1.2.

When in doubt, consult the Controls option to get a map of your particular controller and its respective buttons. Because the Dimensions developers did their best to keep the controls consistent, you'll likely find that the Back, Jump, and Select buttons are in identical positions on your controller, and you'll probably also find identical functionality for the joysticks.

The following controls are used in LEGO Dimension (and this book):

■ **LJ**—Move character
■ **RJ**—Move camera
■ **Y**—Change character, hold for character wheel
■ **X**—Attack, hold to aim
■ **B**—Build/use

- **A**—Jump/double-tap to roll
- **Menu**—Pause/in-game options

NOTE

The Menu Button

On the Xbox One controller, the Menu button consists of three tiny horizontal lines. This button is to the left of the X button. Your controller might have the Menu button in a different location.

For example, to use these controls to drive a vehicle, you press Y when you're near a vehicle to jump in it. Then you use LJ to drive and steer the vehicle in the direction the LJ is pressed. (Pull back on the LJ, for example, to drive in reverse.) Press Y to exit the vehicle.

Vehicles can be upgraded (see Appendix B, "Vehicles and Upgrades," for details), so it's possible that some vehicles will have abilities such as dropping mines or using a winch. To use such abilities, you need to press additional buttons, as the game describes when you do a vehicle upgrade.

Using Vorton and the In-Game Toy Pad

When you begin a new game, the events described in Chapter 2, "The Adventure Begins," occur: Batman meets Gandalf and Wyldstyle, and together they reactivate the damaged gateway. The gateway looks exactly like the physical Toy Pad you have connected to your game console. Characters jump through it to move to the various levels in Story Mode. This gateway is below ground on Vorton, and there's an aboveground area as well that you'll be introduced to shortly.

Figure 1.3 shows Batman, Gandalf, Wyldstyle, and the Batmobile in the gateway room.

The character you are currently controlling is displayed in the upper-left corner. If a second player is playing, that player's character is displayed in the upper-right corner. Notice that a healthy character has four hearts; sometimes the heart icons (to the right of the character's image onscreen) are different shapes or colors, but the important thing is that the number of those icons indicate how much health the character has. When a character is reduced to zero hearts from taking damage or falling, the character returns to life nearby, and you sometimes lose 1,000 studs as a penalty.

You place a character's minifig on the physical Toy Pad to make that character appear onscreen. There are three pads on the Toy Pad: left, right, and center (round). The left and right pads can hold three minifigs each (or two minifigs and a vehicle), while the center pad can hold only a single minifig or vehicle.

FIGURE 1.3   The three heroes are gathered in the gateway room.

If you're currently playing as one character (such as Gandalf, as shown in Figure 1.3), you can change to another character by facing the character you are currently controlling at the character you wish to change to and pressing Y. Sometimes, however, if you're very close to multiple characters, your controls might jump to a character you didn't intend to use. If that's the case, another method is available to change to a different character: Press and hold Y, and you see a wheel appear, like the one in Figure 1.4, showing all the minifigs and vehicles currently on the physical Toy Pad. Use the left joystick (LJ) to select the character you wish to control and release Y. You then see a glow move from one character to another to indicate that you've taken control of a different character.

FIGURE 1.4   The selection wheel is useful for changing characters or finding vehicles.

If you currently have a vehicle selected, using the wheel brings the vehicle closer to you. A portal opens in the ground, and the vehicle appears nearby. This is useful when you need to use a vehicle but it's not visible on the screen or is some distance away (especially if a second player is playing).

While you're controlling a character, you use the LJ to move around and press A to jump. Give it a try. Characters such as Wyldstyle who have Acrobat ability can jump higher if you double-press A.

Every character has one or more special skills that make them special. Batman, for example, has a Batarang that he can fling at targets. To use this special ability, you press and hold X. A yellow target circle appears on the screen (Figure 1.5) that you can move around with the left joystick (LJ) as long as you continue to press and hold down X.

FIGURE 1.5   Use the Batarang to hit distant targets and objects.

As you move the target around, it lights up anything that can be hit with the Batarang with a similar-looking yellow target. Release X to throw the Batarang, and any marked targets (up to three at a time) are hit, typically releasing studs for you to collect or triggering something like a door opening.

NOTE

Special Abilities

Every character has special abilities. You need to experiment with the various buttons to see what each character can do, and you can also take a look at Appendix A, "Character Skills," to learn more about each character's special skills.

So far, you've spent a lot of time in the gateway room beneath the surface of Vorton. It's time to head up and check out what's on the surface. To do this, move a character to the elevator located near the front-left corner of the gateway room (Figure 1.6).

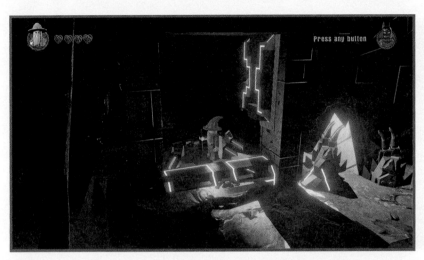

FIGURE 1.6 The elevator takes you to the surface of Vorton.

On the surface, you can see a lower level and an upper level, with strange round gateways in the distance (Figure 1.7).

FIGURE 1.7 The surface of Vorton is where you find world gateways.

You can wander around and inspect all 14 gateways—one for each LEGO world that you can visit if you have the right minifigs. Because you have Batman, Gandalf, and Wyldstyle, you automatically gain access to the DC Comics world (Batman), the Lord of the Rings world (Gandalf), and the LEGO Movie world (Wyldstyle). Notice in Figure 1.8 that the DC Comics gateway has a blue vortex in its center; this means that world is unlocked and can be explored because Batman's minifig is on the Toy Pad.

FIGURE 1.8 The DC Comics world gateway is unlocked.

If you remove the Batman minifig from the Toy Pad (and no other DC Comics minifigs such as Superman or Wonder Woman are on the pad), that gateway locks (Figure 1.9).

FIGURE 1.9 The DC Comics world is locked because Batman isn't on the Toy Pad.

When a gateway is locked, you see one or more images of minifigs appear in the center of the gateway. These are the minifigs that can unlock that world. As you can see in Figure 1.9, one of the characters that can unlock the DC Comics world is Cyborg. Some worlds have multiple minifigs that can unlock them, while three worlds can be unlocked only by a single minifig: the Midway Arcade world (only unlocked with Gamer Kid), the Wizard of Oz world (requires the Wicked Witch of the West), and the Portal 2 world (requires Chell).

If a gateway is open, simply move a character near the portal and press A to jump into it. You're then whisked away to that world. Chapter 17, "Adventure Worlds Overview," covers some of the special features you need to know about before you start exploring the worlds, so feel free to jump over there if you want to visit a world before starting on Story Mode. Each of the 13 chapters following Chapter 17 provides details of a particular world you can visit.

NOTE

Midway Arcade Unavailable

At the time this book was being written, the Midway Arcade world remained locked. This is because there is only a single minifig that can unlock it, and that minifig wasn't released until March 2016, well after this book was completed. The good news is that by the time you're reading this, you'll have a completely new and unexplored world to visit, and you'll be completely surprised by what it contains!

While you're in the gateway room or on the surface of Vorton, you can press the Menu button to find six options:

- **Resume** —Select this option to return to Vorton.
- **Options** —Select this to view and change 11 different options, including turning on and off the vibration of your controller, turning off subtitles, changing the screen brightness, and more. Choose the last option in the list, Back, to return to the previous menu.
- **Show Game Controls** —Choose this option to see a schematic of your controller with button descriptions. (You saw this previously in Figure 1.2.)
- **Help** —Choose this to get the same options as with the Help option on the main menu.
- **Extras** —Choose this option to see special features that can be turned on or off; for example, after you've found all the minikit items, there'll be no reason to leave the minikit finder ability turned on. You can buy these extras only when you've found special red bricks. One red brick can be found in each of the 14 worlds you'll explore.
- **Quit Game** —Select this option and choose Yes to return to the main menu. Choose No to return to the previous menu.

Note that when you press the Menu button and see these six options, you can also see how many red bricks, gold bricks, and studs you have collected so far (Figure 1.10).

FIGURE 1.10   Pressing Menu displays your game status and some options.

Getting to Know the Gateway Options

Take control of a character and head back down to the gateway room. The large in-game Toy Pad that looks like the physical one plugged into your game console is waiting for you, and it has some special abilities of its own that you should know about.

Jump a character onto the left or right glowing pads and press B, as indicated in Figure 1.11.

FIGURE 1.11   Access the Toy Pad computer by jumping on a pad and pressing B.

Six buttons appear (Figure 1.12). Don't panic if one of the buttons appears black; this simply means you've placed a character on the Toy Pad that can't upgrade a vehicle. (Upgrading vehicles is covered in Appendix B, "Vehicles and Upgrades.")

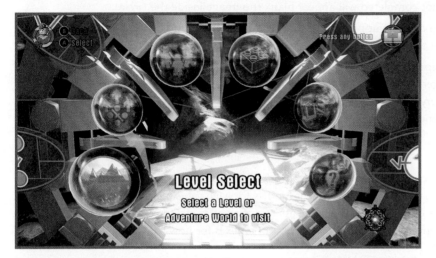

FIGURE 1.12   The Toy Pad computer has its own special features.

The following sections describe each of these buttons, starting with the button in the lower-left corner.

Level Select

Use the LJ to select the Level Select option and press A to go to a screen like the one in Figure 1.13.

FIGURE 1.13   The Level Select screen lets you cycle through worlds and levels.

When you begin the game, you have to start at the first level, Follow the LEGO Brick Road. When you complete that level, the next level unlocks; when you complete that level, the next one unlocks, and so on. The Story Mode levels are on the outer ring shown in Figure 1.13. Levels you've not completed will appear blank (no image inside the circle).

The worlds you can visit appear in the inner ring, and for every world you have already visited, you see a small image of that world. Worlds you've yet to visit will appear blank.

LEGO Dimensions level packs come with special minifigs to unlock five unique worlds, and you also get five bonus levels, one per pack, that you can play in addition to the level included in Story Mode. As you can see in Figure 1.13, you've got over a dozen worlds to explore and almost two dozen levels to play!

Upgrades

For those characters who "own" vehicles (that is, their minifig was sold with a vehicle in the same pack), there are three different models for each vehicle, each with unique abilities. These upgrades come at a cost, but the abilities they offer include enhanced speed, more health/armor, and even weaponry. Consult Appendix B for how to use the Upgrades option.

Characters

Selecting Characters allows you to view every LEGO Dimensions character. A small video shows the character in action, and beneath the video you see a list of any vehicles or special objects the character owns. Press A to select a character, and that character's skills and abilities are displayed. You can reference Appendix A for a complete list of all 44 characters and their abilities.

Red Brick Unlocks

As you explore the 14 worlds, you'll have a chance to chase down a special character you'll meet in Story Mode, named X-PO. In each world, X-PO carries a red brick that you can obtain. When you have red bricks, you can go to the Red Brick Unlocks area to turn them in for special features. An example of a red brick feature is the ability to turn all characters into transparent ghost-like versions of themselves. Another red brick feature lets you build in-game items faster. Go through the entire list of 14 red brick features, and you can see the cost (in studs) beneath the locked icon. Press A to buy the feature, and then you can turn it on by using the Extras menu item described earlier in this chapter.

Minikit Viewer

Hidden in each of the Story Mode levels are 10 minikits. Some are easy to find, while others are cleverly hidden. Collect all 10 minikits for a particular level to unlock a special event in one of the 14 worlds.

NOTE

Assistance with Finding Minikits

There's one item in the Red Brick Unlock area that turns on hints to help you find the minikits. When you purchase this special feature, small arrows appear onscreen that give you hints about the direction of all the hidden minikits on that level.

Extras

Select this option to access the building instructions you've already used to build vehicles and other in-game objects as well as hints and instructions you encounter in the game for solving puzzles, defeating certain enemies, and more. As you progress through more levels, this list grows.

Playing Keystone Puzzles

As you play through the Story Mode, you encounter a number of puzzles that you can solve by using special objects called keystones. There are five keystones in all (see Figure 1.14), and you'll discover them individually in different levels. As you discover a new keystone, you also get an in-game tutorial that shows you how to use the keystone's special ability.

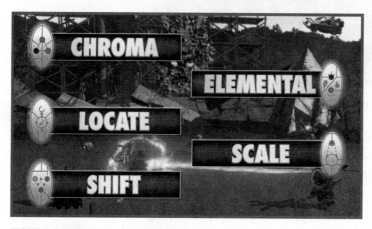

FIGURE 1.14 The Five keystones.

You activate each keystone by using a keystone terminal. As the game progresses and you have discovered multiple keystones, some terminals give you access to multiple keystone abilities to solve more complex puzzles.

These are the five keystones:

- **Shift**—This keystone (see Figure 1.15) allows you to move characters through three colored portals that appear in different locations. When you move a character onto a glowing pad that matches the color of a portal on the screen, that character jumps through the portal on screen, often gaining access to difficult-to-reach areas or locked rooms.

FIGURE 1.15   The Shift keystone.

- **Scale**—This keystone (see Figure 1.16) allows characters to shrink or grow in size. For some puzzles, only a small character (smaller than the standard character size onscreen) can enter. Also, some objects can be lifted and moved only by oversized characters. By placing a minifig on a glowing pad, you can shrink or grow that character.

FIGURE 1.16   The Scale keystone.

- **Chroma**—This keystone (see Figure 1.17) requires good teamwork of three characters. By moving a character onto one of three different colored pads, the characters can "paint" themselves in certain colors that unlock doors and other areas. For example, moving Batman onto the blue pad will turn him blue and moving Wyldstyle onto the yellow pad will turn her yellow. Players need to remember how to combine colors—such as combining blue and red to make purple or combining red and yellow to make orange. If you need to turn one of the toy pads green, for example, you'd move the Batman minifig (blue) and the Wyldstyle minfig (yellow) to the toy pad to combine the two colors and turn that pad green. You need to color certain pads to match a colored map onscreen to solve this type of puzzle.

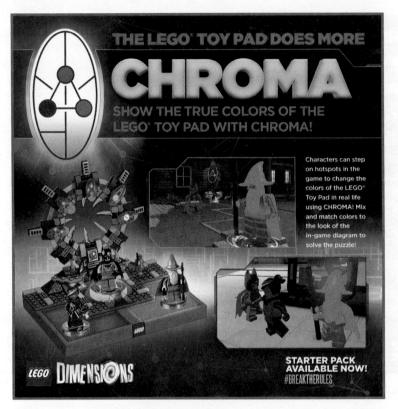

FIGURE 1.17   The Chroma keystone.

- **Locate**—This keystone (see Figure 1.18) requires a character to explore the surrounding area slowly and carefully. When the character nears a special white diamond (that is invisible), the toy pads begins to turn to a dark green as you get very close to it. If you move away from the invisible diamond, the toy pads move from dark green to light green and then into yellows and oranges. Once you find the diamond, you'll need to repeatedly press B. This action unlocks a special vortex that appears and usually offers up a special vehicle or character who comes in and saves the day or provides much-needed help in defeating a tough enemy.

FIGURE 1.18 The Locate keystone.

■ **Elemental**—With this keystone (see Figure 1.19), you can place a character's minifig on one of the three toy pads (left, right, and round) to obtain bonus powers, such as an electrical charge, protection from fire, or a blast of water. The four elements can be used to defeat enemies or provide power or water or other elements to an onscreen object (such as a plant or generator) to trigger a special event.

FIGURE 1.19   The Elemental keystone.

Figuring Out Where to Start

So, where do you begin? I highly recommend starting with Story Mode because there you can earn studs and figure out the keystone puzzles that will be encountered (without the first-time tutorials) in World Mode. Story Mode also requires only the three minifigs you own from the start: Batman, Gandalf, and Wyldstyle. If you don't have any additional minifigs at the moment, only three worlds will be open for you to explore. You can still explore them when you're taking a break from Story Mode, however.

With Story Mode, you quickly start collecting studs that you can use to upgrade the basic Batmobile vehicle with higher speed and some weapons that will be useful against powerful enemies. Story Mode also explains much of the damage that you see as you begin to explore worlds. For example, when you reach the final confrontation with Lord Vortech in Story Mode, you get a first-hand glimpse of what Lord Vortech is attempting to do with all the LEGO worlds. Story Mode also gives you brief glimpses of the various worlds you'll later get to explore in World Mode.

Despite everything I've just said, feel free to start with World Mode! Take Batman and the other two heroes and jump into the DC Comics world; Chapter 19, "DC Comics World," gives some advice on where to go and what to do in that world. Chapter 25, "The Lord of the Rings World," covers the Lord of the Rings world (which Gandalf unlocks), and Chapter 20, "The LEGO Movie World," provides details about the LEGO Movie world (which Wyldstyle unlocks).

Up Next...

Wherever you wish to start, you're going to have a blast with LEGO Dimensions. If you turn the page, you can start reading about Story Mode in Chapter 2.

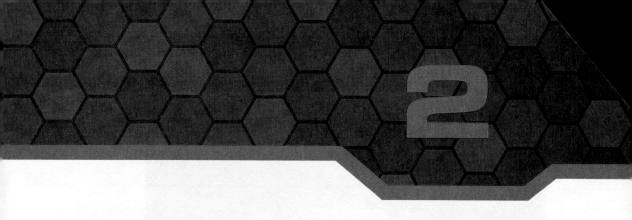

The Adventure Begins

Session Summary

- Help when Batman loses Robin, Gandalf loses Frodo, Wyldstyle loses Metalbeard
- Watch a strange machine explode
- Locate and fix three sections of the Gateway
- Repair the Gateway
- Provide power to the Gateway
- Go find your friends!

Now that you understand how the LEGO Dimensions game controls work, it's time to actually start playing the game. All great adventures start with a hero, but this one actually begins with three heroes meeting for the first time and deciding to take on a villain together. But as you'll soon find out, you're not limited to playing as one of these three heroes—LEGO Dimensions offers up dozens of heroes for you to control and discover their powers. Insert the game disc into your game console and get ready to save the world!

Missing Friends

It's a dark night in Gotham City...

REAL WORLD: Place the Batman minifig on the blue pad (Figure 2.1).

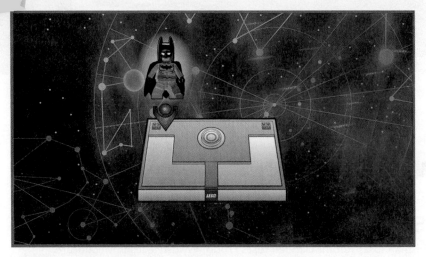

FIGURE 2.1 The Batman minifig on the Toy Pad.

Batman and Robin are chasing Bane through the empty streets of Gotham. It appears that Bane is collecting Kryptonite, a special material that is deadly to Superman. A piece of Kryptonite flies out of Bane's vehicle, and Robin manages to catch it (Figure 2.2).

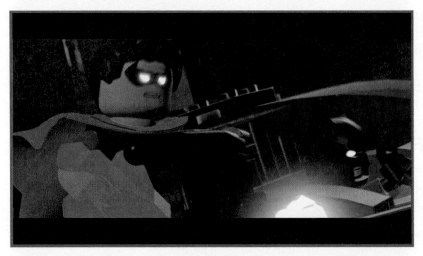

FIGURE 2.2 Robin's got the Kryptonite, but someone else wants it.

But what is this? A blue vortex appears on the side of a building, and Robin, his motorcycle, and the piece of Kryptonite are all sucked into the strange portal! Batman ends his pursuit of Bane, turns the Batmobile around, and jumps through the vortex (Figure 2.3) just as it disappears.

FIGURE 2.3 Batman wastes no time in following Robin into the vortex.

REAL WORLD: Place the Gandalf minifig on the white pad (Figure 2.4).

FIGURE 2.4 The Gandalf minifig on the Toy Pad.

Meanwhile, deep in the mines of Moria, the wizard Gandalf the Grey follows a small group consisting of hobbits, humans, a dwarf, and an elf as they run across a thin stone bridge. Chased by an evil (and gigantic) Balrog, Gandalf turns to face the creature (Figure 2.5) to give his friends time to escape.

FIGURE 2.5   The good and wise Gandalf protects his friends from the evil Balrog.

Gandalf slams his staff into the stone and yells, "You shall not pass!" The Balrog falls into the chasm as the bridge collapses. But that's one sneaky Balrog! It manages to trip up Gandalf, who falls and grabs the edge of the crumbling bridge. He tells his friends to run, and then he falls.

As Gandalf grabs his sword and reaches the falling Balrog, another vortex opens up behind him. The Batmobile comes screaming by him but then hits the stone walls. Luckily, Batman ejects from the vehicle before it explodes—he's good at that. Using his grappling hook, Batman manages to pull himself and Gandalf back up (Figure 2.6) to the group of heroes above.

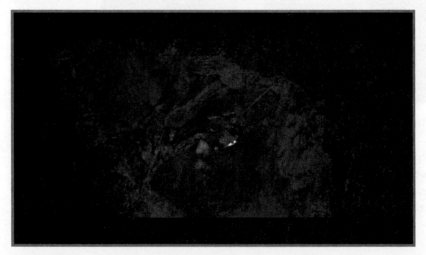

FIGURE 2.6   It's an interesting moment when Gandalf meets Batman.

NOTE

The Works of J.R.R. Tolkien

If you're not familiar with Gandalf, hobbits, elves, or even nasty Balrogs, you might want to keep your eyes open for some famous books. Written by J.R.R. Tolkien, *The Hobbit* follows Bilbo Baggins, a hobbit, on an adventure with a motley crew of dwarves to defeat a dragon deep in the heart of a mountain. On this adventure, Bilbo discovers a strange ring that is central to another set of tales called *The Lord of the Rings*. Bilbo's nephew, Frodo Baggins, takes that ring and goes on his own adventure, part of which is interrupted by the appearance of the blue vortex. Gandalf must rescue Frodo so the two can return to their friends and the adventure that awaits them.

Batman's still looking for his missing friend, Robin, but now another vortex appears, and one of Gandalf's friends, Frodo, gets pulled in (Figure 2.7), along with the special ring he's guarding. Gandalf realizes that he must join Batman and find Frodo, so he and Batman jump into the vortex together.

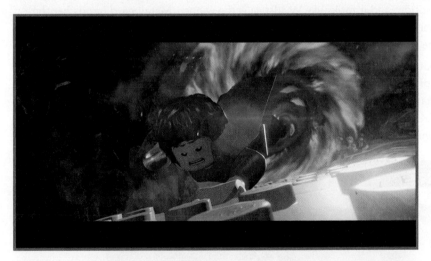

FIGURE 2.7 Someone wants the magical ring that Frodo is carrying.

REAL WORLD: Place the Wyldstyle minifig on the purple pad (Figure 2.8).

FIGURE 2.8   The Wyldstyle minifig on the Toy Pad.

Meanwhile, at a dance party in the LEGO world, Wyldstyle and Unikitty are competing in a dance competition, and it looks like Wyldstyle is the winner. Metalbeard hands her the trophy, but another vortex opens up behind Metalbeard and pulls him in, along with a toolbox and the trophy.

Gandalf and Batman appear a few seconds later, surprising everyone...including the LEGO Movie version of Batman. It's confusing. Gandalf realizes a quest has been placed in front of them and that they must join together to find their friends. Before Unikitty and Emmet (two other LEGO Movie characters) can grab their gear, however, another vortex opens (Figure 2.9) beneath Wyldstyle, Gandalf, and Batman, and the three disappear.

FIGURE 2.9   Wyldstyle, Gandalf, and Batman fall into another vortex.

A Strange Machine

As Batman, Wyldstyle, and Gandalf fly through the strange vortex, Batman uses Wyldstyle's scanner to see if he can find the source of the vortex. He punches a few buttons and locks in on the signal. Deep underground on the planet Vorton, a machine turns on (Figure 2.10).

FIGURE 2.10   What is this strange machine that is powering up?

REAL WORLD: Remove all minifigs from the Toy Pad.

REAL WORLD: Place Wyldstyle on the purple pad.

REAL WORLD: Place Gandalf on the white pad.

REAL WORLD: Place Batman on the blue pad (Figure 2.11).

FIGURE 2.11 Three minifigs now stand on the Toy Pad.

Batman, Gandalf, and Wyldstyle come tumbling through the open vortex, into a strange cavern. Before they can react, however, the strange machine behind them explodes. And now the real adventure begins.

Finding and Repairing Three Parts of the Gateway

The strange machine (called the Gateway) must be repaired, and only Batman, Gandalf, and Wyldstyle have the tools and the skills to get the job done. You'll need all three heroes on the toy pads to make the repairs in the Gateway room.

The Gateway room has three areas to explore and repair, each of them requiring one particular character's unique abilities. Batman has the Batarang and the Grapple ability, Gandalf can use Magic to move objects, and Wyldstyle's Acrobatic ability enables her to access hard-to-reach areas. (Wyldstyle also has a Relic Scanner, which you'll learn about shortly.)

The three challenges described in the following sections can be done in any order. Remember that to change characters, you simply face in the direction of another character and press Y or press and hold Y and use the left joystick (LJ) to select the character or vehicle you wish to use.

Batman's Challenge

Take control of Batman and move to the left side of the cavern. Look for a rotating Help box (Figure 2.12).

FIGURE 2.12 The Help box can provide instructions if you access the box by hitting it.

Move near the rotating Help box and press the X key to access it. In this case, you get details about how to use Batman's Grapple feature. Orange handles occasionally appear in the game and require the Grapple ability. Press and release the B key to launch Grapple when a yellow target symbol appears on a handle. Batman launches the Grapple tool at the handle. Tap B repeatedly to fill up the Grapple power bar. When the Grapple power bar reaches its maximum power, Batman finishes pulling the bar, and something happens. In this case, a staircase appears (Figure 2.13).

FIGURE 2.13   Batman's Grapple ability reveals a staircase.

Move Batman up the staircase and be sure to collect the studs. White studs are worth 10 points each, and yellow ones are each worth 100. Always try your hardest to reach the blue studs before they disappear because they are worth 1,000 points!

Another Help box appears. Press X to access it. This Help box explains how to use Batman's Batarang tool to access Batarang switches. Hold X and use the LJ to move the yellow target over the Batarang switch. Release X to throw the Batarang (Figure 2.14).

FIGURE 2.14   Hit a Batarang switch to reveal a surprise.

After you have Batman hit the Batarang switch, a number of LEGO pieces fall to the floor and bounce around. Move Batman (or any other minifig) near the bouncing pieces and press and hold B. One-third of the Gateway is now repaired.

Gandalf's Challenge

Change to Gandalf and move to the right of the damaged Gateway platform. Blue magical effect stars always indicate a puzzle or action for Gandalf to take, so be on the lookout for the stars as the game progresses because Gandalf is the only one of the trio who can interact with them (Figure 2.15).

FIGURE 2.15   Gandalf's Magic ability lets him interact with the blue stars.

Move to the Help box and press X for instructions on using Gandalf's Magic ability. Move near the stars and hold B to reveal a staircase. Climb the stairs, collect the studs, and interact with the second magical effects item at the top of the stairs (Figure 2.16).

FIGURE 2.16   A second magical area needs Gandalf's attention.

LEGO pieces fall to the floor and bounce around. Go down the stairs or jump down, move near the pieces, and press and hold B to repair one-third of the destroyed Gateway.

Wyldstyle's Challenge

Change to Wyldstyle, move her all the way to the far right of the Gateway, and press X on the controller to access the Help box. Here you need to use Wyldstyle's Acrobatic ability to reach and grab blue ledges.

When Wyldstyle is beneath a ledge (standing on a small glowing target on the floor), press A and then press A again to jump higher and grab a blue bar. Two tall walls with studs appear (Figure 2.17). Wyldstyle must jump up and then continue jumping and climbing up to reach a platform at the top.

FIGURE 2.17 Wyldstyle's Acrobat ability is handy for reaching high places.

TIP

Using Wyldstyle's Acrobat Ability

After a jump, move the LJ to the left or right, and Wyldstyle holds onto a bar or wall for a while. If you release the LJ and let it return to center, Wyldstyle lets go of the bar. This is useful for jumping up and pausing to look around. Holding LJ left/right doesn't keep Wyldstyle holding the bar forever, so look around and then make another jump. Otherwise, she'll start to lose her grip and begin moving down again.

Once Wyldstyle reaches the top of the platform, kick the large blue glowing rock (X), and it breaks into pieces that slowly drop down to the ground near the Gateway. Jump down and approach the bouncing LEGO pieces; hold B and build one-third of the Gateway.

Putting the Gateway Back Together

Once all three sections of the Gateway are assembled, it's time to put the three sections together to create the Gateway. This requires a Master Builder! Thankfully, Wyldstyle has the Master Builder ability!

Access the Help box that appears near the three large sections of the Gateway (by moving near it and pressing X) to get instructions about how to use a Master Builder ability. Move Wyldstyle onto the glowing purple target on the ground in front of the three large portal pieces (Figure 2.18).

FIGURE 2.18 A Master Builder is required to repair the Gateway.

Place Wyldstyle on the glowing Toy Pad panel indicated in the lower-right corner of the screen (Figure 2.19).

FIGURE 2.19   Move Wyldstyle around on the Toy Pad to fix the Gateway.

WARNING

Wyldstyle Must Move Around

If a character other than Wyldstyle is already on the left or right glowing pads (not the circular pad in the middle), leave it in place. If a character other than Wyldstyle is on the round pad, you'll need to move that minifig to the right or left pad to make room for Wyldstyle.

After you have made all three repairs, you get special instructions to build the Gateway from real LEGO bricks (Figure 2.20).

FIGURE 2.20   Follow the onscreen instructions to assemble the Gateway.

NOTE

Build the Bags in Order

You'll use the LEGO parts from Bag 1 and Bag 2 to build the Gateway. Don't open Bag 3 just yet.

Press A to start building the Gateway. Pressing A or moving the LJ to the right moves you forward through the pages. Pressing B or moving LJ to the left takes you back. Page 57 concludes the building instructions. When you get there, press A twice to leave the instructions and return to game.

Congratulations! You've built the Gateway. A strange device (Figure 2.21) appears to its right. What could it be?

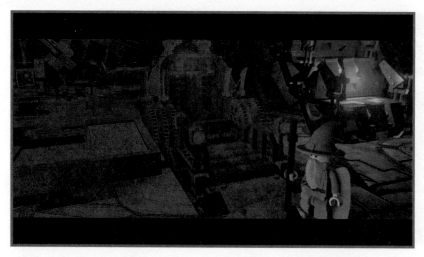

FIGURE 2.21   A strange device appears next to the Gateway.

Providing Power to the Gateway

The Gateway doesn't appear to be working. It must need power! Change to Batman (face another character and press Y), and the building instructions for the Batmobile appear (Figure 2.22).

FIGURE 2.22   Quick! Build the Batmobile!

Once again, press A and follow the onscreen instructions to build the vehicle. Press A or move the LJ to the right to move forward through the pages. Press B or move LJ to the left to go back. When you get to page 15 of the Batmobile building instructions, the Batmobile appears on the screen (Figure 2.23).

FIGURE 2.23   The Batmobile is ready to go and just needs a driver.

Press A again, and the game asks if you want to save the Batmobile to the Toy Tag. Press A to select Yes. (Later, you'll be able to swap between different vehicles.) Place the Batmobile minifig on the center pedestal, and the information is saved to the Toy Tag.

Move Batman (or another minifig) to the strange machine and access the Help box. Instructions on using an Accelerator switch appear. This involves driving a vehicle onto the device.

To enter a vehicle, move near it and press Y. Use the LJ to practice steering the vehicle around.

Drive onto the Accelerator switch, and then push the LJ forward (to drive forward) and watch as the yellow Accelerator power bar begins to fill (Figure 2.24). When the power bar fills up, you know you enough power has been generated and can be sent to a nearby object requiring power (in this case, the Gateway). If you do not fill up the power bar, your vehicle is ejected from the switch, and you must enter it again and drive forward until the power bar is full.

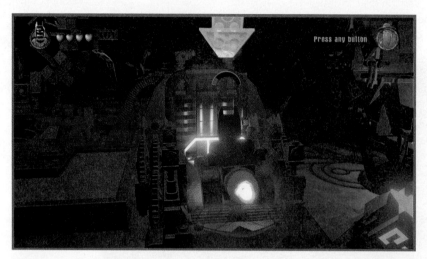

FIGURE 2.24 Power the Gateway using a vehicle on the Accelerator switch.

Once the power bar fills up, the Gateway becomes active, and a blue vortex appears. A blue arrow points to the top of the Gateway. Now you can select any minifig and move into the portal. (Don't forget to collect the studs!) However, you *cannot* drive the Batmobile into the portal. Once one minifig enters the portal, the other minifigs follow—but to where?

Up Next...

Batman, Wyldstyle, and Gandalf have successfully repaired the Gateway, but they have no idea how to use it or where their friends are located. They leap into the vortex, hoping to rescue their friends and maybe find out who is behind the appearances of the strange vortices. (Yes, the plural of vortex is vortices.)

So where will they end up? It's a mystery, but not for long. In the next chapter, you'll guide the heroes down a colorful stone path and confront a cruel black-hatted villainess.

The Wizard of Oz

Story Summary

- Watch Gandalf, Wyldstyle, and Batman arrive in Oz
- Encounter Dorothy and her friends on the Yellow Brick Road
- Meet and battle the Wicked Witch of the West
- Travel through the dark forest to the castle
- Explore the castle and defeat the Wicked Witch of the West

This chapter provides details on solving the puzzles and defeating the Wicked Witch of the West in the Wizard of Oz Story Mode adventure.

"Not in Kansas Anymore"

Wyldstyle, Batman, and Gandalf exit the vortex after repairing and entering the Gateway and find themselves in a very strange world (Figure 3.1). "It's so...colorful!" gripes Batman.

FIGURE 3.1 The trio land in a strange world with a yellow brick road.

When the trio lands on the Yellow Brick Road, they can travel in two directions: either forward (toward the big green castle in the distance) or backward (away from the castle). If the characters choose to go back, they will encounter a large silver fence (Figure 3.2). Every character has special abilities (Batman has the Stealth ability, for example, while Gandalf does not) and only characters that have Silver Blowup ability can destroy Silver objects such as this wall. (The Wicked Witch of the West minifig is sold separately and has the ability to destroy Silver objects.)

FIGURE 3.2 A silver fence blocks Batman, Gandalf, and Wyldstyle.

NOTE

Destroying Silver Objects

If you have a minifig with Silver Blowup ability, press Y and select that character to destroy the silver fence and gain access to a special area containing Munchkin Town (Figure 3.3); you don't need to go there now as doing so is not required to complete the Story Mode, but if you purchase a character who has the Silver Blowup ability, definitely return to this level later and visit Munchkin Town.

Discovering one path blocked by a silver fence, the group must move forward and find a wagon blocking the way forward on the Yellow Brick Road (Figure 3.4).

FIGURE 3.3 After destroying the silver gate, you can visit Munchkin Town.

FIGURE 3.4 There must be a solution for getting around this wagon.

Look carefully at the wagons here—the one that's blocking the Yellow Brick Road and the one that's parked on the grass—and you will spot some glowing LEGO pieces in barrels. Approach the wagon that's parked in the grass and press X to open a barrel and grab the studs. To the left of the wagon blocking the path is a stack of bricks with a barrel at the top. The barrel has some useful LEGO pieces inside. Hit it with X and then press B to build something out of all those bouncing LEGO pieces. An orange handle appears on the side of the wagon that's blocking the road.

Use Batman's Grapple ability to pull on the orange handle until the wagon is moved off the road.

Behind the wagon are purple poppies. Touching or jumping into the purple poppies puts a character to sleep. If you fall asleep, tap B repeatedly to wake up. You can destroy the poppies by driving over them with the Batmobile. Enter the Batmobile by pressing Y and drive through the poppies until they are destroyed. Then proceed on the Yellow Brick Road.

Follow the Yellow Brick Road

In the distance, a young woman is skipping down the road with three companions and a dog. Batman overhears the woman calling one of her friends "Scarecrow," which is the name of one of Batman's famous enemies.

Gandalf, Wyldstyle, and Batman don't recognize (friendly) Scarecrow, Tin Man, Cowardly Lion, Dorothy, or her little dog, Toto (Figure 3.5). Dorothy is happy to have more companions with her on the Yellow Brick Road, but a vortex appears suddenly and pulls in Dorothy, Toto, and her three friends.

FIGURE 3.5   Dorothy and friends greet Batman, Gandalf, and Wyldstyle.

NOTE

Wyldstyle's Relic Scanner

One of many hidden objects (not required to complete the game) can be found in the grass fields to the left and right of the Yellow Brick Road. If you investigate and discover a collection of crates, Wyldstyle can use her Relic Scanner to discover a hidden crate with a special item inside. If you missed the crates, you can easily replay the level after you solve it or restart the game by quitting and returning to the Gateway at Vorton and then jumping back through the vortex.

Continue moving forward on the Yellow Brick Road. You eventually see a purple relic that was part of the Gateway before it exploded (see Chapter 2, "The Adventure Begins"). Before the characters can retrieve it, they spot the Wicked Witch of the West and her flying monkeys attempting to grab the relic (Figure 3.6).

FIGURE 3.6 The Witch and her flying monkeys are not friendly.

The Wicked Witch surrounds the characters with a green flaming circle. Flying monkeys attack at various times as the witch flies around and attacks the players from above. Try to dodge the witch's yellow fireballs to avoid taking damage.

During the battle, the Wicked Witch uses Magic to trap the characters in magical chains. To escape the chains and free all the characters, move one character's minifig to a different pad on the Toy Pad. Immediately after your characters break free, the Witch is vulnerable to attack. Use either Gandalf's Magic or Batman's Batarang to attack the Wicked Witch. You need to knock her down three times to end the battle, and then she will grab the purple relic and flee, with her flying monkeys, back to her castle.

NOTE

All About _The Wizard of Oz_

The Wonderful Wizard of Oz, written by L. Frank Baum, was published in 1900. Yes, the book is more than 100 years old! There have been a number of film adaptations over the years, but the most famous is the 1939 film _The Wizard of Oz_, starring Judy Garland as Dorothy. Many of the characters and scenes found in this LEGO world are based on that film!

After the first encounter ends with the Wicked Witch, the characters find themselves in a dark forest, filled with dangerous creatures and hidden secrets.

The Road Through the Forest

A strange device appears in the forest (Figure 3.7). Move a character near it and press B to use it. This is the Game Save tool.

FIGURE 3.7   The Game Save tool lets you save your progress.

The Game Save tool offers three options:

- **Save and Continue**—Your progress is saved and the game continues.
- **Save and Exit**—Your progress is saved, and you exit the game and return to the Gateway room.
- **Cancel**—Your progress is not saved, and if you quit and return to the game, you start at the last saved point prior to this one.

After you select an option, the Game Save tool disappears. If you wait around this area too long, flying monkeys attack. Fight them off and continue on the path. To the far right, you encounter a silver barricade. Only characters that have the LEGO Silver Blowup ability may pass.

The path continues up (North), and the characters encounter a large tree with a glowing red apple. Target the apple with Gandalf's Magic or Batman's Batarang. When the apple drops, the tree comes to life, and flying monkeys attack. Attacking any monkeys holding LEGO pieces causes them to drop the pieces.

Use a character to build a larger Super Saw (by pressing B) from the dropped pieces and then move it to the right of the tree in the area indicated by the white outline of the Super

Saw. The tree runs away, leaving behind a prickly vine that hurts you if you attempt to cross over it. Use the Batmobile to break through the vine and allow the characters to pass through and continue on the path.

NOTE

Help Boxes and Minifigs

Many Help boxes appear on the other side of the dangerous vine. One Help box informs you that only minifigs with the Cracked LEGO ability can destroy Cracked LEGO Walls, and another explains that only characters with the Suspend Ghost ability can destroy Ghostly Swarms. Check in Appendix A, "Character Abilities," for a list of minifigs and their special abilities to find a minifig that allows you to cross special barriers.

Another solid wall is covered with vines, skeletons, and other LEGO pieces and blocks the characters' path. Be careful to avoid any green spiky vines coming out of the ground; they knock out a character for a few seconds.

Move Wyldstyle to the right of the vine barricade and place her minifig on the purple pad so she can use her Relic Scanner. She uncovers a crate with an orange handle, and you can use Batman's Batarang ability to pull down the crate.

Parts appear that you can assemble to form a boost pad (Figure 3.8). Use any character to build the ramp (by pressing and holding B). You can drive a vehicle over a boost pad to gain speed and jump over obstacles.

FIGURE 3.8 The boost pad can get vehicles over indestructible obstacles.

After you jump over the vine wall, it gets destroyed, revealing a long bridge with another boost pad. Collect the studs on the bridge and then use the boost pad to jump over the next obstacle.

As you approach the castle, the characters see soldiers entering the castle and the drawbridge closing. Collect as many studs as you can and approach the drawbridge. Once you get near the drawbridge, the soldiers attack. Knock them out and collect the studs.

NOTE

Don't Ignore Distant Objects

Hit the gargoyles and torches on the sides of the castle for bonus studs. As you progress through the game, you'll pass by many more objects in the distance that you can hit to reveal hidden studs.

To the left of the drawbridge are a number of containers and weapons. Destroy them, collect the studs, and then press B to build an Accelerator Switch. Drive the Batmobile onto the Accelerator Switch and use it to lower the drawbridge. A closed gate blocks entry to the castle. Place Wyldstyle on the purple pad, and her Relic Scanner reveals a target that Batman can hit with his Batarang. Hit the target, and the gate opens.

The Winged Monkeys

Inside the castle, soldiers attack. Search the room for studs and then move up the stairs on the left side of the room. (A Game Save tool is available in this room; use it if you wish to save your progress.)

After you go up the stairs, flying monkeys attack and light the stairs on fire. Jump down before the stairs collapse.

When Wyldstyle discovers a relic with her Relic Scanner, use the Batarang to pull on the handle and remove the rest of the stairs to reveal parts for a special double wall that Wyldstyle can climb. Destroy the wooden beams blocking the wall and get Wyldstyle up to the higher platform, using her Acrobatic ability.

When Wyldstyle reaches the upper platform, defeat the two guards and move to the right, where you'll find a winch that can lower a rope for Batman and Gandalf to climb. Change to Batman or Gandalf and move toward the rope. Press A to jump on the rope and then push the LJ up/forward to climb the rope. Press A to exit the rope.

After you get both Batman and Gandalf to the top platform, move Gandalf toward the door underneath the blue dragon and press and hold B to use his Magic ability on each of the three blue dots to open the door and enter the next room—the Witch's chamber!

The Search for the Wicked Witch

In the Wicked Witch's chamber, the Witch casts a spell and opens up three portals—blue, purple, and yellow. She can use these portals to move around the room very fast, and you want to seal these portals so she can't use them.

Enter the room and fight off the various guards that attack. In the room are three hidden objects that can be found and built. Once you have built them all, Gandalf can use his Magic to move each object up to one of the portals to block that portal's use.

To the right of the room, destroy the green crates to reveal some bouncing LEGO pieces. Use these with the B button to build an orange handle on one of the wooden cages stacked against the left wall. Batman can use his Grapple ability to pull out a cage. Switch to Gandalf and use his Magic (X) to first destroy the cage (with a flying monkey inside) and then defeat the monkey. Once the monkey is defeated, use Gandalf's Magic to repair the cage (B) and move it over the yellow portal.

The Witch casts a spell that surrounds the characters with chains. Move your character's minifig to another pad on the Toy Pad to break the spell.

Move to the raised platform behind the portals and defeat the two guards. Gandalf finds a special object that needs his Magic ability. Use B to raise the object and then drop it. Destroying the object reveals parts that form a target for Batman's Batarang. If you switch to Batman and hit the target, a chandelier drops. Repair it and press and hold B to use the chandelier parts to block the purple portal.

The final portal is to the left of the room, just beneath the blue portal. Change to Wyldstyle and use her Acrobat ability to jump up to the blue handle and pull it down. This rotates the bookcase to the left and reveals additional parts that must be assembled (B button). Assemble the item and then have Gandalf raise it up to block the blue portal.

Once all three portals are blocked, the Wicked Witch finds herself trapped as she flies around the room. In the center of the room, her crystal ball and table are destroyed, forcing the witch to drop down and remain in the rear of the room. Move to the center of the room and use B to build a water-squirting device. Press Y to sit on the device and then aim it at the witch using the LJ. Press X to fire a stream of water, and the witch melts.

Batman can use his Grappler to grab the purple relic before it gets sucked into the portal that appears. All three characters can then jump into the portal and return to the Gateway.

Up Next...

The heroes have just begun their investigations of the repaired Gateway, and they're about to discover one of the strangest places any of them has ever seen—the city of Springfield, where Homer Simpson and his family live. But all isn't as it seems in Springfield, and Wyldstyle and Batman will both discover familiar villains put to work by Lord Vortech.

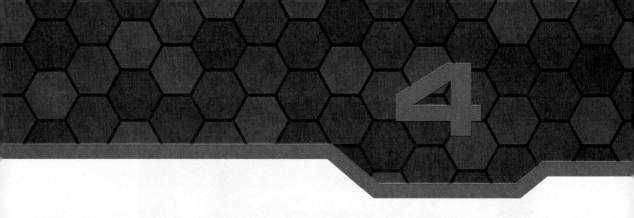

Meltdown at Sector 7-G

Story Summary

- Watch Batman, Gandalf, and Wyldstyle visit Springfield
- Escape the Simpsons' house
- Freefall over Springfield
- Crash-land in the Springfield Nuclear Power Plant
- Face the Joker-Bot

This chapter provides details on solving the puzzles and defeating both Lord Business and The Joker/Joker-Bot in The Simpsons Story Mode adventure.

742 Evergreen Terrace

Batman, Wyldstyle, and Gandalf find themselves freefalling over a city, but before they can figure out where they are, they crash through the roof of a home and land on a rather comfy couch. Use Wyldstyle's Relic Scanner on the couch to reveal an orange handle. Have Batman pull the couch with his Grapple ability (Figure 4.1) to reveal a bunch of LEGO parts. Change to Gandalf and use his Magic ability (Y) on the music player to send it to the music shelf and reveal more bouncing LEGO pieces.

FIGURE 4.1 Batman checks the seat cushions with his Grapple tool.

NOTE

Additional Abilities Not Required

A Help box in the house reveals that only characters with the Rainbow ability can smash Rainbow LEGO objects, such as the obstacle on the right wall. In the backyard, another Help box points out that you need a character with the Dig ability to tackle Dig Spots. These additional abilities are not required to solve this level or to finish Story Mode.

Using the parts, build a boost pad. While controlling any character, place the Batmobile on the Toy Pad and drive it onto the boost pad and through the back window to allow the characters to leave the house.

In the backyard, visit the sandbox, and a peculiar device appears. Press X to access the device (called a keystone device), and three portals appear—a blue one at the treehouse, a yellow one on the lower-left side of the roof, and a magenta one at the top of the roof. You can place a character's minifig on a particular glowing pad (each with its own color) on the Toy Pad to have that character jump to the same-color portal.

Move any character to the blue pad to allow that character to jump through the blue portal that appears just above the treehouse. After the character lands on the top of the treehouse, the treehouse falls to the ground and reveals some parts that bounce. Next, move a character to the yellow pad to jump to the lower-left section of the roof (Figure 4.2).

FIGURE 4.2   Use the yellow portal to get up on the roof.

Push a box of LEGO parts to the end of the checkered path. This involves first pushing the box to the right and then getting behind the box and pushing it in the direction of the backyard. When the box tumbles to the ground, jump down and grab the studs that appear when the doghouse is destroyed. More bouncing LEGO pieces appear.

Change to Wyldstyle and move her to the magenta pad. She appears on the rooftop and slowly falls down. Grab the blue bar and pull (A) to have Wyldstyle fall to the ground and get more bouncing parts. Press B to build a trampoline from the various bouncing parts in the backyard.

Then have Wyldstyle use the trampoline to jump up and hold on to the blue bars that run horizontally across the back of the house, the right side of the house, and the chimney. Use A to grab a bar and the LJ to move horizontally around the house and to the chimney. When Wyldstyle reaches the chimney, use her Jump ability to move to the top of the house (press A while pushing the LJ up).

Wyldstyle reaches the chimney top, but before she can grab the purple relic, cube-shaped creatures grab Batman, Gandalf, and Wyldstyle and fly them to a vortex high in the sky. These same creatures are attacking the city of Springfield. Batman can fling a Batarang to free Wyldstyle, Gandalf, and himself...and then they find themselves falling to the ground again.

> **NOTE**
>
> **What Is *The Simpsons*?**
>
> *The Simpsons* is an animated television show that was created by Matt Groening and follows the Simpson family—Homer, Marge, Bart, Lisa, and Maggie—as well as hundreds more characters who inhabit the city of Springfield. With more than 580 episodes and growing, the show has a large fan base. The Simpsons Story Mode adventure features a number of characters and familiar locales from the show. You can learn much more about the Simpsons by visiting https://en.wikipedia.org/wiki/The_Simpsons.

Attack of the Micro Managers

Use the LJ to move the selected character around the sky and grab the circles of studs that appear beneath the falling characters. The trio lands on the first of three flying square machines. On this first machine, a Game Save tool lets you save your progress.

Change to Wyldstyle and use her relic scanner. Destroying some small LEGO devices to the left and right of a closed section of the machine allows the closed section to open and a computer to appear. Fight off the bad guys (Figure 4.3) that appear on the platform and then move a character to the machine and press B. A message indicates that a relic is at the nuclear power plant, and the machine then self-destructs. The trio once again falls to Springfield. Have the characters collect studs before they land on a second flying machine.

FIGURE 4.3   Use a variety of tools and powers to fight the cube-shaped enemies.

Destroy the various strange objects on this new machine and use B to repair the accelerator pad from the bouncing LEGO pieces. Use the Batmobile and drive up on the accelerator pad to open a panel on the platform and have a device appear. Use Batman's Batarang and hit the flying LEGO enemy that guards the device. The enemy explodes into parts. Use B to build another computer, and use B again to have a character access the computer. The computer reveals that Homer Simpson is someone to look for with regard to the relic. The flying machine explodes, and the characters fall again.

A third (and final) large flying platform appears. Land on it and use Batman's Batarang to destroy the three enemies that attack (Figure 4.3). Change to Gandalf and use his Magic ability to open the closed panel to reveal another computer. When the enemies destroy the computer, repair it again by using Wyldstyle's Master Builder ability. Two orange handles appear.

Use Batman's Grapple ability and pull on both orange handles to open up the flying machine (Figure 4.4) and allow the trio inside. Three areas here require Gandalf's Magic; you can spot them because blue stars surround them.

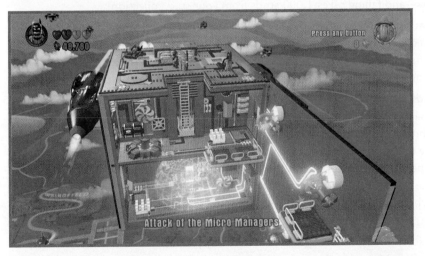

FIGURE 4.4 This platform opens to reveal three challenges inside.

Use any character to jump down to the middle of the open machine and destroy all the objects and reveal some bouncing LEGO parts. Use B to build the machine that creates the three colored portals. Press X to use the machine and open the three portals. The yellow portal appears on top of the machine, the magenta portal appears on the lower level of the machine, and the blue portal appears near the opened door of the machine to the far right.

Place Gandalf on the blue pad to jump through the blue portal. Then use Gandalf's Magic ability to disconnect two of the tubes. One of these tubes is near the blue portal, and the other requires Gandalf to climb down the ladder to the right. After disconnecting these tubes, move Gandalf to the yellow pad to return to the top of the machine. Have Gandalf climb down to the middle platform and then move to the far right, where he can use his Magic ability to disconnect the third and final tube.

Move any character to the lower level by using the magenta portal. Move that character to the computer that appears and press B. Your character hears a message, and then the floating platform crash-lands in Springfield.

Another Day at the Office

The trio has crash-landed inside the Springfield Nuclear Power Plant. Wyldstyle's Relic Scanner indicates that there is something near the other side of the building, so you need to get your characters moving to the right. There is a Game Save tool here that you can use to save your progress.

Look around, and you see a strange-looking man behind a glass window. That's Homer Simpson! Also, you see numerous small fires; do not touch them, or they will hurt you. And be careful where you step, as there are plenty of places to fall down into the dangerous toxic chemicals below—and falling takes 1,000 studs from your stud collection!

Jump to the platform on the right but don't fall into the neon green nuclear waste. Destroy the various objects on the platform for studs to give yourself plenty of room to move around. Move further to the right, and Homer starts pushing buttons on the control panel and starts up some of the power plant's dangerous areas.

Change to Wyldstyle and move to the purple target that appears on the floor to access her Master Builder ability. She needs to be moved to different glowing pads on the Toy Pad to access the three parts needed to build a special contraption that reaches into the green goop. Once the contraption is built, use Batman's Grapple ability to pull on the orange handle that appears. The contraption pulls out the Shift keystone device that creates portals. Activate the keystone device with X, and three portals appear in different areas: Yellow gives a character access to the upper steam pipe room, magenta provides access to the lower room, and blue returns the characters to the platform.

Move any character through the magenta portal first by placing the minifig on the magenta pad on the Toy Pad. Move this character to the white target and press and hold B while rotating the LJ clockwise to turn the yellow handle (Figure 4.5). This turns off the steam in the room above.

Move any character through the yellow portal. Then cross the room and pull the handle on the opposite side. Steam hurts any character exposed to it, so don't cross this room until you've turned off the steam by using the magenta portal. Pulling the handle turns off the flow of green toxic waste from the pipes below, allowing the characters to cross the waste using the floating grates that appear. Move all characters to the blue pad, and they return to the platform.

FIGURE 4.5 Turn the handle to shut off dangerous steam in the room above.

NOTE

Extra Characters Can Join Any Time

Characters who have the Drill ability can access Drill Spots such as the one on this platform. Just place any minifig on the Toy Pad to have that character join the game at any point in a level. You can find out which characters have which abilities by checking Appendix A, "Character Skills."

Cross the green toxic waste by using the floating grates. On the next platform, blue barrels begin to fall to the right. Cross this area carefully, or you will get hurt. Wait patiently for a break in the falling blue barrels so you can safely cross.

Wyldstyle needs to use her Acrobat ability to move up the vertical walls to the higher platform. Two handles can be pulled here, and a third handle must be built from the bouncing LEGO pieces that appear when Wyldstyle destroys the box of parts. Build it and pull it down to cause steam lids to the right of the platform to rise and fall. You need to time your jumps carefully to jump from one steam lid to another.

NOTE

Find a Hidden Minikit

Be on the lookout for five green barrels that can be destroyed in the power plant. These barrels are not hard to spot. Each of them reveals a secret LEGO minikit. Minikits can be collected in certain levels (10 per level) to open up a bonus special event in certain LEGO worlds.

As you jump onto the steam lids and move farther to the right, Homer presses more random buttons that start up more dangerous areas in the power plant.

On the next platform, change to Gandalf and move down the stairs to a lower area. Use Gandalf's Illumination ability (Figure 4.6) to light up the dark area by placing him on the center (round) pad. Gandalf's staff provides a bright light that reveals bouncing LEGO bricks that can be used to build the Shift keystone device. Press X to activate the Shift keystone and open the three colored portals.

FIGURE 4.6   Gandalf can light up extremely dark areas with his staff.

The yellow portal moves a character to an upper staircase. The magenta portal moves a character into a room behind the large glass wall. The blue portal jumps a character to the far right, beneath a dangerous stamping machine.

Move any character through the yellow portal and push the large containers over the edge. Jump down. Press and hold B to build a device in front of the large glass window.

Next, move any character through the blue portal and collect the studs. Hit the two hanging machines on this platform, and a blue door above closes, preventing yellow barrels from coming out. Another door opens to the left of the closed blue door.

Change to Gandalf and move him back to the platform if he's elsewhere. Then move him to the new device in front of the large glass window. Press and hold B to use his Magic ability on this device and move the magenta portal on a track to a higher platform. Place any character on the magenta pad to move through this portal. This character can move out of the open doorway and onto the conveyor belt.

The characters can safely cross the conveyor belt, but they are stopped by a security camera that protects a large door. Batman must use his Stealth ability to approach the door. Move Batman to the blue pad and press B to activate the Stealth ability, and he turns invisible. Move him to the yellow handle and pull it (B) to disable the camera. After the door opens, move a character through the door.

Business Time

The characters must rescue Homer Simpson, who has been grabbed by Lord Business's machines. Lord Business fires a laser at the characters, so don't stand still very long. The characters can hide behind three large machines and let Lord Business fire his laser at them until the machines are destroyed. Once the original machines are destroyed, three permanent blue machines appear, and your characters can hide behind them to avoid Lord Business's laser. When needed, repair these blue machines by using Wyldstyle's Master Builder ability. Move her to the purple target (Figure 4.7), and then move her minifig to a pulsing purple pad on the Toy Pad. Do this three times, and a large machine is built as Wyldstyle jumps and twists quickly to assemble it.

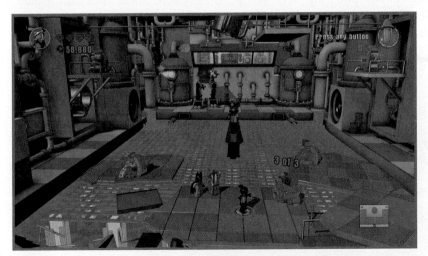

FIGURE 4.7 Move Wyldstyle's minifig from pad to pad to use her Master Builder ability.

Press B to fire a large burst of green toxic waste at Lord Business. Once the toxic waste has been fired, the platform explodes and falls. You can jump from platform to platform—but be careful not to land on the green toxic areas, which can hurt you. (If your character takes too much damage, it will shatter and you'll lose some studs as a penalty before the character reappears with full health.)

Wyldstyle must again use her Master Builder ability, so move her to the purple target and then move her from pad to pad three times. The toxic waste firing machine appears again. Move a character to it and press B to fire another burst of waste at Lord Business.

Lord Business falls again but then stands and destroys the machine one more time. Jump to the platform on the left and use B to build the Shift keystone device that will appear on the middle platform. Use X to access the keystone device and open the three portals.

Move any character through the blue portal. Pull the handle, causing Lord Business to be hit with another toxic waste blast.

Then move any character through the magenta portal. Pull the handle, and another toxic waste blast is fired at Lord Business.

Finally, move Batman through the yellow portal. Use his Batarang to hit the pipe and drop more toxic waste onto Lord Business.

A video sequence plays, with Lord Business having Homer chased around the room until a green glowing nuclear rod is recovered. Once Lord Business has the rod, the trio is attacked and moved to Mr. Burns's office. A Game Save tool appears here, so use it to save your progress if you like.

A number of boxes are stacked in Mr. Burns's office. Destroy them and use B to build three small power pads from the bouncing parts—yellow, red, and blue. These three pads (Figure 4.8) activate a new keystone device called a Chroma keystone in the center of the room, and The Joker appears.

FIGURE 4.8   Power the Chroma keystone device with these three pads.

NOTE

The Hacking Terminal

Only characters with the Hacking ability can access hacking terminals. Consult Appendix A to determine which characters have the Hacking ability. If you have a character with this ability, place that character's minifig on the Toy Pad and access the hacking terminal to play a mini-game for a reward.

The Joker turns on the odd device and then escapes through the window. Before the trio can follow him, however, the monstrous Joker-Bot appears outside the window. It swipes at the building and rips off the roof!

Return of an Old Friend

Use A to jump and avoid the Joker-Bot arms as they sweep across the room. Fight any enemies that appear and destroy the large teeth-shaped boxes that appear. Assemble the bouncing LEGO pieces to form the Shift keystone device and open up three portals (Figure 4.9).

FIGURE 4.9 Three portals provide access to different areas of Joker-Bot.

Move Batman to the magenta pad and fight The Joker. The Joker leaves behind a bomb that you must attack to break it into pieces. Then use B to build your own bomb and jump down before the bomb explodes and damages Joker-Bot.

Avoid the green lasers that fire from the Joker-Bot's eyes by using A to jump. Fight the enemies that later appear and rebuild the purple relic machine from the bouncing parts to open up the portals again.

Move Batman through the blue portal and fight The Joker again. Use The Joker's broken bomb parts to build another bomb and do more damage to the Joker-Bot.

Avoid the Joker-Bot's laser eyes and the purple poison that sprays from the flower on its lapel. When the Joker-Bot fires another round of containers that release enemies when they break open, defeat them and build the Shift keystone device again.

Move Batman through the yellow portal and fight The Joker one more time. Build the final bomb and jump down to the room before it explodes. The Joker-Bot is now disabled.

Change to Wyldstyle and use her Relic Scanner on the Joker-Bot to reveal an orange handle. Move Batman near the Joker-Bot and use his Grapple ability to pull the orange handle that appears. The Joker-Bot collapses, and the heroes jump away just in time to avoid getting hit.

A short video scene begins, with The Joker exiting the Joker-Bot and attempting to escape with a new keystone piece. Gandalf delivers a magical jolt that stuns Joker and causes him to get pulled into a vortex, allowing the trio to retrieve the new keystone piece before they jump into the vortex and return to the Gateway.

Up Next...

The heroes are about to be put to some serious tests of their fighting abilities when they arrive in the Ninjago world and find themselves in the evil Master Chen's arena. But before they can take on Master Chen, they'll have to fight three of Chen's warriors and a famous enemy of Superman.

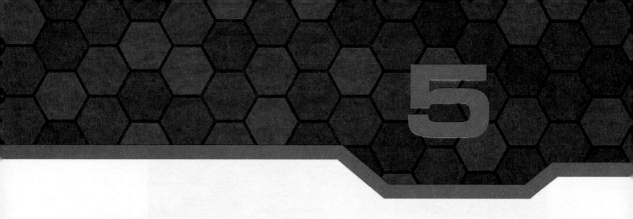

Elements of Surprise

Story Summary

- Prepare yourself for an arena battle
- Defeat Griffin, Gravis, and Karlof
- Jump down into Master Chen's maze
- Defeat Saruman and the giant Snake
- Take on Lex Luthor and his power-armor
- Win the final showdown with Master Chen

This chapter provides details on solving puzzles and defeating a number of mini-bosses as well as Lex Luthor and Master Chen in the Ninjago Story Mode adventure.

Only One Can Remain

Wyldstyle, Batman, and Gandalf exit the vortex and land on a couple of fighters in Master Chen's arena. Master Chen will send three of his best fighters to take on Batman, Wyldstyle, and Gandalf. The first fighter is Griffin Turner, who uses the Speed element to move with super-speed. (You'll fight other characters later that use other types of elements to gain special abilities.)

Destroying Griffin Turner

Change to Gandalf and use his Magic on the pit in the center to build a relic device. Watch for Griffin's attack, and keep in mind that Gandalf's movement slows down as Griffin runs directly at him. When Griffin attacks Gandalf (or any other character), press and hold A to avoid his attacks. Each time Gandalf avoids Griffin's attack, someone in the stands tosses down a box or two of LEGO pieces. From the bouncing pieces, use B to build a blue power pad, when three power pads are built, power will be provided to a keystone device.

Avoid additional attacks from Griffin, and two more boxes are tossed down. Once again, use Gandalf's magic power to assemble a red power pad and a yellow power pad. Once you have these three power pads, you get access to the Chroma keystone device that's in the pit. Move your character into the pit and use X to turn it on, and the three power pads light up and let a character change color by running over a pad (Figure 5.1). You'll be moving colored characters' minifigs to specific pads to solve a puzzle shortly.

FIGURE 5.1 Use the Chroma keystone device to solve color puzzles.

NOTE

One Color per Character

With the Chroma keystone device, only one character can change to a color (red, blue, or yellow). Once a color has been chosen, that color can be selected by a different character only if the Chroma keystone device is turned off and then turned on again.

A snake appears in the center pit, holding a map showing colors on the pads. Make note of the color of the left pad, the right pad, and the round center pad. You must have a character run over a power pad that matches one of the colors on the map and then move that character's minifig to specific pads on the Toy Pad to change the character's colors to match the map. For example, if the map shows a blue left pad, a red right pad, and a yellow round center pad, have one character run over the blue pad and then place that character's minifig on the left pad. Have another character run over the red pad and place that character's minifig on the right pad. Finally, have a character run over the yellow pad and then place that character's minifig in the round center pad. If the puzzle map only shows one pad with a color, then you'll only need to move one character onto that color pad and then move that character's minifig to the proper Toy Pad. The puzzle maps gets more complicated as the game progresses; a purple pad on the puzzle map, for example, will require a blue character's minifig and a red character's minifig to be moved to the same Toy Pad to "mix" the colors to make purple.

After you place the colored characters in the proper Toy Pad locations, the relic device explodes, leaving behind more bouncing LEGO pieces. Use any character to build a handle that can be pushed (rotate LJ in the direction you wish to push) to rotate the snake until it reaches its maximum height and explodes.

When more bouncing parts appear, use B to build a treadmill. Griffin runs into the treadmill and starts powering it up. The treadmill then overheats and explodes, knocking Griffin out of the competition. One enemy down!

Getting Gravis

Gravis, a new enemy, appears. Gravis uses the Gravity element, and he causes three floating platforms to appear. Change to Gandalf and have him use his magic on the center pit again to make the Shift keystone device appear. Press X to turn it on, and the three portals appear: yellow on the left floating platform, blue in the center, and purple to the right.

Change to a character who is not on the blue pad, and then move that character to the blue pad. After the character jumps through the portal, fight Gravis until he flees and the left floating platform falls.

Change to a character who is not on the purple pad, and then move that character to the purple pad. Once again, fight Gravis after jumping through that portal until he flies away and the right platform crashes down.

Change to Wyldstyle (although any character will work) and move her to the yellow pad. (If she's already on the yellow pad, move her to the blue pad or the purple pad and then move her back to the yellow pad.) Have her jump through the yellow portal and fight Gravis until the center floating platform collapses.

Take a Shot at Master Chen

The center pit disappears, and a color map appears on the large doors beneath Master Chen. Have Wyldstyle use her Relic Scanner to the left of the doors to reveal a Batarang target. Change to Batman and hit the target with his Batarang. Fight any enemies that appear, and be sure to collect hearts if you are low on health. After you hit the target, a blue power pad appears.

Change to Wyldstyle and move to the right of the large doors. Use Wyldstyle's Acrobat ability to jump from pole to pole (Figure 5.2) and knock down the red power pad. (It's resting on a small shelf on the wall to the right of the large doors.) Change to Gandalf and use his magic to knock down the yellow power pad that is in the snake's mouth above the large doors.

Move Gandalf back to the center of the arena and use his Magic ability to retrieve the Chroma keystone device. Press X to activate the power pads and use one or more characters to solve the color puzzle shown on the map on the large doors. Remember to move a character over a power pad to change that character to a color (red, blue, or yellow) and then move that colored character to the pad (left, right, or round center) that has that same color indicated on the map.

FIGURE 5.2 Wyldstyle must perform daring acrobatics to find a power pad.

Defeating Karlof

A snake crane explodes through the large doors, and the final fighter, Karlof (using the Metal element) attacks the trio. Have Gandalf hit the snake crane with his magic (B) and then fight Karlof and any enemies as they attack.

Change to Wyldstyle and move her to the purple target just in front of the snake crane. Now use her Master Builder ability by moving her minifig to the first pad that begins to glow purple. Then move her minifig to the next Toy Pad that changes to purple. Finally, move Wyldstyle's minifig to the third pad that flashes purple. She builds a giant magnet from the rubble (Figure 5.3).

FIGURE 5.3 Build a giant magnet using Wyldstyle's Master Builder ability.

Change to Gandalf and use his Magic ability to raise the magnet and attach it to the crane. Two boxes are tossed from above. Use B to build a generator cart and an accelerator switch. Place the Batmobile on the center (round) pad and drive it onto the accelerator switch. Lightning jumps from the cart to the crane, super-charging the magnet!

Attack Karlof, and he turns to metal. Run so he follows you near the giant magnet. The magnet grabs him and prevents him from attacking any further. Congratulations! You've defeated the three fighters!

Before you can deal with Master Chen, however, a new vortex appears, and the evil Lex Luthor jumps through in his power-armor. He tells Master Chen to hand over his staff. Master Chen sends his soldiers to attack Lex Luthor while he disappears down a secret door. Batman, Gandalf, and Wyldstyle follow him down into the tunnel and find themselves in Master Chen's maze.

Master Chen's Maze

There are a number of puzzles to solve in this maze. There is also a Game Save tool near the front of the starting room. If you run through any of the green clouds, you reappear in the same room.

Change to Gandalf and attack the three chests near the back of the room. Use his Magic to assemble a device, and you get a compass-like device in the center of the room (Figure 5.4).

FIGURE 5.4 This compass-like device will help you escape the maze.

NOTE

The New Look of the Chroma Puzzle Map

Look carefully at the device you just created in the middle of the room; you might notice that it looks like the three pads on the Toy Pad. Instead of using a map (like the one stuck to the large doors in Master Chen's arena), you can use this device and its colors to solve the Chroma color puzzle.

Use X to activate the Chroma keystone device and power up the three power pads (red, yellow, and blue). Change a character to a particular color and move that character to the proper pad(s). Fight off any enemies that appear. After you solve the Chroma color puzzle, the strange device starts rotating, and a large green arrow points in the direction the trio should go (Figure 5.5).

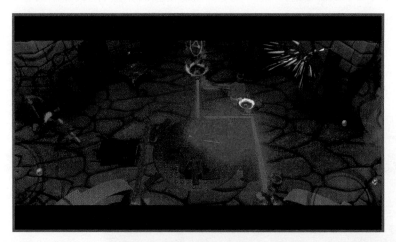

FIGURE 5.5   Move in the direction indicated by the green arrow on the compass.

You enter a second room that has a similar compass device in the middle of the room. Destroy random objects around the room to give yourself room to move around (and fight enemies). Gandalf must use his Light ability to provide light in the dark room to the left and reveal the red power pad.

Change to Batman and pull on the orange handle in the snake's mouth on the left to reveal the pieces you need to build the blue power pad.

Activate the Chroma keystone device and use colored characters placed on the proper pads to match what the strange compass device in the center of the room displays. When the puzzle is solved, the device once again rotates and points in the direction you must travel.

Keep moving from room to room, going where the green arrow points, until you arrive in the third (and final) puzzle room. Once again, you must use the three power pads to find the exit. Wyldstyle needs to use her Master Builder ability here, so move her to the purple target and then move the Wyldstyle minifig to the purple pads in the order that they light up to build the final compass device. Solve the Chroma color puzzle, and then follow the final green arrow to exit the maze.

Saruman's Sneaky Snake Surprise

The trio next encounters the evil wizard Saruman, riding a large snake and guarding a new keystone relic. Saruman can capture and hold a character with his purple lightning, so move that character to a different pad to be freed.

Destroy the many objects to the left and right to build three boost pads from the bouncing LEGO parts (Figure 5.6). You can then use these boost pads and the Batmobile to attack Saruman and the snake. Have a character drive the Batmobile up a boost pad when Saruman's snake is in front of that boost pad. This temporarily stuns Saruman and the snake. After the first attack, the three snake heads at the rear of the room open up and drop bouncing LEGO parts to build the Shift keystone device.

FIGURE 5.6 Build three boost pads and use the Batmobile to stun Saruman.

Build the Shift keystone device and activate it to open the three portals: blue on the left, yellow in the middle, and purple on the right. Depending on where Saruman and the snake have been stunned, move a character through the corresponding portal to attack Saruman and the snake. A button label (such as X) appears, and you must repeatedly press it to attack. After a successful attack, that snake head is destroyed. Perform two more stun attacks, using the Batmobile and a boost pad, and move a character through the correct colored portal to jump up to a snake head so you can attack. The attacks on the snake head can be tricky (and frustrating), but just remember to keep pressing the letter you see appear onscreen until the snake is defeated.

After the third and final attack on Saruman and the snake, Saruman is sucked into a portal, allowing Batman to grab the new relic. The trio rushes in to the next chamber to find Master Chen being attacked by Lex Luthor in his power-armor as he tries to steal Master Chen's staff.

Elemental Showdown

Fight off any enemies Lex sends your way, and avoid his missiles. Targets appear on the ground where the missiles will hit, so don't stand near them or you'll get hurt. Three large boulders fall to the ground after Lex's attack. Destroy them and use a character to find and build the three power pads and then activate (X) the Chroma keystone device.

The solution to the Chroma puzzle defeats Lex and his power-armor, so look for it on the back of the power-armor (Figure 5.7). When Lex turns to run away from you, you can spot the map right there on the back of the power-armor. Take a good look because Lex will turn around and attack again. You'll have to solve the Chroma puzzle three times using three different puzzle maps; the maps change each time you solve a puzzle and the Chroma keystone fires a blast at the power-armor. Hit the armor three times to destroy it.

FIGURE 5.7   The Chroma puzzle solution is on the back of Lex's power-armor.

When the Chroma puzzle is solved, Lex and his power-armor are flung back against the rear wall, and he's sucked into a vortex—but the fight isn't over. Master Chen is still not happy about you defeating his three warriors in the arena. Watch as the new relic keystone joins with Master Chen's staff, giving him even more powers!

Master Chen lands six large ice pedestals in the center of the room. Change to Batman and jump from pedestal to pedestal, and then cross two walkways until you reach an orange handle embedded in a stone on the left side of the room (Figure 5.8). Use Batman's Grapple ability to pull on the handle to reveal some bouncing LEGO pieces.

FIGURE 5.8 Pull the handle to access the higher platform where Master Chen waits.

Jump down, build a ladder from the pieces, and then climb up onto the large stone. Jump over and climb up a second ladder. Get close to the line and then press A to jump—you'll automatically grab the line and slide down to the middle platform, where Chen is waiting. Fight him until he teleports you back to lower ground.

Master Chen announces that he'll defeat you using a number of elements. The first is Earth, and he creates a large ramp with boulders rolling down it. Use the small alcoves cut into the stone as places to hide and use a combination of running and hiding in the alcoves to make your way to the top of the ramps. Fight Chen again, but once again he knocks you back to the ground and then jumps higher before changing the room to use the Fire element. (Another option is to use the Batmobile to drive to the top of the ramps. If a boulder destroys the Batmobile, it simply respawns in the same location, and you can continue moving up from that point.)

When the Shift keystone device appears, activate it, and three portals will arrive: blue on the left, yellow in the back, and purple to the right.

Move a character first through the blue portal and drop down onto the safe bit of ground beneath it. Then move the same character through the yellow portal and drop safely down to the ground underneath. Finally, move through the purple portal, and then run to the left and jump up on to the stairs and fight Chen.

Chen next uses the Water element and electrifies the floor, so you cannot walk on the lower ground. Above Chen, a small map gives you the color code for the Chroma puzzle to solve. Place the Batmobile on the left or right pad (not the round center pad, which you need free for the Chroma puzzle) and drive a character to the proper power pad to change that character to a specific color. Activate the Chroma keystone to provide power to the three power pads.

Solve the Chroma puzzle to drop a snake head on Chen, forcing him to release his staff. The purple relic breaks off, and Chen gets sucked into a vortex. Your trio of characters grabs the purple relic and the staff and jumps into the vortex to return to the Gateway. You'll see a keystone that's been left behind, so follow the building instructions to place the third purple keystone onto the toy Gateway.)

Up Next...

The heroes have never met anyone like The Doctor. Lord Vortech may be powerful, but The Doctor has his own secrets and abilities that can help level the playing field. Up next, the heroes will meet his mysterious traveler (and his strange machine called the TARDIS) and have to deal with some very scary enemies.

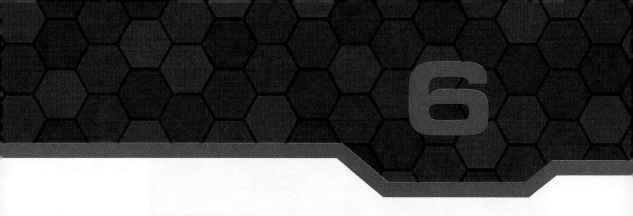

A Dalektable Adventure

Story Summary

- Meet The Doctor
- Arrive at a dark and dangerous facility
- Fight off the CyberKing
- Solve a lot of puzzles in a mysterious cemetery
- Meet some unfriendly angel statues
- Defeat the Dalek Emperor with some help from The Doctor

This chapter provides details on how to solve the puzzles and defeat the Cybermen and Daleks in the Doctor Who Story Mode adventure.

An Unwanted Upgrade

Wyldstyle, Batman, and Gandalf have been in the vortex for a bit too long and are starting to get worried. They should have found an exit by now. All of a sudden, they hear a voice through Wyldstyle's Relic Scanner and spot a police call box in the vortex with them! A man pulls them into the open door, and they find themselves in a much larger space...strange!

The Doctor knows the trio, but they don't know him. How is that possible? The Doctor provides his phone number to Wyldstyle in case they get into trouble and need him, and then he hops in the call box (called the TARDIS) and disappears.

The nearby walls are covered with ice. Do not touch them, or they will freeze you temporarily and steal a heart or two of your health. Destroy any objects you can and collect studs. Move to the right, and you see a bunch of parts floating around a clear container. Farther to the right, you find some blue bars that Wyldstyle needs to pull down (A) to form a ladder. Climb up the ladder (LJ) and move out to the circular path that surrounds the glass enclosure. Destroy the objects on the path and use the bouncing parts to build (B) a Batarang target (Figure 6.1) at the top of the enclosure. When you hit the target, a bunch of bouncing parts fall to the lower level.

FIGURE 6.1   Build a target to open the enclosure and release the parts inside.

Drop down and use the bouncing parts to build (B) the Elemental keystone device. When you activate the device, a graphic appears in the lower-right corner of the screen, showing various colors on the pads. Placing a character on the red glowing pad provides one character with the Fire element, and the character is surrounded by a sphere of flames and can shoot fire and perform a few other tricks (Figure 6.2).

FIGURE 6.2   Provide a character with real fire power.

The Fire element can melt the ice blocks blocking the large doors that lead out of this room. If you place a character's minifig on the Toy Pad that glows red, that character can then stand next to ice and melt it. Another option is to press and hold X and use the LJ to move a target that provides a beam of fire that can be directed at objects (as well as enemies) such as the ice walls.

After all the ice is melted in the area, one section of wall to the right of the doors has an area that only Gandalf can fix with his Magic ability. Change to Gandalf and approach the wall filled with stars and repair it.

On the left side of the doors is an orange handle for Batman's Grapple tool. After pulling the handle (by repeatedly pressing B), a fire starts. Fortunately, a minifig placed on the Toy Pad glowing dark blue can get the Water element.

A character with the Water element is surrounded by a sphere of water. Place a character on the dark blue Toy Pad and move and touch the fire or press X and direct a stream of water to the fire. After you put out the fire, you can assemble (B) a bunch of bouncing LEGO pieces to repair part of the wall and create an energy coil (Figure 6.3).

FIGURE 6.3 Charge up an energy coil by standing near it while using the Electric element.

Finally, putting any minifig on the teal (round) pad gives that character Electric powers, which can charge coils. A character with this power is surrounded by a sphere of lightning. Charge the coils by moving very close to them or pressing X to fire a lightning beam with the LJ at the coils. A door opens, revealing an evil Cyberman! Defeat the Cyberman, and then head down the hallway and into a new room.

NOTE

What (Not Who) Is *Doctor Who*?

Doctor Who is a television show from Great Britain that has a worldwide following. The show started in 1963 and is still on the air today. It follows the exploits of The Doctor, a mysterious figure from the future who frequently changes appearance and travels through time in his TARDIS (Time and Relative Dimension in Space), usually with a companion or two. The Doctor has a number of enemies who are quite terrifying, and a few of them make an appearance in the LEGO Dimensions game. You can find much more information about Doctor Who at https://en.wikipedia.org/wiki/Doctor_Who.

The trio needs to move to the far right of the room. There is a Game Save tool to the right of the door the trio just entered. Use it if you'd like to save your game's progress.

Have Batman use his Stealth ability (B) by placing his minifig on the Toy Pad that glows blue to activate this power. Green laser beams move along the far-right side of the room; don't get too close to them without first using Batman's Stealth ability, or they will shut down the green handle that must be pushed on the circular machine on the raised platform. Push the green handle around until the covered section opens and reveals the Elemental keystone device. Activate the device (X).

Place a character's minifig on the red pad and move to the left to melt the ice that is blocking the large doors. Destroy the boxes around the door and use Gandalf's Magic (B) on the bouncing parts that are revealed. Raise the four pieces to complete the puzzle on the door to open it. This also triggers a Cyberman to create a fire to block the stairs to the right.

Use Gandalf's Magic ability (B) to assemble more bouncing parts that appear near the unfrozen large doors to build a focusing machine. Three focusing machines in all must be assembled, as indicated by round icons at the top of the screen (Figure 6.4). You must find the other two and build them.

Change to Wyldstyle and move to the left, where you see the fans spinning behind a grate. Press B to use her Relic Scanner to reveal an orange handle. Pull the handle with Batman's Grapple tool (by repeatedly pressing B). When you see more bouncing pieces, use B to build the second (of three) power focusing machines.

Move to the far right and place a character's minifig on the Toy Pad that glows dark blue to get the Water element. Put out the fires on the stairs (either by walking up the stairs or pressing and holding X while using LJ to fire a stream of water) and head to the upper platform.

When bouncing boxes appear, destroy them—but be careful because they contain Cybermats (that behave like snakes) that can attack you. When some bouncing parts appear to the right, use B to build a blue handle for Wyldstyle to jump up and grab. This opens up windows that let you see outside. What is this strange place where the heroes have landed?

FIGURE 6.4 You must build three power focusing machines.

Change to Gandalf and walk toward the drone (on the other side of the window). Use Gandalf's Magic ability (B) to raise the drone and move it to the far right. The drone lands on a platform and then moves inside the facility.

Go back down to the lower level and move to the far right, where a character needs to use the Electric element to apply power to a coil (Figure 6.5). This brings the drone down where Batman can use his Grapple tool to pull (by repeatedly pressing B) on the orange handle on the side of the drone.

FIGURE 6.5 Use the Electric element to power up the coil.

When the drone breaks apart, use the bouncing parts to build the third (and final) power focusing machine. Change to Wyldstyle and move her to the purple target in front of the three machines. Use her Master Builder ability by moving her minifig to each of the three glowing purple pads in the order that they light up. She builds a new device on the door, and the device has an unpowered coil.

Place a minifig on the teal round pad, and use the Electric element to provide power to the coil. This activates CyberKing! Run from his lasers and defeat the Cybermen as they attack. Keep fighting the Cybermen until CyberKing gets his arm stuck in the metal flooring: Run to him and repeatedly press X to attack his metal arm. CyberKing is released, but he is missing one arm. Continue fighting Cybermen and the CyberKing until the CyberKing gets his other arm stuck, and then repeat the attack using X.

From the destroyed pieces of CyberKing's arms, build a boost pad and use the Batmobile to launch straight at CyberKing. His body is destroyed, but his head runs for an exit. The trio follows him into a dangerous hallway (there's a Game Save tool here). When Cybermen block the way, defeat them. (The Batmobile is an excellent tool for destroying Cybermen!)

Continue down the hallway and defeat any Cybermen that appear. At the end of the hallway, use the bouncing pieces to build a Batarang target, and then use Batman's Batarang to hit it. Quickly run through the door that opens. Cybermen attack indefinitely, so get out quick!

A Puzzle of Perception

The heroes find themselves in a cemetery. Weird! A Game Save tool is here, so use it if you wish to save your progress. (Fans of the *Doctor Who* TV show will recognize the angel statues guarding the cemetery.) Destroy the vines holding the two gate doors closed, and then proceed through the gates.

TIP

Valuable Studs Are Hidden Away

Gandalf can get a lot of extra studs by using his Magic ability on certain tombstones scattered all over the cemetery. Keep an eye out for blue stars, which mark these tombstones.

Destroy tombstones on the lower level (just inside the open gates). One of them in particular provides some bouncing bricks. Use B to build the Elemental keystone device. If you get too close to one particular tombstone, a couple Cybermen attack. Where they originate, you can find a new elemental power, Earth, which allows you to grow objects at Earth Spots, places where you'll see a little greenery that can be encouraged to grow with the right power (Figure 6.6).

FIGURE 6.6 Use the Earth element to grow a strange mound of dirt called an Earth Spot.

Activate the Elemental keystone device, and then move a character to the green pad; look in the lower-right corner of the screen to see which pad corresponds to green. Once that character has the Earth element (surrounded by a sphere of leaves), move the character to the Earth Spot and target it by holding X. A few circular platforms appear in the lake, along with an area that only Gandalf can control with his Magic (after turning off the Earth power). Change to Gandalf and press B to reveal the CyberKing's head (which runs away) and start a fire to the left of the small lake.

Use a character that has the Water element to put out fires. Gandalf can then use his Magic to toss a statue into the crypt and reveal some bouncing parts. Use B to build a strange device with the parts. Several Cybermen wake up and attack, and you also see a number of areas that need Gandalf's Magic and Wyldstyle's Relic Scanner.

On the top of the hill to the right, use Wyldstyle to jump up: Go around near the right rear corner and jump up. Destroy some objects and collect the bouncing LEGO pieces that appear. Build a special drone, and then enter its green beam to float up and grab the bonus studs.

To the right of the entry gates, use Gandalf's Magic to raise the statue and place it on the blue pedestal. Notice that the crypt on top of the hill is now open but dark. Move Gandalf into the drone's green beam; he floats up and can then jump over and use his Light ability inside the crypt. Move inside, and you find a blue power pad. Use Gandalf's Magic ability to move the pad (B) out of the crypt.

Next, change to Wyldstyle and move her to the front-left of the cemetery, where you can use her Relic Scanner inside a locked crypt. When an orange handle appears, have Batman pull it (B) with his Grapple tool and reveal the red power pad.

Finally, change to Gandalf and move around the back area of the cemetery. Use his Magic at a couple locations, one of which reveals the yellow power pad and the Chroma keystone device!

Activate the Chroma keystone device and solve the Chroma puzzle. The correct color/pad assignments are shown inside the open crypt just to the left of the Chroma keystone device. When you solve the puzzle, the three statues on top of the Chroma crypt disappear, revealing another strange machine (Figure 6.7).

FIGURE 6.7   A strange machine sits on top of the large crypt.

Head up the circular stairs and destroy the three coils powering the machine (X). The illusion of the cemetery disappears, revealing a hidden Batarang target near the very rear of the cemetery. Head back there and destroy the vines covering the target. Hit the target and head into the hallway when the door opens.

Quantum Lock Chaos

Inside a clear tube, it's very dark. A Game Save tool is just to the right, inside the malfunctioning door. Head into the room and destroy as much as possible to free up room to move around. You find some canisters (Figure 6.8) that Gandalf can levitate with his Magic (B). This turns on the room's lights and reveals two new areas to explore—one to the left and one to the right.

Change to Wyldstyle and move to the left until she can activate her Relic Scanner. (Notice the angel statues! Are they moving?) Have Batman use his Grapple tool on the orange handle that appears. From the parts that fall, build a shuttle that can be pushed on the track.

FIGURE 6.8   These three canisters can light up the room.

CAUTION

The Angel Attacks Require a Minifig Shuffle

If an angel statue successfully attacks, your character is disabled until you move the minifig to another pad.

The shuttle must swap places with the large pedestal with the angel on top on the right side of the room. Alternate between pushing the shuttle and the pedestal, and use the fact that the track has two paths going in different directions from the far-right side. Once the shuttle has swapped sides, push it into the machine with the large red light to open a door to the right.

When your characters walk through the door, they find themselves in another room. Change to Batman and use his Stealth ability (B) to get by the laser beams and move into the next room. Batman needs to move to the far side of the room and pull the yellow handle (B) to disable the lasers.

Change to Gandalf and use his Magic (B) to unlock the door. Enter the dark hallway and RUN RUN *RUN*! At the end of the hall, a door opens and lets the heroes into another strange room. (There is a Game Save tool here, just to the left of the door.)

Move up the ramp to the second level and use Gandalf's Magic (B) to lower a ladder. Go up and collect some studs and clear out the area.

Move to the far right of the second level and destroy some objects to reveal parts to build a Batarang target. When you hit the target, a large metal block drops some bouncing pieces on the lower level. Drop down to the lower level and build an accelerator switch for the Batmobile. Use the Batmobile (Y) to drive up on the switch. Then push forward on the LJ to raise a platform with a shuttle to push along the track. This also triggers attacks from the angel statues.

Move the angel statue pedestal toward the red light (to the back of the room) and push it into the extra space (Figure 6.9) so it's out of the way of the main track and gives the shuttle room to be pushed into the special machine. Then go back and push the shuttle into the machine—but be quick and keep pushing while the angels attack!

FIGURE 6.9   Moving the statue to the proper location can be tricky.

Once the shuttle is pushed all the way to the machine, an arm on the upper level lifts up a large container containing the Shift keystone device. A purple portal appears high up to the left, and the yellow portal appears in the middle. (The blue portal lets you return to the platform where the Shift keystone device rests.)

Move a character first through the yellow portal by accessing the crank and rotating LJ clockwise to turn it; don't panic when your character appears upside down because this is normal. Two tracks now change position. Make sure the checkered track on the left is visible first. Then move your minifig to the magenta pad and jump through the magenta portal. Push the shuttle along the ceiling (while you're upside down!) until it's all the way to the right. Then move the minifig back to the yellow pad and turn the tracks (by using B and rotating LJ clockwise) with the crank again.

Move the minifig *back* through the magenta portal and run around the perimeter of the fan. If you attempt to run over the fan, the air pushes you down to the ground. Once you're around to the shuttle, continue pushing it along the track to the far right side until it joins with the machine (with the red light). A door opens to the far right, on the middle platform. Move any character through the door, and Batman saves the trio (momentarily) when they are surrounded by the terrifying statues.

Rise of the Daleks

Batman, Wyldstyle, and Gandalf fall down to a platform, where they meet a very special enemy of The Doctor. They are surrounded by Daleks, The Doctor's greatest nemesis—evil tiny creatures housed inside a tall, round mechanical shell with weapons and the ability to fly! And then the Dalek Emperor arrives...uh oh! The Dalek Emperor has three Giant Daleks created, and they attack from above. You must defeat these three before taking on the Emperor.

Avoid the Giant Daleks' death rays that hit red targets on the ground as well as their laser beams, which will follow blue lines. Also use a combination of jumping (A) and fighting (X and B) to defeat the smaller Daleks that attack until some bouncing parts appear. Then build a remote control device and use Gandalf to turn it on. It overrides the first Giant Dalek and sends it crashing into the strange floating machine that emits a shrink ray. You're temporarily shrunk down to a tiny size and are easy for the surrounding Daleks to defeat—so run and jump!

The effects of the Shrink Ray wear off, and you need to fight more Daleks until some new bouncing parts appear that can be built into a strange electronic device on the left side of the platform. Build it and keep watching for an orange handle to appear on the floating platform to the right. Use Batman's Grapple tool (B) and pull on it. Activate the Elemental keystone, give a character the Electric element, and go stand near the electronic device on the left to power it up—and destroy the second Giant Dalek.

The final Giant Dalek appears on a floating platform and starts a number of fires. Activate the Elemental keystone and give a character the Water element. Put out the fires and build a dangerous-looking weapon from the parts. Pull on the orange handle on top with Batman's Grapple tool, and the gun fires a Batarang target that attaches to the Giant Dalek. Use Batman's Batarang to hit that target and defeat the Giant Dalek.

Keep fighting more standard Daleks and use the next set of bouncing parts to build a new vehicle. Jump into it (Y), and then aim for various areas on the Dalek Emperor (using the LJ). The Dalek Emperor is enraged and fights back by sending more Daleks to attack as well as dropping bouncing parts to the platform.

Change to Wyldstyle and move to the glowing purple target. Then move her minifig from toy pad to toy pad in the order that they light up purple. She can use her Master Builder ability to build a Super Telephone (Figure 6.10)!

Change to Gandalf and use his Magic to make a phone call. Just when things look their worse, the TARDIS appears, and The Doctor shrinks down the remaining Daleks. He doesn't know the trio, but they know him! In they go to the TARDIS!

The Doctor returns the trio to the Gateway room, where he examines the device. He is able to fix the Gateway so that the heroes cannot be tracked—and the heroes obtain a new keystone.

FIGURE 6.10   Make a call to The Doctor!

Up Next...

Superman is powerful, and he protects the city of Metropolis against all enemies. But when he's pulled into a vortex and captured by Lord Vortech, it's up to Batman, Wyldstyle, and Gandalf to rid the city of the evil Sauron and his minions.

Painting the Town Black

Story Summary

- Solve puzzles to make your way through the streets of Metropolis
- Defeat Two-Face in a street battle
- Meet Sauron and discover another keystone

This chapter provides details that will help you solve the puzzles and defeat Two-Face and Sauron in the DC Universe Story Mode adventure.

Lex Tech Lockdown

The trio land in Metropolis and watch as Sauron drops his tower into the heart of the city. A keystone has also dropped, and Sauron takes it and blocks off various parts of the city. The heroes need to make their way to the LexCorp building to retrieve the relic.

Move down the street and into the parking lot to the right of the abandoned car.

Destroy the nearby objects and build an accelerator pad (Figure 7.1). Use the Batmobile to power the accelerator pad and raise the garage door. Inside the garage is dark, so use Gandalf's Illumination ability to light it up by pressing B when he's inside the opened garage. Inside are a vehicle and an orange handle.

Use Batman's Grapple ability to pull open the door and reveal the Scale keystone device. When the Scale keystone device is activated, two pads glow. The left pad glows orange and shrinks a character when that character's minifig is placed on the orange pad. The right pad glows green and makes a character much larger than normal when that character's minifig is placed on the green pad. Moving a character's minifig to the white (round) pad returns the character to normal size (as does turning off the Scale keystone device). Fight off any enemies who attack. Now you need to shrink a minifig and deal with a tube puzzle (Figure 7.2).

FIGURE 7.1   An accelerator switch is needed to open the garage.

FIGURE 7.2   You must solve the tube puzzle on the wall to lower the energy field.

Move a minifig to the orange pad to shrink that character. On the back of the building (just to the left of the energy field) is a tube puzzle. A tube puzzle has a tiny entry door that allows only a shrunken character to enter. Once inside, the character climbs tiny ladders and moves left or right to navigate obstacles.

Change to the small character and enter the tube puzzle through the small door and climb the ladder inside. Then walk through the tube to the container on the right and push the button (B). The energy field is now disabled. Exit the tube puzzle and then have the heroes move right and enter the area previously blocked by the energy field.

One of Sauron's guards is firing arrows at you from a tower. Hide behind the truck in the middle of the road and disable him with Gandalf's Magic or Batman's Batarang. You can also destroy the truck to reveal a boost pad (B). You can use the Batmobile to ram the guard tower to disable the guard and collect the studs after the tower is destroyed.

Change to Batman (by moving him to the blue pad) and use his Stealth ability (B) to approach the fire truck to the left of the destroyed tower. Enter the fire truck and push the big red button (B) to disable the lasers and drop out the Scale keystone device again.

To the left of the fire truck is another tube puzzle that can only be solved by a character shrunk using the Scale keystone. Have a small character enter the tube—but don't go too far, or you'll fall out of the tube. Instead, move another minifig to the orange pad and then move that character to the small orange square beneath the tube puzzle. Move that same minifig to the green pad, and the character grows in size and pushes up the missing section of the tube puzzle (Figure 7.3). Move the small character in the tube puzzle all the way to the left and then move that minifig to the white (round) pad to return the character to normal size. Pull the handle (B) to disable the purple energy field to the left.

FIGURE 7.3 A large character must push up the missing section of the tube puzzle.

Fight any enemies that approach as you move left. Change to Gandalf and move to the far left and use his Magic on the large tank-like vehicle.

The rear of the vehicle opens, and the Shift keystone relic appears. Activate it, and the yellow portal allows a character to examine the roof, while the magenta portal lets a character explore the dark offices. You can skip using this Shift keystone if you're in a hurry, but you'll miss an opportunity to grab some valuable blue and purple studs on the roof using the yellow portal.

Farther down the road is a large barricade. Destroy the red truck near the big barricade and use it to build a boost pad. If you stand far enough back, you can also use Batman's Batarang or Gandalf's Magic to knock off the enemies who are sitting on the barricade. Drive the Batmobile to blast through the barricade and proceed down the road.

You see a roadblock of fire, with flowers to the right. Move the heroes to the right, through the flowerbeds, and you hear Sauron's voice taunting you.

Continue moving to the right, and you see a green laser beam. Use Batman's Stealth ability to move through the open door and turn off the laser (B) using the handle on the left side of the room. Now Gandalf can use his Magic ability on the machine inside the room to recover the Scale keystone relic.

Use Wyldstyle's Acrobat ability to jump up on the roof above the laser. Use her Relic Scanner to find a semi-invisible block. To the left of the tube puzzle, find and destroy the box of parts and then build a ladder. Activate the Scale keystone relic (X), and then move Batman and Gandalf up to the roof, where Wyldstyle waits.

Shrink one character (by placing its minifig on the orange pad) to go into the tube puzzle. Another character needs to be large (so place its minifig on the green pad) to pick up the invisible block (B). Then walk the big character to the tube puzzle (Figure 7.4) and use X to toss it into place so the small character can continue moving through the tube.

FIGURE 7.4   The tube puzzle can be repaired by placing blocks in the empty areas.

When the small character reaches a hole in the tube, make another character small by walking him/her onto the orange pad and then move that character's minifig to the green pad to make it large. This pushes up the final portion of the tube so the small character can enter the chamber and push the red button and disable the next purple energy barrier.

Oliphaunt in the Gloom

The heroes continue on to LexCorp and find a number of prisoners inside a large wall surrounding the tower. A vortex appears, and out drops a large elephant carrying one of Batman's biggest enemies, Two-Face! His elephant is carrying some weapons, and you must defeat Two-Face to stop the attack. (A Game Save tool is here, so use it if you wish to save your progress.)

Two-Face fires a weapon that can ensnare you, so move any trapped character minifigs to a different pad to break out. Move down the street (and toward Two-Face). Fight off enemies until Two-Face launches a green truck that lodges over a pit of fire. Use Batman's Batarang to pull on an orange handle on that truck. The Elemental keystone device appears.

Place a minifig on the red pad to give that character the Fire element. Use LJ and X to fire a stream of fire at the cannons on the left and right just beneath Two-Face. When the cannons are knocked out, move a character to the teal (round) pad to give that character Electric power (Figure 7.5). Use LJ and X to throw electricity at the two coils (or stand very close to them) that are exposed when the cannons are destroyed. Move Wyldstyle closer to the elephant and use her Relic Scanner to locate a Batarang target that Batman can hit with his Batarang (B). Gandalf then needs to use his Magic to pull Two-Face down off the elephant.

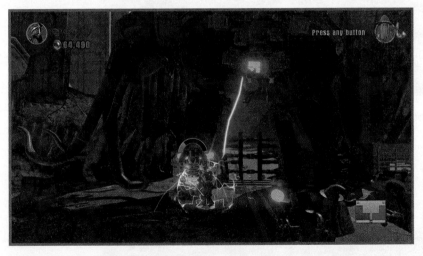

FIGURE 7.5   Use the Electric power to help defeat Two-Face.

Two-Face disappears into a vortex. Move Wyldstyle to the purple target on the ground and use her Master Builder ability to assemble a large energy cannon. Repeatedly press X to fire the cannon at the large gate. Then go through the gate to enter the tower and reach Sauron's throne room.

The Dark Lord Restored

Sauron's throne sits on a round platform that begins moving up the tower. The trio must fight off many enemies while Gandalf moves around the circular platform in a clockwise or counterclockwise manner. As Gandalf moves by a hatch in the platform, a Dalek rises up from the hatch and attacks. Defeat the Dalek and use the bouncing parts from the hatch to build an accelerator switch. Use the Batmobile to power the switch (Figure 7.6) and raise a lighting device. Exit the Batmobile, approach the lighting device, and shine its light on Sauron's throne by moving to the lighting device and pressing B and rotating LJ clockwise to turn the wheel (Figure 7.7).

FIGURE 7.6   Locate the lights using the accelerator switch.

FIGURE 7.7   Turn the crank to point the lights at evil Sauron.

Locate two more hatches and perform the same steps—build the accelerator switch, power it with the Batmobile, and shine the lighting device on the throne—two more times. When three lights have been pointed at the throne, the circular platform exits the tower and flies up near a floating eye in the sky.

Move Wyldstyle to the purple target and use her Master Builder ability to build a massive spotlight. Use the LJ to move the spotlight so it shines on the floating black LEGO pieces over the dome.

When Sauron attacks, fight him off while waiting for a vortex to appear. If you get caught in Sauron's energy trap, move your minifig to a different Toy Pad. When a wagon flies out of the vortex, destroy it and build a fireworks cannon for Gandalf to fire at the floating black LEGO pieces. Press Y to jump on the firework cannon and aim it at the floating black LEGO pieces, and then press X to fire.

When Sauron attacks again, fight him off and wait for a second vortex to appear. A school bus comes out of the vortex. Repair the bus by adding lights to it, and then use Gandalf's Magic ability (B) to connect power to the bus lights. Shine the lights at the floating black LEGO pieces one final time to defeat Sauron!

Up Next...

Up next, you'll be headed back to the future... or is it the past? Both, actually. You'll meet Doc Brown and Marty McFly, who use a DeLorean sports car that's been converted to a time machine to travel through time! You'll get to do the same as you visit 1885 Hill Valley and meet a very special enemy for the first time.

Once Upon a Time Machine in the West

Story Summary

- Arrive in Hill Valley 1885 and help out some citizens
- Find Doc Brown and help him get to his DeLorean time machine
- Meet a dastardly villain who keeps dropping obstacles in your path
- Defeat the giant Lord Vortech with help from Doc Brown

This chapter provides details about solving puzzles and fighting Lord Vortech in the Back to the Future Story Mode adventure.

The Good Samaritans

Welcome to Hill Valley. A number of activities in town must be accomplished to gain the trust of the townsfolk. Start by using Batman's Grappler tool (B) on the orange handle on the left (just beneath the water tower) to open the crate of parts. Change to Wyldstyle and use her Master Builder ability to help one of the townfolks, Joe, to build his giant camera. After the camera is built, use Wyldstyle's Acrobat ability to pull on the bar and take a photo. The camera, unfortunately, breaks. Apparently, the Wild West isn't ready for large photographs just yet.

Continue moving to the back of the street, and you're asked to help fix the railroad track. Destroy all the various boxes around the tracks to clear the area, and a locked box appears. Use Gandalf's Magic to open it and reveal some bouncing pieces. Use B to finish the track—and then get out of the way of the train!

Continue moving to the far right, where someone has gotten stuck in a pile of bricks inside the fence. Next to the fence is the Location keystone. You'll use it to locate a rift diamond—it's an invisible diamond that can open up a vortex, but first you have to find it. Activate the Location keystone, and the screen glows green. Wander around and look for the small white rift diamond to appear onscreen (Figure 8.1). At first, the white rift diamond is invisible, so keep moving around. As you get nearer to a white rift diamond, the glowing pads on the Toy Pad become more green. As you move away from an invisible diamond, the pads becomes more yellow. Move near a diamond and repeatedly press B to open it.

FIGURE 8.1 As you near the invisible diamond, the pads change to green.

The first rift diamond you'll need to find is just to the left of the poor fellow stuck in the pile. Stand near the diamond, and then repeatedly press B to open a portal; out will come a giant crane. Climb in it (Y) to rescue the person stuck in the pile of bricks. Use the LJ to rotate the crane until it's over the pile of bricks, and the crane pulls the townsperson from the pile.

Move toward the town entrance, and a strange flying vehicle appears. It's Doc Brown from the future, in his DeLorean time machine! You'll need to help him get his DeLorean car unstuck and onto the wagon. Use Batman's Grapple tool (LJ and B) to pull the boxes out of the wagon and build part of a ramp. (There's a Game Save tool on the right side of the wagon if you'd like to save your progress.)

Change to Gandalf and use his Magic to lift the large saw (to the right of the wagon) and move it to the right to cut the wood. Use the bouncing parts to add more parts to the ramp.

Now change to Wyldstyle and move to the left, where she can use her Acrobat ability to jump up to the bar (Figure 8.2) and onto the second-story balcony. Attack the rocking chair and use the bouncing parts left over to repair the track at the end of the balcony.

Push the large box on the track until it crashes to the ground below. Use B to use the remaining bouncing pieces to finish building the ramp. Doc Brown drives up, puts the DeLorean into the wagon, and then disappears! Looks like you'll need to explore more of the town.

FIGURE 8.2   Wyldstyle needs to get up to the second-floor balcony.

NOTE

What Is *Back to the Future*?

Doc Brown invented a time machine ("...out of a DeLorean?") that lets him and Marty McFly (and a few other people) travel to the past and to the future. The *Back to the Future* movie trilogy has Marty and Doc traveling to 1885, 1955, and 2015. Wait, 2015 has already passed, so how can that be the future? Well, the original *Back to the Future* movie came out in 1985, so 2015 was 30 years in the future. It's hard to believe that movie is more than 30 years old! You can find out more information about the trilogy by visiting https://en.wikipedia.org/wiki/Back_to_the_Future.

A Test of Skill

The trio continues into town and discovers a new enemy, Lord Vortech, disguised as a cowboy. Before the trio can react, Lord Vortech drops the *Daily Planet* down into the streets of Hill Valley. The trio runs, and Lord Vortech then drops the Kwik-E-Mart into the street (with Homer Simpson inside). The heroes turn to fight but are cut off from Lord Vortech.

Fight off any enemies that appear (and use the Game Save tool on the right side to save your progress). Attack the car to reveal the red power pad. Use Gandalf's Magic on the dumpster (to the right of the Kwik-E-Mart) to reveal the blue power pad. Change to Wyldstyle and move near the Kwik-E-Mart sign; then use her Relic Scanner (B) to locate an orange handle that Batman can pull with his Grapple ability (B) to reveal parts to build (B) the yellow power pad. These pads are needed to solve the next puzzle.

Activate the Chroma keystone device (Figure 8.3) and use the puzzle map on the front doors of the Kwik-E-Mart to solve the puzzle and open the front doors of the Kwik-E-Mart.

FIGURE 8.3   Open up the Kwik-E-Mart using the Chroma keystone.

TIP

Mixing Colors

Remember as you play the game and use the Chroma keystone that blue mixed with yellow makes green. You need to move both a blue character and a yellow character to any pad requiring the color green. Similarly, use an orange pad by moving both red and yellow characters, and use a purple pad by moving both blue and red.

Use the bouncing parts that tumble out the front door to build a boost pad and blast the Batmobile through the back wall of the Kwik-E-Mart.

Lord Vortech blocks the heroes by pulling more items out of vortices, including a Helicarrier (from the Marvel Superheroes universe) that tumbles over and blocks the way forward. Fight off any enemies that appear. Then move Wyldstyle to the purple target and use her Master Builder ability by moving her minifig from pad to pad, going to each one as it lights up purple. When she builds the weapon shown in Figure 8.4, use Y to jump onto the weapon, and then move the LJ while pressing X to fire at the various parts on the Helicarrier that are twinkling with stars.

FIGURE 8.4   It takes a big weapon to knock parts off the Helicarrier.

Parts of the Helicarrier explode and drop down. Use the bouncing LEGO pieces to build a ladder and some handles for Wyldstyle to climb on the left side of the building. Use the LJ and A to move and jump up to the top of the building, where you activate the Shift keystone device. This opens up the three colored portals: The yellow portal appears on the same rooftop as the Shift keystone device, the blue portal is on the roof of the building across the street, and the magenta portal appears at the top of the Helicarrier, where Lord Vortech waits.

Move a character into the blue portal first if you're collecting studs. Then move a character through the magenta portal. When Lord Vortech jumps down from the Helicarrier, follow him by jumping down.

Lord Vortech pulls the Statue of Liberty out of a vortex, followed by Metalbeard's ship. Fight off any enemies that attack. Use B on the bouncing parts near the flames to build an accelerator switch.

Use the Batmobile on the accelerator switch to power up the large fan on the side of the ship. The fan explodes, revealing the Elemental keystone device. Activate the device (X) and place a character on the blue pad to gain the Water element. Then fire a stream of water (LJ and X) or simply walk over the flames to extinguish the flames on the ship.

Change to Wyldstyle and move her up to the deck of the ship and then climb the ladder. Have her use her Relic Scanner (B) to reveal a power coil (with Lord Vortech hiding behind it). Move Wyldstyle to the teal (round) pad to gain the Electric element. Use the LJ and X to fire a beam of electricity at the coil (Figure 8.5). This powers up the ship and rotates a ladder. Have Wyldstyle climb the ladder and then jump (A) to grab onto the blue bars that allow her to climb to the very top of the ship. Lord Vortech jumps down again, and the trio now faces off with him.

FIGURE 8.5   Fire electricity at the coils to power up the ship.

A Show of Strength

Fight off some of the enemies that Lord Vortech sends to you if you need health hearts. After you've handled a few of them, get in a vehicle and drive toward Lord Vortech; he will change to a Giant Lord Vortech. Get away from him and drive onto the accelerator switch to the far left. Lord Vortech swings his sword down to hit it but not before a vortex opens and Marty McFly drives the flying DeLorean into the fight to distract Giant Vortech.

The Location keystone relic device now appears. Activate it and find the white diamond— to the far right. Open the white diamond by repeatedly pressing B, and a flying machine comes out of the vortex and attacks Giant Vortech. Lord Vortech is stuck inside a ball of ice. Activate the Elemental keystone device and place a minifig on the red pad to give that character the Fire element. Use the LJ and X to point a stream of fire at Lord Vortech and melt the ball of ice. When Lord Vortech is freed, run and fight off the enemies he sends your way. If Lord Vortech manages to trap you, move your minifig to a different pad. Keep fighting, and eventually Lord Vortech grabs your character and moves him/her to the top of the tower before changing into Giant Bird Vortech.

Have Gandalf use his Magic to bust open the containers to the far right. Use the parts inside to build a vertical wall that Wyldstyle can then move up (Figure 8.6) to access the Location keystone device.

The white diamond is on the top walkway on the far left, just after the two wooden planks (Figure 8.7). Find it and repeatedly press B to open it.

FIGURE 8.6   Climb the vertical wall to access the Location keystone.

FIGURE 8.7   The diamond is way up high on the platform.

A flying creature exits the vortex and attacks Giant Bird Vortech, destroying the platform you are on and causing the heroes to drop to the ground. Lord Vortech surrounds himself with a fire sphere. Activate the Elemental keystone device to the right and move a minifig to the blue pad to give that character the Water element. Fire a stream of water (LJ and X) at Lord Vortech to put out the fire sphere. Fight any enemies Lord Vortech sends, and if he manages to trap you, move your minifig to a different pad.

Move Gandalf to the far left and attack the various sparkly boxes and other items, including the cylinder objects on the platform above the ground. You'll need to use LJ and X to aim Gandalf's magic and release X to fire at anything that's up high and can't be reached by climbing. Use Gandalf's Magic on the bouncing parts to build an accelerator pad. Drive the

Batmobile onto the new accelerator pad to lower the Location keystone device, and then activate the device.

The white diamond is against the wall on the far right. Activate it (by repeatedly pressing B) to open a new vortex. Out comes a giant battering ram from Middle Earth (Gandalf's home), pulled by trolls! The trolls attack Lord Vortech, who is now surrounded by another sphere of ice.

Move a minifig to the red pad and use the Fire element to melt the ice surrounding Lord Vortech. This guy just doesn't seem to give up!

The action is over, and a video reveals Marty rescuing Doc Brown, and then flying off in the DeLorean. The heroes also realize they are not powerful enough to fight Lord Vortech and run and jump through a new portal to escape.

When the heroes arrive back on Vorton, Gandalf discovers some new LEGO pieces on the ground. Use the onscreen instructions to build X-PO (Figure 8-8). X-PO explains that the heroes must recover a number of elements from various worlds, including the ones that were stolen already by Lord Vortech. If the heroes can recover them, they might just be able to defeat this extremely powerful enemy.

FIGURE 8.8   Batman speaks to a new robot ally, X-PO, about Lord Vortech.

Up Next...

The heroes have been to some new and unique worlds and time periods, and things are about to get a little crazier when they encounter a not-so-friendly artificial intelligence (AI) named GLaDOS who manages a series of challenges at the Aperture Sciences Laboratory.

GLaD to See You

Story Summary

- Meet GLaDOS and enjoy the challenge of Test Chamber 01
- Survive the challenges of Test Chambers 02 to 05
- Find a secret maintenance area and try to escape the facility
- Find yourself back in Test Chamber 09
- Defeat GLaDOS and find out whether the cake is a lie.

This chapter provides details about how to solve puzzles and how to defeat GLaDOS in the Portal 2 Story Mode adventure.

Test Chamber 01

Batman, Gandalf, and Wyldstyle are welcomed to the Aperture Science Enrichment Center by a cheerful voice. That voice belongs to GLaDOS, who insists that there is no cake, that the cake is a lie. Hopefully this is not the case, as cake is one of the elements needed to defeat Lord Vortech.

Explore Test Chamber 01 of the Enrichment Center, and you spot a few things. You find two portals (very similar to the vortices), orange and blue, and a blue power pad sitting on top of a raised platform on the right side of the room.

Move Wyldstyle to the center of the room and use her Relic Scanner (B) to locate the hidden boost pad. Drive up the boost pad in the Batmobile (Y) and enter the orange portal. The Batmobile flies through the orange portal, pushing the Shift relic device through the blue portal on the left side of the room. Activate the Shift relic device, and three portals appear: a blue portal on the floor near the relic device, a yellow portal on a wall high up near the celling, and a magenta portal that allows a character into a small room overlooking Test Chamber 01.

Go through the magenta portal first and collect all the studs. Approach the small pedestal with the red button. Press B to push the red button and activate the yellow line running to the room's exit; you know the yellow line is complete when you see the check mark.

Move a character through the yellow portal, and the character falls onto the raised platform. Press another button by using B, and a cube falls to the ground in the glass-enclosed room in the back of Test Chamber 01. You must move the cube to the small platform on the opposite side of the room. Only Gandalf can move the cube, so change to him and move him through the yellow portal (Figure 9.1). The players can then exit Level 1 to the right. An elevator appears behind a blue energy shield. Move a character through this shield and onto the elevator to proceed to Test Chamber 02.

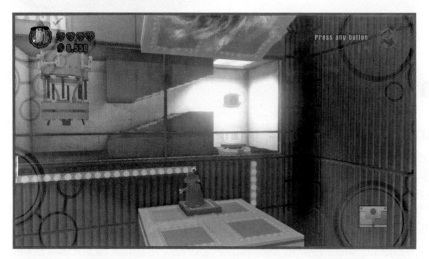

FIGURE 9.1   Gandalf needs to move the cube to activate the exit.

NOTE

The Portal Game Series

GLaDOS is one of the main characters in the Portal 2 game (and the original Portal). In Portal 2, you control the actions of Chell as she navigates a series of puzzles (at the Aperture Science Enrichment Center) that can be solved only by using a special device called the Portal Gun. To create portals, use the Portal Gun to put a portal on the floor and another on the ceiling, and you can then drop through the floor portal and come out the portal on the ceiling. You can learn more about Aperture Science and the two Portal games by visiting https://en.wikipedia.org/wiki/Portal_(series).

Test Chamber 02

There is a Game Save tool in this room and in each of the remaining test chambers. The test chambers are dangerous, so use the Game Save tool to save your progress.

TIP

Collecting Studs Can Be Dangerous

You can find extra studs by destroying the safety rails, but be careful not to fall off the edge once the rails are gone.

If you go through the first door on the left on the back wall, you can see a pedestal and a red button. Destroy the crates to the left of this doorway and build the orange handle over the door so Batman can use his Grapple ability (B). Pull the handle and unlock the door. Enter the small room and press the red button (B) to activate the yellow line and drop a red power pad to the floor.

Destroy the items in the center of the room and build an accelerator switch. Drive the Batmobile onto it, and the accelerator switch self-destructs and reveals the blue power pad.

Change to Wyldstyle and use her Relic Scanner on the second door from the left to reveal a Batarang target. Hit it with Batman's Batarang (LJ and X) to reveal the yellow power pad. A vertical wall is also in the back for Wyldstyle to climb up to find 1 of the 10 special items for this world.

To open the exit door for Test Chamber 02, activate the keystone device. When you activate this device, you can choose between the Chroma keystone power and the Elemental keystone power; note that there will be times in the game when you will have up to four keystone options displayed when you open a keystone device. Use the LJ to move up or down and select the Chroma keystone power by pressing B. Find the Chroma puzzle map on the right side of the room.

When you solve the puzzle, the map disappears and is replaced with a device that launches a character to the other side of the room, over the toxic waste. Before a character can use the launcher, however, activate the keystone relic and choose the Elemental keystone power. Move a minifig to the red pad, and a protective sphere of fire surrounds that character as he/she flies through the flames near the top of the ceiling (Figure 9.2).

Next, move the same character onto the launcher to move to the opposite side of the room. Be careful, however, as there's another nearby launcher where you land that will fling you into another dangerous area if you aren't careful. This other launcher can launch you through an electric field toward the rear of the room! When a character lands on the first platform, move that same character to the teal pad to get the Electric power and then move onto the platform. Your character is launched to another platform that has a launcher. Step onto that launcher, and it flings you to the left platform, where you see two coils and a small pedestal with a red button.

FIGURE 9.2 Heroes need to be protected as they launch across the room.

Move your character to the pedestal, where you can push the button (B) to have a small cube dropped inside a vertical maze (Figure 9.3). You need to power up the two coils to perform two different actions. One coil causes a kicker to push the small cube. The other coil provides power to a set of rails that the small cube may cross without falling into toxic waste.

FIGURE 9.3 Power up the coils to move a cube through wall maze.

After the small cube is dropped, move your character's minifig to the teal pad to obtain the Electric element. You can charge the coils by standing near them, but they charge too slowly, and the cube falls into the toxic waste. Instead, charge the left coil by using LJ and X and then, as quickly as possible, switch to charging up the right coil. This allows the cube to be kicked across the top of the maze, where it drops down to the middle portion.

Once the small cube is in the middle part of the maze, quickly charge the right coil to kick the cube over to the lower-right corner of the maze. Once the cube is in the lower-right corner, quickly charge the left coil and then quickly charge the right coil. This kicks the cube into the holder on the lower-left side and opens the exit to Test Chamber 02. If you're having trouble with this puzzle, try using Gandalf and his Magic ability. Proceed inside to the elevator and move on to Test Chamber 03.

Test Chamber 03

Before you do anything in Test Chamber 03, use the Game Save tool to save your progress. If you attempt to enter the room in the back, the guard turrets point their red lasers at you and fire. Don't go in there yet.

You'll find guard turrets scattered in many upcoming test chambers; they're never really friendly and you'll usually need to find a way to sneak by or disable them. Proceed to the right until you can see the orange handle high up on the wall. Use Batman's Grapple ability (LJ and B) to pull on it. You get a keystone relic that offers up the Location power and the Scale power. Activate it and select the Location keystone first.

Move to the left again, and the white diamond appears near the entrance to the room that is guarded by turrets (Figure 9.4). Repeatedly press B to activate a vortex in the room, and a giant tree appears that attacks and destroys the turrets. It is then safe to enter and explore the room. Move to the right—but don't go too far! When you see the red lasers, don't get any closer, or a new set of turrets will fire on you. Instead, send a character back to the keystone relic and activate the Scale keystone.

FIGURE 9.4 Find and activate the diamond to open a vortex that can help you.

Shrink a hero down (by moving the character's minifig to the orange pad) and enter the tube puzzle (mounted to the wall) through the tiny door on front; there's a small orange emblem on the front of the door. Move through the chamber until you reach the raised platform, and then move that character's minifig to the green pad to make the character large. The turrets rise up and tip over into the toxic waste!

Move your character's minifig back to the orange pad (to shrink him/her) and then exit the tube puzzle. If you keep moving to the right, you find your way blocked by a giant turret firing blue energy. Put Gandalf's minifig on the green pad to make him large. Then use his Magic (B) to move the giant turret to the left blue platform and then to the right blue platform to break the glass surrounding the two platforms and expose two pedestals (each with a red button). This also disables the giant turret, but now there's a tricky puzzle to solve.

You must press both the red buttons to activate the yellow lines that open the exit to Test Chamber 03. This is a tricky puzzle to solve that requires careful timing as the yellow lines will turn off after 5 seconds once you push a red button. You need to move one character onto each of the two pedestals (Figure 9.5). Have one character push the red button (B). Swap quickly with the other character at the other pedestal and push the other red button (B). If you do this quickly, the two yellow lines light up, and the exit staircase appears. If you're having trouble doing this and have a second controller, you could have another player join the game and assume control of the second character so you can both push your red buttons simultaneously. Once the exit is open, move a character into the elevator to exit Test Chamber 03.

FIGURE 9.5 This tricky puzzle requires fast reflexes and swapping between two characters.

Test Chamber 04

Explore Test Chamber 04, where a pedestal (with a red button) is enclosed in each of two square cubes. Save your progress first with the Game Save tool, and then you're ready to proceed. There are also three small rooms on the back wall that are a bit higher than you can jump. Finally, there is a relic device here that offers up three keystones: Location, Elemental, and Chroma.

Use the Location keystone first. The white diamond is to the left side of the room, close to the entry door. Activate it by repeatedly pressing B to open a portal from which a train enters and breaks the two enclosures, allowing access to the pedestals and buttons.

You see an energy ball fired from a device on the left wall. You need to get that energy ball to a matching device on the right wall. To do this, you first need to move the platform the energy ball is bouncing off of so that it angles the energy ball toward the ceiling. You do this by pressing the red button on the left. But don't do this until you activate the Elemental keystone device and place a minifig on the blue pad to give that character the Electric element. That character can safely walk onto the electrified platform and push the red button (B). Notice that this flips the platform so that the energy ball now bounces up to the ceiling and then back down (Figure 9.6).

FIGURE 9.6 Rotate the platform to reflect the energy ball toward the ceiling.

Next, move a minifig to the red pad to give that character the Fire element. The character can then safely walk onto the platform that's on fire—but don't push the red button (B) yet. Wait until the energy ball has reflected toward the ceiling and then press it. The platform flips so that the energy ball reflects in the direction of the device on the right wall. This activates another energy ball inside the left rear wall. You need to get that energy ball into the device on the right rear wall.

Activate the relic device and select the Shift keystone to open up three portals: blue in the alcove on the left, yellow in the center alcove, and purple on the alcove on the right.

You need one character to move through the yellow portal, another through the purple portal, and a third through the blue portal. When you move the characters through these portals, various platforms rotate so the energy ball correctly bounces from the left side to the right side. The exit to Test Chamber 04 opens.

Test Chamber 05

In this test chamber, you'll discover a special object called a Companion Cube that is often used to press and hold buttons as well as serve as a place to jump on to access higher areas in a test chamber. But not this time. Move to the far right and destroy the two Companion Cubes. Be careful of the laser beam that is running from left to right and don't jump into it. It is safe, however, to walk under it at normal height.

From the bouncing parts that remain, build an accelerator pad. Drive onto the pad with the Batmobile, and a platform moves out of the right wall. Use Gandalf's Magic ability (B) to move the cube to the left, where the laser beam is located. A green handle appears, and you can use it to rotate the laser beam. Don't rotate the handle yet, though.

Activate the keystone device and choose the Scale keystone. Shrink a character (by placing that character's minifig on the orange pad) and move that character into the tube puzzle to the left of the relic device. Move through the tube maze and into a small room. Stand on the green tile and move that character's minifig to the green pad until he/she becomes large. When the yellow power pad drops out onto the floor, move the character onto it to go out the open window.

Activate the relic device again and choose the Location keystone. When you see the white diamond to the right of the yellow power pad (Figure 9.7), open it (repeatedly press B). A vortex opens, and Homer Simpson falls through it, breaking open a container in the rear left of the room and revealing another green push handle as well as the blue and red power pads. Before you can use the Chroma keystone device, however, you have to destroy the turret guarding the red power pad.

Move a character to the first green handle (in front of the blue power pad) and rotate the laser around until it's pointing to the device with the other green handle (just behind the yellow power pad). Next, go to the second green handle and rotate it until the laser beam enters a small window to the left of the turret and destroys it.

Next, activate the relic device and choose the Chroma keystone. Solve the Chroma puzzle by using the pattern shown on the map at the very rear of the room, behind the blue power pad. Solving the puzzle destroys the machine at the back of the room and reveals another larger cube and another push handle.

FIGURE 9.7 Find and open the diamond, and a familiar character provides assistance.

Go to the second push handle (behind the yellow power pad) and rotate it so the laser beam now enters the new cube at the rear of the room. Go to the new cube and push the third handle and rotate that laser beam until it goes through the opening and destroys two turrets in the other room. Enter this new room and go through the door at the rear and into a smaller room. You'll find a new robot ally (named Wheatley) behind a large grate. Use Gandalf's Magic ability to open the grate and then enter the new tunnel that opens up.

You're now entering the maintenance areas for the facility. Change to Wyldstyle and use her Relic Scanner to reveal an orange handle on the ceiling. Use Batman's Grapple ability to pull, causing a set of platforms to be created. Use these platforms to move to the other side of the room and find one of the 10 minikits for this level.

Use Gandalf's Magic ability to clear the debris over a pipe that you presume leads out of the facility. Jump into the pipe.

Test Chamber 09

Use the Game Save tool to save your progress and then wander around Test Chamber 09 until you find the blue, red, and yellow power pads, which are protected by some dangerous traps and turrets. There's a tube maze here that needs solving, so start by accessing the keystone device and choosing the Scale keystone. Make a character small by placing his/her character's minifig on the orange pad, and then move that character into the tube maze on the left rear wall through the small opening with the orange emblem on the front. Follow the maze to the end, change the character to normal size by moving that character's minifig to the green pad, and press B to push the red button and release the yellow power pad from where it is currently stored. Move that character's minifig back to the orange pad so it shrinks and have him/her leave the tube maze.

Next, activate the Elemental keystone and move a character's minifig to the red pad to get the Fire element power. Move over the flames on the left side. Once inside the flames, move that same minifig to the green (round) pad and direct a stream of leaves (LJ and X) onto the grow pad (Figure 9.8). Vines grow and destroy the container, revealing the blue power pad (and extinguishing the flames).

FIGURE 9.8   Hit the grow pad with a stream of leaves to reveal the blue power pad.

Activate the Shift keystone, and the yellow portal appears near the top of the room (moving back and forth), the blue portal appears in the middle of the rear wall (providing a way to return to the room), and the magenta portal leads to a room filled with poisonous gas (a neurotoxin, according to GLaDOS). Move a character through the yellow portal first—but *only* when the yellow portal is in the middle so the character lands on the platform. If you don't time it right, you fall onto the spikes! Push the red button (B), and the poison gas is sucked out from the other room. Move that character through the blue portal.

Move a character to the magenta portal and press B to push the red button. Move that character through the blue portal.

Now you need to get to the red power pad, but it's guarded by two turrets. Activate the relic device and select the Location keystone. The white diamond is just to the left of where the turrets' lasers are leaving the small room (Figure 9.9). Open the diamond (by repeatedly pressing B), and a Dalek appears that destroys the turrets. Use Gandalf to reveal the red power pad with his Magic ability.

Now activate the Chroma keystone and find the puzzle map solution to the left of the exit door. Solving the puzzle opens a door with another red button that you should push (B). Remember that blue and red make purple, and red and yellow make orange.

When the exit to Test Chamber 09 opens, move a character into the elevator.

FIGURE 9.9 Find the diamond to pit a Dalek against the turrets.

Take on GLaDOS

Now it's the heroes versus GLaDOS. Avoid her stomping machine by watching where the shadow is located on the ground. You have only a few seconds to move before the stomping machine comes down. After you avoid it three times, GLaDOS drops the Shift keystone. Activate it and get ready to start moving your character from portal to portal.

At first, the room is divided into three chambers, two of them filled with poison gas. Quickly move all the minifigs to the blue pad. Use Wyldstyle's Relic Scanner to find an orange handle. Have Batman pull on it (B) to get rid of the poison gas canister.

Quickly move all three heroes through the magenta portal. Once again, use Wyldstyle's Relic Scanner to reveal a turn handle on the floor. Push on the handle to rotate it, and spikes destroy another poison gas canister.

Next, move Wyldstyle through the yellow portal. Use her Relic Scanner to find a red crank. Move her back through magenta portal, and then move Gandalf through the yellow portal. Use his Magic to turn the crank and destroy the third poison gas canister.

GLaDOS removes the partitions and drops another relic device. This one has the Location keystone and the Chroma keystone. Use the Location keystone first to find the white diamond located near the right rear of the room (Figure 9.10). A vortex opens, and HAL 9000, another somewhat misguided computer intelligence, appears along with three power pads.

While HAL and GLaDOS have a conversation, quickly activate the Chroma keystone and solve the puzzle. Find the map on a back panel on GLaDOS as she turns to speak to HAL.

After you solve the Chroma puzzle, collect the parts that fall off GLaDOS. Quickly build a boost pad, and use the Batmobile to launch at and hit GLaDOS.

FIGURE 9.10 Find the diamond, and HAL distracts GLaDOS.

TIP

What Is HAL 9000?

A famous science fiction writer named Arthur C. Clarke wrote a novel called *2001: A Space Odyssey* that was also made into a very famous science fiction movie. In it, an astronaut in deep space finds that the computer controlling the ship, HAL 9000, may not be functioning properly. Bad things happen. Fortunately, HAL 9000 is more interested in GLaDOS than you in this game.

The platform lowers as GLaDOS tries to repair herself, revealing a cake in a small alcove. There's another test to pass, however, and it involves the flames shooting from igniters on the left and the right. Access the Elemental keystone and place a minifig on the blue pad to give that character the Water element power. Use water to extinguish all the flames. When the fires are out, rush to the back of the room and grab the cake.

GLaDOS tries to defeat the heroes with electricity, but a vortex opens, and the heroes escape just in time—with the cake!

Up Next...

The heroes are going to find themselves transported next to a world of elves, dwarves, orcs, and wizards (both good and evil). Fortunately, Gandalf knows this place well, and you'll race with the heroes to a gigantic castle with a showdown against one of Batman's most famous villains.

10

Riddle Earth

Story Summary

- Find a way through the Great Gates of Minas Tirith
- Fight Brainiac and Digital Overlord inside the castle
- Battle The Riddler and Balrog in the courtyard
- Defeat The Riddler and send him back to Lord Vortech

This chapter provides details on solving puzzles and defeating The Riddler and a handful of mini-bosses in the Lord of the Rings Story Mode adventure.

The Great Gates

The Riddler and an army of orcs have taken over the city of Minas Tirith. The great gates to the city are blocked, and Wyldstyle, Gandalf, and Batman are going to need to fight off orcs and find a way into the city if they are to defeat The Riddler.

Fight off any attacking orcs until a horn sounds. You see a keystone device fly from within the castle and fall into a larger tower on the left. Use Gandalf's Magic ability to break apart the objects near the large tower, and then use Wyldstyle's Relic Scanner to reveal an orange handle that Batman can pull with his Grapple ability (B). Then have one of the characters use the parts that appear to build an accelerator pad. Drive the Batmobile onto it (Y) to lower a door on the tower and reveal the keystone device.

TIP

Search the Tower

Inside the tower is a vertical wall that Wyldstyle can climb to grab a special LEGO minikit after using the Elemental keystone to put out the flames at the top.

Activate the keystone device to reveal the Elemental keystone and the Location keystone. Use the Location keystone to find a diamond to the right near the opposite tower (Figure 10.1). If you activate the diamond (by repeatedly pressing B), a giant turret comes out of the vortex. Change to Wyldstyle and climb to the top of the tower to the right of the turret; you can use a ramp that's leaning against a box to get higher. Press Y to enter the turret, the LJ to move the laser beam, and X to fire. Hit the debris blocking the entrance to the city.

FIGURE 10.1 Find the diamond to pull a special weapon from the vortex.

The orcs at the gates fight back and throw debris to destroy the turret. You must rebuild it. Activate the Elemental keystone and move a minifig to the blue pad to give that character Water element. Put out the fires from the burning pieces of the turret by moving over the flames or using the LJ and X to fire a stream at the fires. Once the fires are out, move Wyldstyle to the purple target and then move her minifig from one purple pad to the next, as each begins to glow, to activate her Master Builder ability and rebuild the turret. Climb the small tower again and climb into the turret (Y) and finish clearing the debris at the gate entrance (LJ and X) and then destroy the gates to the city. Fight any enemies that appear and then enter through the main gate.

NOTE

What Is *The Lord of the Rings*?

The castle city of Minas Tirith is located in Middle Earth, the setting for J.R.R. Tolkien's *The Lord of the Rings* trilogy. While many will be familiar with the story from the famous Peter Jackson film trilogy (*The Fellowship of the Ring*, *The Two Towers*, and *The Return of the King*), if you enjoy this world's setting and its characters (including Gandalf), you might want to grab a copy of the three books and read about the evil Sauron's attempt to take over Middle Earth and how the dwarves, elves, humans, hobbits, and other races band together to fight Sauron. You can find more information on *The Lord of the Rings* at https://en.wikipedia.org/wiki/The_Lord_of_the_Rings.

You Shall Not Pass

Move down the stairs to the lower courtyard area. Take advantage of the Game Save tool available here if you'd like to save your progress.

The Riddler has managed to secure himself behind a set of very large doors. You can see a green energy shield protecting the doors. Look around and notice three smaller sets of double doors scattered around the courtyard as well. Notice that there are three icons at the top of the screen; these indicate how many of The Riddler's power cables must be cleared in order to take down the energy shield.

TIP

Look for The Riddler's Mark

Look for five green glowing question marks scattered around the courtyard and attack them. Finding them all gets you a LEGO minikit.

If you examine any of the three sets of smaller double doors, you'll spot a blue handle to the left of each set of doors. Use Batman or Gandalf (not Wyldstyle) to jump up and pull down on the handle. While the character keeps pulling down on the handle, press Y to change to Wyldstyle and then move her to the purple target to the right of the doors. Then jump up and grab the handle above her head to open the doors and run into the room beyond.

Double Doors 1 (of 3)

The three sets of double doors can be opened in any order, but start with the set of doors to the far right of the courtyard.

Inside the room behind the double doors to the far right of the courtyard, GLaDOS appears inside a vortex. She's not happy about the heroes escaping her testing facility, so she's brought a test to the heroes. Fight off any enemies that attack and move the heroes to the left. Carefully walk across a board to the roof of a small tower. To the left of the tower (on the walls) are two small platforms with blue lights around the edges (Figure 10.2).

FIGURE 10.2   Jump left using the platforms and stand on the big red button.

Time your jumps to move to the left and jump onto a platform that has a big red button. Stand on the button to activate it. Press Y to change to another character. When you clear off the platform of boxes and other debris just above the first red button, a second large red button appears. Move a character onto that button to make two large cubes drop.

There is a keystone device to the far left. Activate it and select the Scale keystone. There are two tube puzzles, one to the left of the large doors and one to the right. Move a character's minifig to the orange pad to shrink him/her, and then move the character into the tube puzzle on the left.

Move another character's minifig to the green pad to make him/her bigger than usual and then move that character to the right and grab one of the blocks (double-tap or hold down B). Move to the left and press X and use the LJ to place the block into the tube puzzle (Figure 10.3).

Get the second block and place it above the first block in the tube puzzle (using B to pick up and the LJ and X to place the block). Make a character tiny again (place that character's minifig on the orange pad), climb into the tube puzzle, and move all the way to the top. Then move that character's minifig to the green pad to make him/her large. Jump up to the left of the large statue and push (LJ) it off the pedestal. Doing this removes half of the poisonous gas blocking one of The Riddler's three power generators.

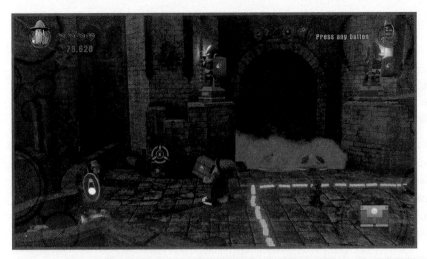

FIGURE 10.3   Use two blocks to repair the tube puzzle.

Move a tiny character to the tube puzzle to the right of the poisonous gas and climb to the top. Once again, move that character's minifig to the green pad to make the character large, and then push the statue off the pedestal.

Find the orange handle on the front of the power generator. Use Batman's Grapple ability (B) to pull on it. Parts break off, revealing a yellow handle. Have a normal-sized hero pull the handle (B) to disable one of the three generators that powers the green energy shield. Move the heroes to the right and exit through the open doors.

Double Doors 2 (of 3)

Move the heroes away from the set of double doors on the right and to the middle set of double doors. Have either Gandalf or Batman (but not Wyldstyle) jump up and pull the handle on the set of double doors. Press Y to change to Wyldstyle and have her jump up while standing on the purple target to grab another handle to open this second set of doors and proceed in.

Move the heroes down the stairs and to the right. The evil Brainiac appears, blocking the heroes' path to the right with a large box and dropping stone statues down on the heroes. Change to Gandalf and press and hold B to grab one of the statues when Brainiac throws it. Continue holding down B until Gandalf throws the statue back at Brainiac. Then use Gandalf again to build a boost pad. Drive the Batmobile up it to destroy the large box.

Fight off any enemies that appear, and then move down the street toward where Brainiac is waiting in the distance.

TIP

A Minikit on the Roof

Destroy some of the items in the street to find bouncing pieces. Use them to build an orange handle, and then press B for Batman to use his Grapple ability (B) to climb to the roof. Destroy three crates on the roof to find a secret item.

Brainiac continues to toss statues at the heroes. Change to Gandalf and press and hold B to catch and toss three statues back at Brainiac (Figure 10.4) to scare him away. You must hold down B until a statue is tossed back at Brainiac. Avoid his blasts in between catching statues. After defeating Brainiac, use B to build an orange handle on the front of the power generator to bust it open, and then pull (B) on the yellow handle.

FIGURE 10.4   Catch the statues and toss them back at Brainiac.

When you've disabled the second generator, move the heroes back to the start and go through the doors to return to the courtyard.

Double Doors 3 (of 3)

The green energy shield still surrounds the final set of doors. You need to disable the last green power generator by moving all the way to the left of the courtyard and opening the doors using the handles, as you did for the other sets of doors with Wyldstyle and the other character. Use Batman or Gandalf to jump and grab the first handle, and then press Y to change to Wyldstyle and have her jump up and grab the second handle. The heroes then enter a rubble-filled courtyard.

Explore the area until Digital Overlord appears and moves a damaged section of castle to block the heroes from moving to the right. Destroy the strange vehicle on the ground and use Gandalf's Magic ability to build an orange handle to pull that section of castle away and move into the next area. You'll need to fight off some enemies that appear.

Digital Overlord then moves three large gold statues to block access to his current location. Fight off any enemies that appear and use Gandalf's Magic to move the three statues.

Digital Overlord sits on top of a box with gold chains surrounding it. When a keystone device appears, activate it and use the Shift keystone to open three portals: the blue portal, which appears to the left of Digital Overlord (up on the roof above), the yellow portal, which appears to the right of Digital Overlord, and the magenta portal, which brings a character back down to where the relic device is sitting.

Have Batman go through the blue portal. Fight off any enemies that appear, and then use his Grapple ability (B) to pull on one of Digital Overlord's legs and expose a weak area. Next, hit that same spot with Batman's Batarang (LJ and X) to destroy the leg (Figure 10.5).

FIGURE 10.5 Hit Digital Overlord's leg to destroy it.

Move Batman to the yellow portal. Once again, use his Grapple ability to pull on a leg to expose a weak area, and then hit that spot with the Batarang (LJ and X). After you destroy two legs, Digital Overlord falls down into the area beneath and is destroyed. A fire then surrounds the power generator.

Activate the Elemental keystone next. Move a minifig to the blue pad to give that character Water element. Move the character around the power generator to extinguish the fires. Batman's Grapple can once again pull (B) on the orange handle to reveal the generator and the yellow handle that disables the generator.

Move the heroes back out into the original courtyard and then up the staircase to the large double doors guarded by the green energy shield. The green shield drops, allowing the heroes to run in.

Riddle on the Citadel

The Riddler taunts the heroes and comes out riding the gigantic Balrog that Batman saved Gandalf from in the game's opening video sequence.

Run around the Citadel courtyard and keep your eyes open for a number of things: a Chroma puzzle map to the right, a yellow power pad, a large statue near the right rear, which hides a red power pad, and a statue to the left, which hides a blue power pad. Find and activate the Shift keystone device in the far left rear of the Citadel courtyard. Three portals appear: magenta on a second level, yellow to the left (which returns a character to the relic device), and blue on the very top level (the third floor).

Move Gandalf through the blue portal and use his Magic on the three chimneys (Figure 10.6). The Balrog catches the first two chimneys, but the third one knocks him silly. The Balrog kicks the relic device away and disables the portals.

FIGURE 10.6 Toss the three chimneys to the Balrog; he has only two hands so can't catch them all.

Move to the keystone device in the center of the courtyard and activate the Chroma keystone. Solve the puzzle (using the map on the door to the right), and a door opens, releasing three stone statues that attack the Balrog. The Balrog grabs the relic device and tosses it to the far right-front corner of the courtyard, near a tube puzzle. Rush over there and activate the Scale keystone.

Place Batman or Wyldstyle's minifig on the green pad to grow that character, and then grab the special box and place it in the tube puzzle. Move Gandalf's minifig to the orange pad to shrink him, and then move Gandalf into the tube puzzle and to the roof. Use Gandalf's Magic on the roof to attack the Balrog with some loud speakers (playing "Everything is AWESOME!"). Unfortunately, the Balrog destroys the speakers and tosses the keystone device to the left, near the center of the courtyard.

Activate the Location keystone and find the diamond fast! It's located near the far-left wall (Figure 10.7). When you activate it (by repeatedly pressing B), a vortex opens, and a Chima vehicle appears and runs over the Balrog before disappearing into another vortex.

FIGURE 10.7 Activate the white diamond's vortex to release a new attack on the Balrog.

The Riddler flies the Balrog away, so have the heroes follow him to a new section of the castle. Activate the Elemental keystone and move a character's minifig to the blue pad to gain the Water element. Hit the Balrog and Riddler with a blast of water until the Balrog runs away. If the Balrog attacks the players and captures them with energy spheres, move the minifigs to other pads to free them.

Move toward the Balrog and use Wyldstyle's Relic Scanner to locate a power coil on the Balrog's back (Figure 10.8). Move a character's minifig to the blue pad to gain the Electric element, and then hit the coil with a blast of electricity (LJ and X). Once again, The Riddler and the Balrog run away.

FIGURE 10.8   The Balrog has a power coil on its back.

Move a character's minifig to the blue pad again and use the Water element to hit the Balrog with another water stream until it runs away. Follow the Balrog and hit the coil on the Balrog's back again with the Electric element (LJ and X).

You need one final attack with the Water element and one final hit with the Electric element to the coil to defeat the Balrog. The Riddler is knocked off the Balrog, and the creature falls from the castle. The Riddler and Gollum fall from the castle as well, but a dragon catches them and flies into a vortex. The heroic trio is also picked up by a dragon and flown into a vortex, along with a glowing golden eye in a glass jar.

Up Next...

When New York City is being swarmed with spooks, spectres, and ghosts, who do they call? That's right: Ghostbusters! But what happens when the Ghostbusters have been captured by one of Lord Vortech's minions, the evil General Zod? It's up to Wyldstyle, Batman, and Gandalf to not only clean up NYC but also rescue the Ghostbusters.

11

The Phantom Zone

Story Summary

- Chase the Ghostbusters through the streets of New York City
- Defeat some pesky ghosts who are causing trouble
- Rid Ghostbusters HQ of enemies and ghosts
- Defeat Zod and release his prisoners, the Ghostbusters

This chapter provides details on solving puzzles, rescuing the Ghostbusters, and defeating General Zod in the Ghostbusters Story Mode adventure.

Who You Gonna Call?

Gandalf, Wyldstyle, and Batman have arrived in New York City, but they're not feeling too welcome right now. The city is being attacked by ghosts. They're everywhere, and they're covering buildings and streets with a horrible purple ectoplasm that hurts you if you touch it! The ghosts like to jump out and surprise you around every corner. To deal with this, when you get trapped by ghostly arms coming up out of the sewers, just press B repeatedly until you escape.

TIP

Find All the Ghostbusters Minikits

There are 10 hidden minikits in this world. One is in the far-left corner when the game begins. Another is hidden inside the truck with the orange handle on it. Batman can use his Grapple ability to pull on the handle and get the item. Also be on the lookout for signs with the Ghostbusters logo; there are 5 of them to collect.

Take control of a hero and move him/her to the right to find the boost pad, which launches you over the purple ectoplasm covering the street. (You can drive through it, but ectoplasm slows a vehicle down to half speed.) The other two heroes will find their own way over the ectoplasm. You may spot the Ghostbusters vehicle (ECTO-1), but it quickly leaves the area.

NOTE

What Is *Ghostbusters*?

The movie showing at the theater is titled *Ghost Smashers*, which is one of the original suggested titles for the movie we now know as *Ghostbusters*. You can find out all about the movie and the equipment used by the Ghostbusters at https://en.wikipedia.org/wiki/Ghostbusters.

Continue moving down the street and use Gandalf's Magic ability to create a ladder underneath the building's balcony on the right. Move Wyldstyle up the ladder to the second-floor balcony, and use her Relic Scanner to locate an orange handle. Change to Batman and use his Grapple ability (B) to get up to the third-floor balcony. Have Batman push the cage off the track (Figure 11.1) so it crashes down to the ground and reveals the red power pad.

FIGURE 11.1   Get to the third-floor balcony and push this cage over the edge.

A pair of pesky ghosts are messing with the traffic lights and have managed to create a massive vehicle pileup. Destroy the random LEGO objects around the street and use the parts to build an accelerator switch.

Move to the left and change to Wyldstyle. Use her Acrobat ability to jump up on the poles. Jump to the second pole and then onto the top of the diner entrance. Jump to the roof of the diner and use Wyldstyle's Relic Scanner to locate another handle on the chef's plate (Figure 11.2). Jump up and pull down the plate to reveal the yellow power pad.

FIGURE 11.2 The yellow power pad is in the chef's plate.

TIP

Never Ignore Purple Studs

A purple stud (worth 10,000 regular studs!) is behind the chef. Don't miss it!

Change to Gandalf and move toward the car pileup at the end of the street. Use Gandalf's Magic (B) to open the car's trunk and build the blue power pad from the parts that come out.

Next, get in the Batmobile (Y) and drive onto the accelerator pad. A hook lowers down and pulls out a relic device. Be careful not to fall into the open hole in the street.

Activate the Location keystone and find the white diamond located to the right, near the large pool of purple ectoplasm (Figure 11.3).

When you open up the white diamond (by repeatedly pressing B), a vortex opens and a large platform appears. Use Wyldstyle's Master Builder ability on the platform and have her use these parts to build a large speaker that can be powered up by the ectoplasm. When the speaker walks itself over to face the car pileup, you see a Chroma puzzle solution on its back.

Activate the Chroma keystone and solve the puzzle. The speaker activates, blasts out the *Ghostbusters* theme song, and clears away the pileup! Continue moving up the street as it turns to the left. (To the right, however, is an area you'll want to explore if you're into collecting studs; plenty of them here if you destroy all the objects in the area.)

FIGURE 11.3   Find the white diamond but don't get too close to the ectoplasm.

Move left down the street. If you like, you can drive the Batmobile onto the boost pad to destroy a scaffolding and reveal studs. All the way to the left is an area blocked off and filled with purple ectoplasm. You can safely drive the Batmobile over the ectoplasm to collect studs—but don't walk through it or you'll take damage and lose a heart or two of health! Farther up the street, ECTO-1 once again goes flying by. Get in the Batmobile and drive across the ectoplasm to the other side of the street.

Once you're safely on the other side of the purple ectoplasm, the other two heroes follow. Now begin moving to the right. There are two boost pads—one toward the top of the screen and one near the bottom. Drive through both of them with the Batmobile to reveal a *lot* of studs. After you collect them, move down the street.

Farther down the street are two more boost pads. You can drive through the farthest one, but the nearer one is covered in ectoplasm and isn't working.

After jumping the boost pad, you see the Statue of Liberty's feet messing up the street and ECTO-1 barely getting away. Get in the Batmobile and move down the street (to the right). When you come to the next boost pad, drive over it with the Batmobile.

A flying police cruiser appears out of a vortex, and a large billboard sign falls to the ground and blocks further progress up the street. The police cruiser fires laser beams at you, so move quickly to an alley to the right of the police cruiser and fight off any enemies that attack. When you see the large Octon Energy sign (Figure 11.4), use Batman's Grapple ability on it (B) to reveal a tall vertical wall that Wyldstyle can repair (B) and then climb up (LJ and A).

On the rooftop is a keystone device. When you use it to activate the Shift keystone, three portals appear: a yellow portal on the rooftop (so a character can return to the relic device), a blue portal on the opposite side of the street on a large crane, and a magenta portal directly over the police cruiser.

FIGURE 11.4 Pull down this sign to reveal a way to get to the rooftops.

Move a character first through the blue portal. Run around the top of the crane and pull down the handle (B) to rotate the crane so it is over the police cruiser.

Next, move Gandalf through the magenta portal. Use his Magic (B) to lower the crane's hook, grab the police cruiser, and fling it away. ECTO-1 rushes in, and out come the Ghostbusters!

General Zod, one of Superman's arch enemies, appears, however, and kidnaps the Ghostbusters. Batman manages to damage Zod's ship before he can fly away. The ship crashes on top of the Ghostbusters' headquarters (an old fire station), and the heroes rush in to confront Zod and rescue the Ghostbusters.

Haunted Headquarters

Inside the Ghostbusters' headquarters are a number of robotic police officers sifting through the Ghostbusters' equipment. A ghost attacks the stairs and destroys them. Find the Game Save tool along the right wall if you want to save your progress.

As you fight off any enemies that attack, change to Wyldstyle and move her to the purple target to use her Master Builder ability to build a laser cutter. Push on the green handle, and the laser cuts a hole that leads to the basement.

The heroes drop down into the basement. Move Wyldstyle to the rear of the room and use her Relic Scanner on the red machine on the right wall (Figure 11.5).

Use Batman's Grapple ability (B) on the orange handle that appears, and the keystone device appears. Select the Elemental keystone and move a character's minifig to the green pad to give that character the Earth element. Use LJ and X to shoot a stream of leaves at the grow pad, and a vine grows, lifting the door to the large red machine near the left wall. Change to another hero and push the large object into the opening in the red machine. The red machine opens, revealing the red power pad.

FIGURE 11.5 You need the Relic Scanner to find a relic device.

Activate the keystone device and select the Scale keystone. Shrink one character (by placing the character's minifig on the orange pad) and enlarge another character (by placing that character's minifig on the green pad). Use the large hero to pick up the box near the tube puzzle on the rear wall. Use LJ and X to insert it into the tube puzzle.

Move the shrunken hero into the tube puzzle. When the character is in the box on the end, move that character's minifig to the white pad (round) to make it normal size. Pull the handle (B) to power up a machine that opens and reveals the solution to a Chroma puzzle.

Move to the front of the basement and change to Gandalf. In front of the swarm of ghosts is an object that Gandalf needs to use his Magic on (B). When he does, he builds a large boom box that plays some music that makes the toaster dance. Use Gandalf's Magic on the toaster (B), and then use the parts that spill out to build the yellow power pad.

Continue moving to the right until you see the blue power pad. When the ghostly librarian who is guarding it starts a fire, activate the Elemental keystone and move a minifig to the blue pad to give that character the Water element. Put out the fire, and the blue power pad is now ready to use.

Activate the Chroma keystone and use it to solve the puzzle. When the puzzle is solved, the ghosts are sucked back into the storage unit, and you now see a staircase leading up. Head back up to the first floor where you'll have to defeat some enemies who attack.

To the rear of the building, find another keystone device. Activate the Location keystone and find the white diamond to the left, just between the (broken) stairs going up and the stairs leading to the basement (Figure 11.6).

FIGURE 11.6 Find the white diamond to find the amazing double couch.

If you open the diamond (by repeatedly pressing B), a vortex opens, and a very familiar structure (to Wyldstyle and fans of *The LEGO Movie*) appears: a double couch!

Climb up the double couch by using the ladder on its side (or have Wyldstyle simply double-jump up on it). It acts like a trampoline, allowing the heroes to jump up to the unbroken section of stairs leading up and to the confrontation with General Zod.

Kneel Before Zod

General Zod attacks the heroes with his ship. Fight off any enemies that appear. While the laser on the bottom of Zod's ship is firing, the green dot (power core) above the laser is vulnerable (Figure 11.7). Hit it three times with Gandalf's Magic or a Batarang.

FIGURE 11.7 Hit the power core above the laser twice to disable it.

Zod's ship crashes into the rear building, and he surrounds himself with a swarm of ghosts that protect him from attacks. Change to Wyldstyle, and run toward his ship, and use the Relic Scanner. An orange handle appears on the front of Zod's ship. Use Batman's Grapple ability (B) to pull it—and release the Ghostbusters! The Ghostbusters deal with the ghost swarm, leaving you to fight General Zod.

Fight any enemies that appear. The roof eventually collapses, revealing the Elemental keystone device. If Zod manages to capture the heroes, move them to different pads to free them.

General Zod flies around the roof, trying to hit the heroes with his laser vision. When Zod is over the right or left machines with the round crank handles (near the front of the building), use the LJ and B to turn a crank on the machine beneath him.

When General Zod is flying above the machine on the left, use the LJ and B to turn the crank and release a water stream. Once the water stream has General Zod captured, move a minifig to the blue pad to give that character the Electric element. If you hit Zod with a beam of electricity, he is injured but escapes.

When General Zod is flying over the machine on the right, use the LJ and B to turn the crank and release a strong blast of steam. When the steam captures Zod, hit him with the Fire element (by moving a minifig to the red pad).

These two attacks weaken Zod, and he flies to the rear of the building. Beneath Zod is a grow pad. Move a minifig to the green pad to give that character Earth element. If you use LJ and X to aim a stream of leaves at the grow pad, a giant Venus flytrap plant grows. The plant grabs Zod and flings him into a collection of Kryptonite.

The fight is now over and a short video will play. Zod is pulled into a vortex before he can be questioned. The heroes jump in to follow him, leaving the Ghostbusters to clean up the town.

Up Next...

If you've ever seen or been into an arcade, you know it's full of games that can be played for a few quarters or tokens. Up next, the heroes are about to discover a world where video games are real, and Batman, Gandalf, and Wyldstyle will chase a thief through a handful of real video games to try to retrieve a special LEGO token.

12

All Your Bricks Are Belong to Us

Story Summary

- Rescue five astronauts from evil aliens in Defender
- Escape the Gauntlet video game maze
- Race the Blue Thief in Super Sprint
- Fight off swarms of enemies in Robotron

This chapter provides details on solving puzzles and defeating Blue Thief in the Midway Arcade Story Mode adventure.

Defender

The trio lands on an unusual planet, where they are being attacked from above. Just as the trio spots a Foundation Element (an arcade token), it's taken away by a fast-flying spacecraft. The heroes are inside the classic 1980s video game Defender!

The heroes are standing in front of a building, and they can only run left or right. At the top of the screen is a counter for the five astronaut characters that must be rescued. To the right is a Batarang target. If you hit the target with Batman's Batarang (LJ and X), a door opens, revealing objects that should be destroyed. Use the bouncing parts that are left over to build a keystone device. Activate the Scale keystone and place a minifig on the orange pad to shrink that character down. Enter the small doors on the left side of the building and look for a handle. Move the shrunken character's minifig to the white (round) pad to return to normal size and pull the handle (B). The front door of the building opens, releasing one of the captured astronaut characters.

Next, activate the Elemental keystone device and get in the Batmobile. You can drive left or right, and if you drive far enough, you return to your starting point, in front of the building.

Drive the Batmobile to the left. Don't skip the boost pads; if you drive on them, you can jump and grab valuable blue studs. Watch for the grow pad and stop when you find it (Figure 12.1). Move a minifig to the green (round) pad to give that character the Earth element. Press and hold X while using LJ to direct a stream of leaves at the grow pad. When you do this, a large hand grows and rescues another captured astronaut from the attackers in the sky.

FIGURE 12.1 Use the grow pad to save another captured astronaut.

Continue moving to the left and find another keystone device. Activate it and select the Location keystone. Find the white diamond to the left of the relic device (Figure 12.2), just beyond the structure with the orange light on top. Activate the white diamond (by repeatedly pressing B) to open a vortex and reveal Doc Brown's DeLorean, which flies in and destroys the structure, freeing another captured astronaut.

FIGURE 12.2 Find the white diamond to rescue another astronaut.

Continue moving left until you discover a new building. Inside the building, find another captured minifig and an object surrounded by stars. Change to Gandalf and use his Magic (B) to destroy the object and free another minifig.

Continue left. Along the way, you encounter a couple special areas that you can access using Hire-a-Hero to purchase a character temporarily with studs that you can use for 30 seconds or more, or additional minifigs with special abilities (but ignoring these won't prevent you from finishing the level). The Defender ship is destroyed. It crashes and starts a fire, trapping a minifig inside the flames. When the keystone device appears to the left of the flames, activate it and choose the Elemental keystone. Move a minifig to the blue pad to give that character Water element. Walk over the flames and rescue the fifth (and final) minifig.

The Defender ship appears and destroys the enemy ship holding the arcade coin; the coin falls to the ground. Before the heroes can grab the coin, however, the sneaky Blue Thief jumps out of a vortex, grabs the coin, and then goes back into a vortex. The heroes follow him in and find themselves in a dangerous-looking maze—they're in a classic video game called Gauntlet!

NOTE

What Is Defender?

Defender is a classic arcade game released in 1981. The player controlled a ship that could fly left or right; this is called a side-scroller game because the background and gameplay move left or right only. The player needed to shoot at aliens trying to capture astronauts from the planet's surface. You can read all about the history of Defender at https://en.wikipedia.org/wiki/Defender_(1981_video_game) or play a version of it online at http://www.classicgamesarcade.com/game/21638/defender.html.

Gauntlet Level 17

The heroes have been teleported to a maze and must find their way out. They are surrounded by all sorts of enemies, including ghosts, grunts, lobbers, and many more—and these enemies don't seem to stop! They are often spawned by piles of bones and nearby generators, which look like rectangular boxes (Figure 12.3), so keep your eyes open for them and destroy them as quickly as possible.

FIGURE 12.3   Destroy bones and generators to reduce enemy numbers.

Playing Gauntlet is a little different from working through the other worlds the heroes have encountered. Here are some play tips to keep in mind as the heroes attempt to locate Blue Thief and escape the maze in this part of the game:

- The heroes lose hearts if they get hit by the various monsters in this maze, but they can restore hearts by destroying food objects. The food object is a stack consisting of a chicken leg, a banana, and a loaf of bread stacked in a pile.

- The heroes need to collect keys that allow them to get through the metal doors that occasionally block their path. Try your best to grab any keys you spot.

- Destroy chests to collect studs—but be careful with this because chests are often used to block a horde of monsters from rushing at you. After you destroy a chest, run back to give yourself room to use your weapons. If you run far enough back, the enemies don't attack the other two characters, and you have a chance to plan your attack.

- Batman's Batarang and Gandalf's Magic can fire at monsters from a distance, destroying multiple monsters with one shot! It's fun to play Wyldstyle, but she can only fight up close and takes a lot of damage during fights, so watch for food objects to restore hearts.

- You often need to just rush into a room and fight as fast as possible, trying to destroy the generators and bones that spawn enemies. Keep an eye on your hearts and fight from a distance whenever possible.

- One particularly nasty enemy is immune to damage. It's Death, a black hooded figure. When you see Death, run and hide!

- Monsters often cannot run around corners, and you can take advantage of this and pull a few down at a time to destroy and then run back behind a wall to plan your next attack.

- Be on the lookout for the word EXIT on the ground; there's a vortex beneath it that allows you to escape the current maze.

- Blue Thief typically hides near the EXIT for a quick escape (Figure 12.4).

When you reach the EXIT, Blue Thief jumps in and escapes with the coin. Follow him into the vortex.

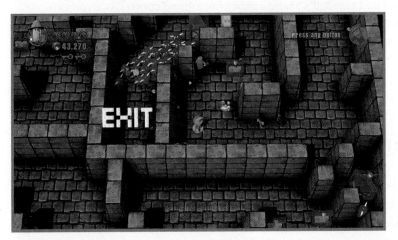

FIGURE 12.4   Blue Thief hides near the EXIT, holding the arcade coin.

> **NOTE**
>
> **What Is Gauntlet?**
>
> Gauntlet is a four-player video game that was released in 1984. Four players could take on the roles Warrior, Wizard, Thief, and Valkyrie, each with its own powers to fight enemies in the endless mazes. You can learn more about Gauntlet at https://en.wikipedia.org/wiki/Gauntlet_(1985_video_game) or try your hand at playing it online at http://www.sega.com/play/gauntlet-arcade-version/2892.

Gauntlet Level 28

You've got to get through one more level of Gauntlet, and here are some more tips for surviving and locating Blue Thief in this level:

- Whenever possible, explore the surrounding areas and get a look at what's beyond doors and at what's being blocked by chests and generators. Often you'll discover both a fast path to the EXIT and a longer path.
- The Batmobile can sometimes be used, but it is also occasionally blocked from entering certain areas. If you've upgraded the Batmobile (see the section "Upgrading Vehicles" in Appendix B, "Vehicles and Upgrades"), you can use its weapons to fire from a distance or even lay down mines. But don't depend on the Batmobile to get you through the entire level.

- Be careful around corners. Some enemies can fire through the narrow gap between wall blocks.
- Batman's Batarang and Gandalf's Magic cannot fire around corners, but you can sometimes fire at an angle without triggering a rush of enemies.
- Always target bones and generators first when entering a room. If you don't, enemies continue to spawn, and you take much more damage than usual.

When you finally track down Blue Thief, he once again manages to jump into a vortex to escape. Follow him and get ready for a different type of arcade game: Super Sprint!

Super Sprint Track 1

The heroes land in a completely new game: Super Sprint. Batman immediately recognizes the race track, and two accelerator switches appear. Drive the Batmobile onto one of the switches and get ready to race!

Super Sprint's rules are fairly easy:

- To win a race, you must be the first to finish three laps and cross the finish line before the other racers.
- Use the LJ to steer your vehicle.
- Watch out for hazards such as water, oil, and even a small tornado. These hazards cause your vehicle to spin and make you lose control momentarily.
- Collect blue studs whenever possible; they're worth 1,000 points each!
- There are often shortcuts (small gaps in the walls) that let you bypass corners and shave off a few seconds of your race time.
- Before each race, you get a quick look at the entire course. In case you miss it, Figure 12.5 shows the course for Super Sprint Track 1.

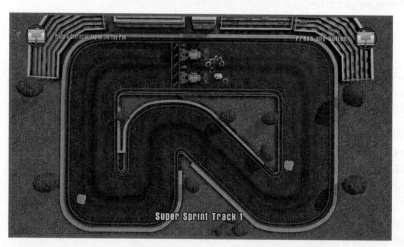

FIGURE 12.5 Super Sprint Track 1 is a simple track to follow.

Win the race, and you discover that you must race—and win—three more times.

Super Sprint Track 2, Track 3, and Track 4

The heroes must win races over three more tracks. Figures 12.6, 12.7, and 12.8 provide overhead views of these three tracks.

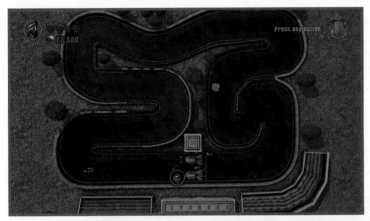

FIGURE 12.6   Super Sprint Track 2 overhead view.

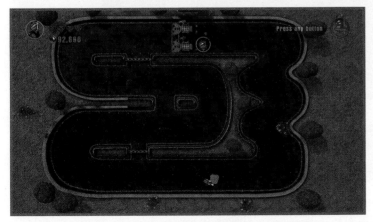

FIGURE 12.7   Super Sprint Track 3 overhead view.

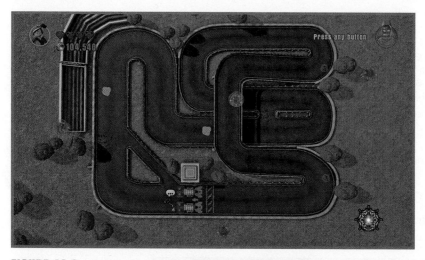

FIGURE 12.8 Super Sprint Track 4 overhead view.

After winning the final race, the heroes win the trophy—the arcade token! But before they can return to Vorton with their prize, Blue Thief races his own car in their direction, grabs the token, and enters a new vortex. Have the heroes jump in to follow him.

Robotron

Batman, Wyldstyle, and Gandalf find themselves in a large dark room (Figure 12.9). Suddenly, enemies appear all around them; welcome to the game called Robotron.

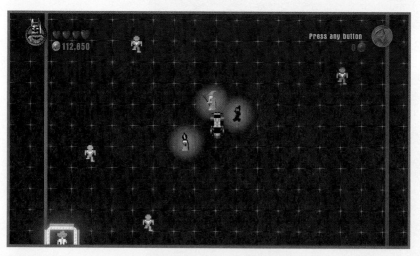

FIGURE 12.9 The heroes need to fight enemies that rush toward them.

The rules to Robotron are simple: Survive an endless wave of enemies who rush toward the heroes. Here are some tips on surviving Robotron:

- Never stop moving!
- Batman and Gandalf have advantages in this game: Batman can fling his Batarang at enemies from far away, and Gandalf can do the same with his Magic. Wyldstyle, on the other hand, must fight up close.
- After one wave of enemies is beaten, you have a few seconds to catch your breath before another wave appears.
- Be on the lookout for Blue Thief. When he appears, hit him three times with Batman's Batarang or Gandalf's Magic to defeat him and end the game.

NOTE

What Is Robotron?

Robotron is a single-player video game that was released in 1982. A player fought against an endless wave of robots by controlling movement with one joystick and controlling the direction of fire with a second joystick. You can read all about the original arcade game at https://en.wikipedia.org/wiki/Robotron:_2084 or play the original version online at https://archive.org/details/arcade_robotron.

When the heroes defeat Blue Thief and recover the arcade token, a vortex opens. Have them jump in and return to Vorton.

Up Next...

Scooby-Doo! Where are you? Up next, the heroes are going to follow the Scooby Gang into a haunted house and discover its secrets, take a ride in a mine cart, and fight off an ancient mummy. Solve the mystery and you'll be one step closer to defeating Lord Vortech.

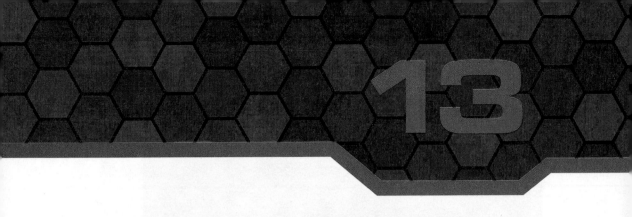

13

Mystery Mansion Mashup

Story Summary

- Find a way into the mansion and join the hunt for the diamond scarab
- Investigate the mansion's rooms for clues
- Meet the mummy and spot the diamond scarab
- Ride in a mine cart as you chase the mummy
- Battle the mummy under the big top tent

This chapter provides details on solving puzzles and defeating the mummy in the Scooby Doo Story Mode adventure.

A Mysterious Mansion

The heroes arrive at a spooky-looking house and observe Scooby Doo, Shaggy, Fred, Velma, and Daphne approaching the front door. The trio overhears something about the team looking for Uncle Arthur, a mummy, and an ancient diamond scarab. Sounds like a Foundation element! The trio hears Fred convince Shaggy and Scooby to go investigate the Big Tent Circus in the distance while he, Daphne, and Velma investigate the house.

When you reach the front doors of the house, the doors suddenly lock. Above the doors is a Chroma puzzle solution. Start looking for the power pads. To the right is a small shed that you should open by using Gandalf's Magic ability (B). The inside of the shed is very dark, so move Gandalf's minifig to the white flashing pad to use his Illuminate ability. When you see the orange handle, have Batman grab it with his Grapple ability (B) and reveal some bouncing parts. Assemble the parts (B) from the shed to repair the hose that waters the fountain on the front lawn and reveal a keystone device.

Activate the keystone device and select the Shift keystone device. Three portals open: a blue one in the gated garden to the left of the house, a yellow one on the roof, and a magenta one to the lower right of the house (which returns characters to the fountain).

Move a character through the blue portal. Clear out the debris to reveal the yellow power pad and open the gate. Next, move a character through the yellow portal to discover the blue power pad.

Activate the keystone device and select the Location keystone. Find the white diamond sitting in front of where the purple portal was located (Figure 13.1). Open up the diamond (by repeatedly pressing B), and a gardener jumps out and waters the plants, revealing the red power pad.

FIGURE 13.1 Find the red power pad by locating the white diamond.

Once all three power pads are revealed, activate the Chroma keystone and solve the Chroma puzzle (whose solution is located above the main doors) to open up the front doors. Remember that you can use the Shift keystone to open up a blue portal to get a character onto the roof where the blue power pad is located. Proceed into the house.

> ## NOTE
>
> **What Is Scooby-Doo?**
>
> Who doesn't love Scooby-Doo? Scooby and friends first hit television screens in 1969, with *Scooby-Doo, Where Are You?* Today, they continue to face mysteries in new shows such as *Mystery Incorporated* and *What's New, Scooby-Doo?* Throughout the years, Fred, Shaggy, Velma, Daphne, and Scooby-Doo have remained friends and traveled the world with the Mystery Machine van. You can learn all about Scooby and friends at https://en.wikipedia.org/wiki/Scooby-Doo.

A Good Old-Fashioned Investigation

Up on the second floor, Fred, Velma, and Daphne continue their investigation of the house. Daphne is captured behind a revolving wall, and the other two enter through a door that locks behind them. If you want to save your progress, look for the Game Save tool on the first floor.

TIP

A Hidden Minikit

Near the fireplace, destroy a few objects to reveal some bouncing parts. Use these parts to build (B) a grandfather clock. Use Gandalf's Magic (B) on the clock to reveal another secret LEGO minikit.

Move up to the second floor and then to the left. Use Gandalf's Magic on the candle hanging on the wall to open a hidden section of wall and reveal a keystone device. Activate the Elemental keystone and move a minifig to the blue pad to give that character the Water element. Use Water on the fireplace on the first floor (LJ and X) and use the parts in the fireplace to assemble (B) a Batarang target. Change to Gandalf and use his Magic to hang the target on the mechanical device at the top of the stairs to the right (Figure 13.2). Change to Batman and hit the target with his Batarang (B) to unlock the door. Go through the door and into the next room.

FIGURE 13.2 Activate this mechanical device to unlock the door.

Use the Game Save tool in this new room if you'd like to save your game's progress. Move to the right and destroy the giant crossbow in the center of the room, and then use the bouncing parts to build (B) a green handle that you can push and turn (Figure 13.3).

FIGURE 13.3 Push this rotating tool to stretch the skeleton on the table behind it.

Pushing and turning the green handle causes a skeleton in the far-right corner to stretch and shatter, revealing some bouncing parts. Use them (B) to build a handle that Wyldstyle can use to jump up and grab. Move her onto the purple target and double-jump (A) to grab the handle. A small cage to the left rises up, revealing a Batarang target. Hit the target to unlock the door, and then move through that door and into the next room. In this next room, there's a Game Save tool against the right wall. Use it if you wish to save your progress.

Use Batman's Grapple ability (B) on the orange handle on the left side of the room. The statue topples, revealing a blue pressure pad inside. A character must be standing on the pressure pad to activate it, so move a character (other than Batman) onto this pressure pad and then change back to Batman (Y).

Destroy the display cases in the center of the room and build another orange handle on the statue to the right. Use Batman's Grapple ability (B) to pull the orange handle and reveal another pressure pad.

If you move a character onto each of the pressure pads, a coffin drops from the ceiling and explodes into parts. Use these parts to build (B) a large hammer. Then have Gandalf use his Magic (B) to move the hammer into the white outline three times to break open the stone sarcophagus resting near the rear wall. Moving the hammer until the entire sarcophagus is broken reveals a keystone device.

Activate the Location keystone. Open the white diamond located near the pressure pad on the left side by repeatedly pressing B (Figure 13.4). A vortex opens, and Superman flies out and uses his laser vision to cut away the rear wall and reveal a secret room. When you move into this room, the mummy steals the diamond scarab and causes the heroes to fall down into a basement.

FIGURE 13.4 Open the diamond, and a friend appears to help you.

Mummy's Mine Cart Madness

In the basement, there's a large tube puzzle (Figure 13.5) on the rear wall. This tube puzzle is missing some sections, however, and you need to start looking for a large cube to insert (LJ and X) into the puzzle.

FIGURE 13.5 The tube puzzle has three clear boxes with buttons to push in each.

A Game Save tool is to the right of the staircase, so use it if you'd like to save your progress. Farther to the right are a bunch of LEGO boxes that you can destroy to reveal a keystone device.

TIP

A Valuable Purple Stud Is Hiding Nearby

There is a purple stud hidden behind the relic device—worth 10,000 points—so be sure to grab it!

Activate the Scale keystone and then move to the far right of the room, where you can see a vertical wall. Change to Wyldstyle and use her Acrobat ability to jump up to the platform above (LJ and A). When you see the large cube up here, move Wyldstyle's minifig to the green pad to make her large, and then press B to grab the block and jump or walk off the platform. You drop the block and need to quickly grab it again (B) and walk it to the tube puzzle. Place the block in the first space from the left by using LJ and X.

Move the Batman minifig to the orange pad to shrink that character. Move shrunken Batman into the tube puzzle and climb the first ladder. Do not move to the right until Wyldstyle (large character) has removed the block (B) and placed it in the second orange spot (LJ and X). Once the block is placed, change back to Batman and climb down and move to the right. Once again, have Wyldstyle grab the block (B) and move it (LJ and X) to the far-right orange space.

Change to Batman and move all the way to the highest clear box. When inside, move Batman's minifig to the white (round) pad to return to normal size, and then pull (B) the handle to unlock the door to the clear box on the far-right side.

Move Batman from inside the clear box back to the orange pad to shrink down. Climb down and change to Gandalf. Move Gandalf's minifig to the orange pad to shrink down. Walk Gandalf onto the orange square on the floor, and then move Gandalf's minifig to the green pad to make Gandalf large. A section of the tube puzzle pushes up, allowing Gandalf inside the tube puzzle to access the clear box on the far right. Enter that box and pull the handle (B) to unlock the door to the clear box on the far left.

Move Wyldstyle's minifig to the green pad to make her large, and then grab the clear box and move it back to the middle orange square in the tube puzzle (LJ and X). Then have Gandalf inside the tube puzzle climb up and enter the clear box on the left and pull the handle (B).

When the two mine carts rise from the floor, get all characters out of the tube puzzle. Enter the Batmobile (Y) and drive up onto one of the carts. When you enter the mine, you can see the mummy in a mine cart ahead of you.

You need to hit the mummy's cart with your own cart six times. To do this, watch for the four lights that appear at various times (Figure 13.6). Only one of the lights is green at a time, and the others are all red. The green light indicates which track you need to follow to bump the mummy. (For example, if the lights are red-red-green-red, you steer onto the third track from the left when the track splits.) You steer with the LJ, so when you see the lights and the track splits, get ready to move your cart to the appropriate track.

FIGURE 13.6 Watch the lights to figure out which track to follow to hit the mummy.

After you knock the mummy's mine cart six times, the chase ends as the mummy's cart is knocked into the big circus tent.

Unmasking the Villain

Inside the tent, the mummy uses the power of the diamond scarab. Fight off any enemies that attack you and watch out for the snake skeletons the mummy fires at you; they steal a heart if they hit you, so attack and jump to make it hard on them to hit you.

Move to the front-left corner of the tent and build a trampoline (B). Jump up and grab the blue bar (A), and then climb up on the platform and activate the Elemental keystone. Change to a different character (one that isn't standing near the keystone device) and move that character's minifig to the red pad to give that character the Fire element. Have that character melt the ice on top of the front-right platform. Switch back to the character at the keystone device and activate the Shift keystone to make three portals appear: the yellow portal on the platform where the ice was melted, the magenta portal on the platform that is currently on fire, and the blue portal on the front-left platform.

If you move a character through the yellow portal, the mummy rams this platform with his scarab vehicle and is temporarily stunned. Jump in the Batmobile and ram him to overturn the scarab vehicle and pin the mummy. Fight off any enemies that attack you, and use the bouncing parts near the scarab vehicle to build a grow pad.

Change back to the character near the keystone device, and activate the Elemental keystone. Move another minifig to the green pad to give that character the Earth element. Hit the grow pad with a blast of leaves (LJ and X), and a statue rises from the ground (Figure 13.7), falls onto the mummy, and releases him.

FIGURE 13.7   You need to build three grow pads to defeat the mummy.

Fight off any enemies that attack until the mummy again enters his scarab vehicle. Once the mummy is back in the vehicle, use the character near the keystone relic to activate the Shift keystone. This time, move another character through the blue portal. Once again, the mummy attacks that platform with his scarab vehicle. He stuns himself again, so get in the Batmobile and ram the scarab vehicle. While the scarab vehicle is upside down, use the bouncing parts near the vehicle to build another grow pad. Activate the Elemental keystone, give a character the Earth element, and hit the grow pad with another leaf blast (LJ and X). A large group of vines attack the mummy, but once again, he breaks free.

Fight off another wave of enemies until the mummy gets in his scarab vehicle one more time. This time, activate the Elemental keystone and give a character the Water element to put out the flames on the front-right platform. Once the flames are out, activate the Shift keystone and move a character through the magenta portal.

When the mummy rams the platform and stuns himself, hit his scarab vehicle with the Batmobile, build a grow pad with the bouncing parts, and hit it with a blast of leaves (LJ and X) after activating the Elemental keystone. A mini-volcano erupts, hitting the mummy with lava. The mummy drops the diamond scarab and is unmasked. What? It's not the Funfair owner? It's Lord Vortech!

In a short video scene, the heroes escape through a vortex so they can return another Foundation element to Vorton and continue their search for their missing friends and Lord Vortech.

Up Next...

When the heroes jump through the gateway again, they're going to find a world that's new to everyone, including you! This is Lord Vortech's realm, and in the distance you'll spot his citadel. Lots of puzzles await the heroes, who will have to cross a vast distance to reach that citadel.

14

Prime Time

Story Summary

- Discover Lord Vortech's Citadel in the distance
- Cross the endless seas to reach the Citadel
- Solve numerous puzzles to keep moving forward
- Get a glimpse of The Tri, Lord Vortech's ultimate weapon

This chapter provides details on solving puzzles and fighting Lord Vortech in his citadel in the Story Mode adventure.

Endless Sea of Possibilities

The heroes land on a vast purple surface, and they can see a large structure in the distance. Do not attempt to have them go back, left, or right.... If you fall off the structure, you lose all your hearts.

Begin moving forward, toward the large building, and the purple surface continues to expand. As you move forward, you see floating platforms that give you access to additional areas. A keystone device is to the right. Activate the Scale keystone, and then go back and climb up the structure on the left. It contains a tube puzzle that must be solved.

Move one character's minifig to the orange pad to make it small and another character's minifig to the green pad to make it big. Use the big character to pick up the large block (B) and place it (LJ and X) into the orange section on the far left of the tube puzzle. Have the shrunken character enter the tube puzzle, climb to the upper-left box, and push the button inside (B). This unlocks a door that leads into the other half of the tube puzzle.

Now move the shrunken character out of the box and into the tube puzzle to the left of the second orange space. Have the large character grab the big box (B) and place it in the second orange space (LJ and X). Move the shrunken character just to the left of the opened door; then move the large character's minifig to the orange pad (to shrink), and then move that character onto the orange spot on the ground. Next, move that character's minifig to the green box to grow it. A section of the tube puzzle pushes up, allowing the shrunken character to access the right side of the tube puzzle. Move the shrunken character into the box on the right, and push the button (B) to make the tops of the three floating cubes (between the tube puzzle on left and the keystone device on right) rotate. You will now see pressure pads (Figure 14.1) that you'll use shortly and can exit the tube puzzle.

FIGURE 14.1 These pressure pads must be triggered by the heroes.

TIP

Go After That Valuable Purple Stud

To get the purple stud on top of the tube puzzle, you need to move the shrunken character on top of the moving section before growing a character and pushing that section up. Then change the shrunken character to a large version, and you can jump up on top of the puzzle and grab that 10,000-point stud.

Move to the floating platform on the right and activate the Shift keystone. A portal opens above each of the floating cubes. Move a character through each of the portals and be sure to have him/her step on the pressure pad on each cube to activate it. When all three pressure pads have been stepped on, the Stay Puft Marshmallow Man appears, holding a platform on its head. A series of moving platforms appear near the keystone device. One is on fire, one has steam, and the other is filled with electricity.

You must activate the Elemental keystone first. Then select a pad and jump on the corresponding floating platform. (For example, move a character's minifig to the red pad to give it the Fire element, and then it will be safe to jump on the moving platform that has fire on it.)

You need to pick only one floating platform to jump on. Wait for it to get near the platform on top of Stay Puft's head, and then jump across and continue on the purple surface in the direction of the citadel in the distance. (The other two characters join you.)

You see a series of floating square platforms that act as walkways. When you move onto a square, it turns green or red. The red squares fall away, and the green squares remain in place, so if you're on a square that turns red, quickly jump back to the safe surface. You must find a safe path for crossing by locating all the green squares. Test squares all around you until you find a safe green square, and keep moving forward or in the direction of the citadel in the distance.

As you discover safe green squares, more floating square platforms appear, allowing you to move forward. Once you've crossed enough green squares, the solid purple platform appears again. Fight off any enemies that appear. When you've defeated the enemies, a new puzzle appears in the distance (Figure 14.2).

FIGURE 14.2 You must locate all three power pads to solve this puzzle.

Move down the center walkway and use Gandalf's Magic on the piece that falls to the ground. A door opens, revealing the yellow power pad and one part of a Chroma puzzle solution.

TIP

Write Down the Puzzle Map Solution

When the Chroma puzzle solution is revealed in pieces, you might want to write it down on a piece of paper so you don't have to return to the area if you forget what color and pad it references. For example, if you only see the left pad and it's blue, write down "left pad—blue."

Next, tackle the left side of the puzzle. Look carefully and notice that the walkway to the door on the left is covered in flames. Activate the Elemental keystone and move Gandalf to the red pad to give him the Fire element. Gandalf may safely walk over the left walkway, but watch for a moving section of the walkway that changes color (indicating that it's electrical); jump over this section as it moves from the rear of the walkway to the front. Move Gandalf to the second door and use his Magic to repair the door and reveal the blue power pad.

Next, move Gandalf to the right walkway. This one is covered in electricity, with a section of fire moving from back to front. Change Gandalf to the blue pad to give him the Electric element and then cross the walkway, jumping over the red fire section if it approaches. Use Gandalf's Magic to repair the door and reveal the red power pad and another piece of the Chroma puzzle solution.

Return to the keystone device and activate the Chroma keystone. When you solve the puzzle, you get steps that can be climbed to reach the top of the platform.

Watch for the visual clue that appears at this point, because the order of the arrows is important for solving the next challenge. A yellow arrow points first to the right floating box, then a magenta arrow points to far left box, and then a blue arrow points to the center box.

Move to the top of the platform and activate the Shift keystone. A character needs to move through the portals in the correct pattern. Remember the pattern of the arrows in the visual clue? First move a character through the yellow portal to activate the yellow button. Then move the same character through the magenta portal to activate the purple button. Finally, move the same character through the blue portal (Figure 14.3).

FIGURE 14.3 Trigger these three portals in the correct order.

Doc Brown's DeLorean races down a section of the purple surface and disappears. It leaves some parts that you can build into an accelerator switch, however. Build it and then drive the Batmobile on to it.

You now see another section of the green squares that must be crossed. Again, try to find the green ones and avoid or quickly jump back away from red. Find the safe green path that lets you continue moving in the direction of the large citadel. (Hint: The correct path isn't always straight toward the citadel.)

CAUTION

Only One Path Leads to the Citadel

There is a section of green that leads you to a special cracked wall that requires Hire-a-Hero or another minifig (other than Batman, Gandalf, or Wyldstyle). If you reach this point, you need to backtrack because you missed a green square that would have moved you in the direction of the large citadel.

Find your way across the square puzzle pathway, and you once again reach a large solid purple surface. Fight off all the enemies that attack, and a new tube puzzle appears in the distance (Figure 14.4). Go to it and activate the Scale keystone on the right side.

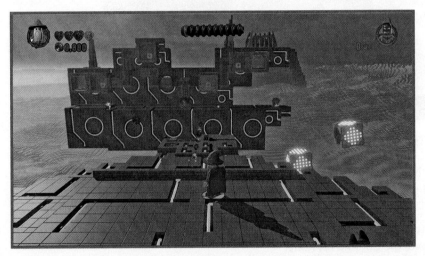

FIGURE 14.4 Solve this tube puzzle to get the power pads.

Move one minifig to the orange pad (to shrink) and another minifig to the green pad (to grow). Move the shrunken character into the tube puzzle, and then change to the large character. Grab the large box (B) and place it on the orange section just to the right of the entrance to the tube puzzle. The shrunken character can now climb up and move to the right into the clear box. Push the button in the clear box (B), and then continue moving into the next clear box (to the right) and push the button inside. The red power pad eventually drops to the surface.

Use the large character and remove the large block (B) and place it in the orange section to the left of the tube puzzle entrance (LJ and X). Change back to the shrunken character, and then move to the left but stop before reaching the section that must be raised up.

Move the large character's minifig to the orange pad (to make it small) and then move that character under the section to be raised (onto the orange section). Then move that character's minifig to the green pad to make it large and push up the missing section of the tube puzzle.

Change back to the small character in the tube puzzle and climb to the clear box at the very top of the puzzle. You now see a Chroma puzzle solution in the background to the left (Figure 14.5).

FIGURE 14.5   The Chroma puzzle solution floats to the left.

Inside the clear box, push the button (B) to unlock the left section of the tube puzzle. Climb back down and proceed left. Push the button in the clear box, and the yellow power pad is released.

A small set of stairs to the far left leads up to the blue power pad. Return to the keystone device and activate the Chroma keystone.

When you solve the Chroma puzzle, a pathway appears to the far right and you see revolving cubes. Pay attention to each cube because there is a color associated with each one. At the end of the pathway, when another keystone device appears, activate the Shift keystone.

You need to move a character to each cube while the button is on the bottom. If you move a character to a cube while the button is on the sides or top, the character falls and loses all hearts.

Activate the Shift keystone and move the character through a portal *only* when that color button is pointing down (Figure 14.6). The character exits a portal and activates a button. While the button is activated, the character is safe and cannot fall as the cube rotates.

FIGURE 14.6   Move through a portal only when the button is on the bottom of a cube.

Move the character through the other two portals when it is safe to do so. After all buttons have been activated, a pathway is added, but it's on fire. Activate the Elemental keystone and give a character the Fire element (by moving that minifig to the red pad). That character may now safely proceed forward.

Move forward until a solid purple platform appears. Then change to a different character and activate the Location keystone. Change back to the character who ran ahead, locate the white diamond (Figure 14.7), and open it (by repeatedly pressing B) to open a vortex. A section of the yellow brick road appears!

FIGURE 14.7   Find the white diamond and open it to keep moving forward.

Get in the Batmobile and drive onto the boost pad at the end of the small section of yellow brick road until you land on another section. Activate the Location keystone. This time, the white diamond is located on the new section of solid purple platform that appears. Open it, and a vortex provides three platforms for you to move up.

On the top of the platform are two launchers (Figure 14.8). If you step on one, you are launched closer to the large structure and land on another bit of solid purple platform.

FIGURE 14.8   Step on a launcher to get a little closer to the citadel.

TIP

A Minikit Is Nearby

You can change to Wyldstyle (by pressing and holding Y and selecting Wyldstyle if you didn't use her on the launcher) and use her Relic Scanner at the back of the platform to find a secret minikit.

Continue moving forward (toward the large citadel), and the puzzle squares appear. Once again, look for green (safe) squares and avoid the red ones. Find a safe way forward, and eventually more solid purple platform appears, connecting to the citadel. Fight off a swarm of enemies and then enter the citadel.

High-Tension Dimension

Fight off all the enemies that appear, and then cross to the large structure. When Lord Vortech's minions attack, fight them off and wait for the Elemental keystone to appear and then take on the powers you need to fight Lord Vortech.

This is a very difficult fight: Minions attack from the ground, and machines attack from the air. Keep moving and jumping, and wait to attack Lord Vortech with an Elemental power when he surrounds himself with ice or fire. If he surrounds himself with fire, hit him with water, and he falls and remains stunned. If he surrounds himself with ice, hit him with flames (LJ and X). After you successfully attack him three times, Lord Vortech is pulled toward a vortex. He builds a giant spider web (Figure 14.9) to keep him from falling into the vortex.

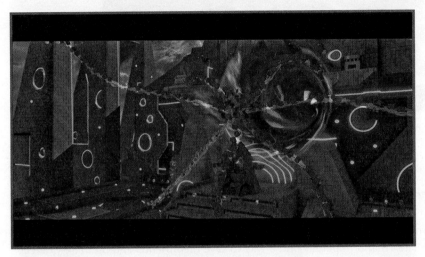

FIGURE 14.9 When Lord Vortech builds the web, look for a keystone device to appear soon.

X-PO sends in a Location keystone. Activate it and find the white diamond in the center of the room. When you activate the diamond, a Dalek appears and shoots at Lord Vortech, freeing him from the spider web. Lord Vortech shows the heroes their friends, trapped in cages, and then his villains rush in and capture the heroes.

X-PO informs the heroes that he is under attack, and then the missing Foundation elements appear. Lord Vortech combines them into a single Foundation element and uses it on the caged prisoners.

The Tri forms, with Robin, Metalbeard, and Frodo combining with other elements to form one massive enemy (Figure 14.10). Before The Tri can attack, Batman, Gandalf, and Wyldstyle escape through a vortex.

FIGURE 14.10   The Tri is Lord Vortech's ultimate weapon.

Up Next...

Lord Vortech has taken the hero friends—Robin, Frodo, and Metalbeard—and changed them into a horrible giant creature called The Tri! But there's still hope: Up next, the heroes will fight The Tri and hopefully find a way to save their friends and ultimately defeat Lord Vortech.

15

The End Is Tri

Story Summary

- Meet The Tri at Octan Tower
- Visit Middle Earth and face The Tri once again
- Rescue three friends from inside The Tri
- Discover the source of The Tri's power

This chapter provides details on solving puzzles and facing The Tri in the LEGO Movie Story Mode adventure.

Destruction of the Dimensions

The heroes have arrived at Octan Tower, but for some reason the gravity is out of whack. The Tri arrives, landing on the side of the building. It shoots a blast at the trio and destroys part of the building. The heroes must make their way across a debris-filled section of the wall (Figure 15.1) in order to take on The Tri, who waits on the opposite side of the building.

FIGURE 15.1 You must cross some dangerous areas to reach The Tri.

The Tri activates its own version of the Elemental powers, and then you can place the heroes' minifigs on the colored pads to give them powers. Change to Batman and carefully walk across the beam to the platform that has small fires on it. Fight any enemies that appear. If you destroy the various objects that appear, you can use them to build an orange handle on the bookcase. Then use Batman's Grapple ability on it (B) to tip the bookshelves over and reveal a flowerpot.

Change to Gandalf and destroy two flowerpots—one that is out in the open, and one that is revealed by Batman's Grapple ability. Then use the bouncing pieces to build a grow pad. Move Gandalf's minifig to the green (round) pad to give him the Earth element and hit the grow pad (LJ and X) with a blast of leaves. Three large vines grow (Figure 15.2), and the heroes can use them to cross over to the next section of the building.

FIGURE 15.2   You need these vines to cross to the next section of the building.

Cross to the next section and fight off any enemies that appear. Destroy the Octan Energy container at the back-left section of the platform and use the parts to create a Batarang target. Hit the target with the Batarang (B) to open up a panel in the floor to the right and reveal a handle. Pull the handle (B) to turn off the electricity that is surrounding the stairs to the left.

Place Batman's minifig on the red pad and move him up the stairs. The small fires will not hurt you.

A Hidden Minikit

To the far right of the walkway, hit the floating object on the right wall with your flames (LJ and X) until you see an orange handle. Lift Batman's minifig from the red pad and place it down again to disable the Fire element. Use Batman's Grapple ability on the handle (B) to reveal a secret LEGO minikit.

Lift Batman's minifig again and place it down on the red pad to gain the Fire ability again. Move to the right of the thin platform and jump across the flames to the next section of the platform. Destroy the objects here and use the bouncing parts to build a device that launches a line across (Figure 15.3) to the section of building where The Tri is located. Jump up (with Batman), grab the line, and slide across to the other side. The Tri opens up a vortex that pulls in the heroes.

FIGURE 15.3 Slide across the line to reach The Tri.

Worlds are starting to merge. The heroes find themselves in a mine, with The Tri taunting them in the distance from Sauron's tower. Fight off any enemies that attack. There is a Game Save tool here, so use it if you'd like to save your progress.

And Another Hidden Minikit

Move to the right and fight off any enemies that appear. Use Batman's Grapple ability on the orange handle to the left of the vertical wall to pull down another section of vertical wall that Wyldstyle can climb (A) to find a secret LEGO minikit.

The Tri's strange power is still in effect, and it appears to be similar to the Scale keystone's power. Move a minifig to the orange pad, and then move that shrunken character through the tiny door near the cage at the back of the mine.

Inside the cage is a handle you must push to raise a bucket—you'll have to move that minifig to the round pad to return to normal size to push the handle. Change to Gandalf and use his Magic on the bucket. Bouncing parts appear. Once again, use Gandalf's Magic to build a ladder that allows the heroes to move up. Jump on the clouds to get to the higher platform and fight off any enemies you find there.

Destroy any objects on this platform and use the bouncing parts to build a ladder. Take one character up the ladder, and then move that character's minifig to the orange pad to shrink it. Move that character onto the orange section on the floor, and then move that same character's minifig to the green pad to make it large so it can push up a section of the tube puzzle.

Change to a second character and drop down to the platform below. Move that character's minifig to the orange pad to shrink it, move onto the orange section, and then move that same minifig to the green pad to make it large so it can push up the other missing section of the tube puzzle.

Change to the third character and shrink him/her on the orange pad and then enter the tube puzzle. Climb up and into the clear box on the left and push the button (B) to open the door. Then have the shrunken character enter the center clear box and push a button inside the box (that requires moving that character's minifig to the round pad to return to normal size to push the button). The final door to the clear box, on the far right, opens. Before moving the shrunken character out of the middle clear box, change to the large character on the lower level and move that character up the ladder to the higher platform.

To the right of the upper platform is a large box. Move the large character (not the one still holding up a section of the tube puzzle) and pick up the box (B). After placing this first box in the first missing section, move to the right again (past the water wheel), until you find a second large box that you should pick up and place (LJ and X) in the second missing section. Move the shrunken character into the clear box, move that same character's minifig to the white (round) pad to return to normal size, and pull the handle (B).

A door opens beneath the tube puzzle, revealing an accelerator switch. Drive the Batmobile onto the switch to start the water wheel spinning.

Move a character onto one of the small sections of the water wheel. Being careful not to fall off, wait until the water wheel has spun and your character sees a walkway on the opposite side. Jump over (A) and run all the way to the far right and fight any enemies that appear.

TIP

And Yet Another Minikit

Move Gandalf's minifig to the white (round) pad to use his Illuminate power to light up the cave to reveal a secret LEGO piece.

Against the back wall is a wooden elevator. Move a character onto the wooden section to lift the elevator and reveal a new room (Figure 15.4). With The Tri watching from high above, defeat any enemies that appear.

FIGURE 15.4   Get on the elevator to move up and into this new room.

Explore this area carefully. To the left is one of three pieces of the puzzle map solution to a Chroma puzzle. Make note of the color and which pad it shows. Use Gandalf's Magic (B) to rotate the crank and raise up the blue pad used for an upcoming Chroma puzzle.

Beneath the caged skeleton are some bouncing parts. Use them to build an orange handle on the bottom of the cage. Then use Batman's Grapple ability on the crank (B) to reveal the red pad. Look behind the red pad to find the second piece of the Chroma puzzle map solution. Make a note of its color and which pad it shows (left, right, or round).

Change to Wyldstyle and move her onto the far-right purple target. Use LJ and A to jump up to the top of the platform to reveal the third piece of the puzzle map solution as well as the yellow pad.

When you solve the Chroma puzzle, a vortex appears at the top of the stairs, and once again, the heroes are pulled in.

NOTE

What Is *The LEGO Movie*?

The LEGO Movie, released in 2014 (with a sequel scheduled for 2018), introduced a number of new characters, including Wyldstyle and the bad guy Lord Business (seen in The Simpsons Story Mode adventure). In the movie, the hero, Emmet, discovers that the world he knows comes from the imagination of a young boy in "the real world." You can learn more about the movie at https://en.wikipedia.org/wiki/The_Lego_Movie.

Not-So-Nice Tri

High in the sky of Gotham are two vortices. LEGO parts from each vortex fly into the other. The heroes find themselves on the roof of a large skyscraper.

Move toward the middle of the skyscraper, and The Tri falls from a vortex and traps itself in the roof. When The Tri swings its sword, press A to jump and avoid it. Also watch for its freeze beam (shooting from Robin's eyes), which traces a path on the roof and freezes you like an ice cube.

Fight off enemies as they appear from numerous vortices that open. As objects fall to the left side of the building, destroy them. Use the bouncing parts to build a boost pad (Figure 15.5).

FIGURE 15.5 This boost pad gets you inside the giant robot called The Tri.

Drive the Batmobile onto the boost pad, and it blasts through the chest of The Tri and into a room with three boxes on the back wall protected by energy shields. Metalbeard is trapped in a strange energy cage to the far right. Near Metalbeard, examine the machine trapping him to find a Chroma puzzle map solution.

Change to Gandalf and use his Magic on the object on the back wall to reveal a Batarang target. Hit it with Batman's Batarang to reveal a red pad (for a Chroma puzzle) in the right side box. Each time you hit the Batarang target, one of the energy shields drops and gives you access to a different Chroma pad.

At the far left side of the back wall, destroy the two objects there and use the bouncing parts to build an orange handle for Batman to pull with his Grapple ability (B). When the vertical wall appears and while the energy shield is down, have Wyldstyle climb (LJ and A) to the top and access the yellow pad.

Solve the Chroma puzzle, and a handle appears near Metalbeard's energy cage. Pull the handle (B) to free Metalbeard, who is then pulled into a vortex and taken back to the Gateway on Vorton.

Move a character through the opening on the left side of the room to return to the rooftop. The Tri is angry, and after a few enemies attack, it slam its fist down and creates a pile of rubble. Change to Wyldstyle and move her to the purple target so she can use her Master Builder ability to build a giant cannon (Figure 15.6). Move to the cannon, press Y to jump on it, and use the LJ to aim it at a spot just beneath Frodo's head to reveal an orange handle.

FIGURE 15.6 Fire this cannon at The Tri to make an orange handle visible.

Change to Batman and use his Grapple ability on the orange handle (LJ and X) to pull him up and into a new room inside The Tri. There is a huge tube puzzle here to solve. Note that Frodo is being held prisoner inside another energy cage to the far right of the room.

Starting on the rear-left wall, use Batman's Grapple tool (B) on the orange handle high above to release a large box. Change to Gandalf and use his Magic high above the center of the tube puzzle to release a second large box. Change to Wyldstyle and use her Relic Scanner to the far right of the tube puzzle to locate another orange handle for Batman to pull (B) that releases a third large box.

Move a minifig to the green pad to make this character large. Place the three large boxes in the three missing spaces (orange squares) on the back wall. Use B to pick up a box and LJ and X to place it. Look carefully at the boxes and notice the orange lines on them. Each box works only in one particular location. The box with the two lines running horizontally must go in the center orange section. The box with the two lines running vertically must go in the far-right missing orange section, and the box with the curved orange lines must go in the far-left missing orange section.

Move a minifig to the orange pad to shrink this character. Move the character into the tube puzzle, climb up to the first large box on the left, and pull the handle. A green light on a device in the center of the room lights up (Figure 15.7).

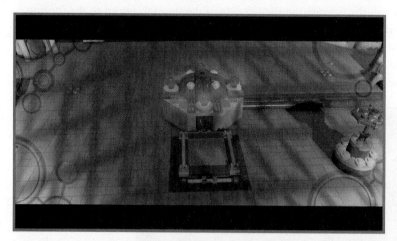

FIGURE 15.7   This device can free Frodo from the energy cage.

Move the minifigs for the two characters outside the tube puzzle to the orange pad to shrink them. Then move these two characters onto the small orange squares on the floor. Move these two minifigs to the green pad to make them large so they can push up the two missing sections of tube puzzle.

Now the shrunken character can move to the middle clear box. Pull the handle, and another green light appears on the strange device. Exit the center clear box and then move the shrunken character into the tube puzzle, using the small doors on the far right. In the top clear box, pull the handle until you see a third green light. Drop down to the clear box below and pull that handle until the fourth green light is lit. Then pull the handle (B) that appears.

Frodo is freed, and X-PO pulls him into a vortex and back to Vorton and the Gateway. Head back out the exit on the left to return to the rooftop.

Fight off another wave of enemies until The Tri drops some more debris in the center of the roof. Use those parts to build a new contraption aimed at The Tri. Hit the Batarang target on the back of the device to fire some projectiles just above The Tri's belt. A hole appears, along with some boxes beneath the hole that you can destroy and then use to build a bridge. Run across the bridge and enter The Tri's body again. (If you get really close, you can also try to jump across without the bridge, but it's risky!)

Robin is trapped by an energy cage to the far right. Move Gandalf to the right and use his Magic on the computer against the back wall. When you see a gold wall, move a character to the red pad to activate the Fire element, and then use LJ and X to cut around the outline on the wall (Figure 15.8).

FIGURE 15.8 Cut through the gold wall with the Fire element.

When you see a power coil, move a character to the blue pad to get the Electric element. Then hit the coil with electricity (LJ and X) to activate one of the blue lights on the machine in the center of the room.

Change to Wyldstyle and move her minifig to the red pad to give her the Fire element. She can now safely climb the stairs on the left side of the room. Move her to the purple target, and then jump up (A) to grab the blue handle and reveal another coil. Once again, give a character the Electric element and hit the coil with electricity to activate another blue light on the machine and raise a handle. Pull that handle to free Robin, who is then pulled into a vortex and returns safely to Vorton with Metalbeard and Frodo.

When a fire starts on the rear wall, move a character to the blue pad and put out the fire to reveal a passage deeper into The Tri's robotic body and a video scene starts.

Batman spots a single block from Lord Vortech's body, and hits it with his Batarang. Deep inside The Tri, the walls shake, the ground rumbles, and alarms are going off. The heroes jump into a vortex and join their friends back on Vorton, but they know defeating Lord Vortech is going to take a lot more help—so they open up vortices and pull in the Ghostbusters, Doctor Who, the Defender spaceship, GLaDOS (!!), and a repaired X-PO (thanks to The Doctor!). What will the heroes do next? They actually discuss it over coffee (see Figure 15.9)!

FIGURE 15.9 A coffee break before the final battle.

Up Next...

It's all come down to this—the final battle with Lord Vortech. You'll have to take all the skills you've mastered with the various keystone elements to defeat him, but you won't be alone. Batman, Wyldstyle, and Gandalf will have some friends they've helped out on this adventure show up to provide some much needed assistance. Time for the showdown....

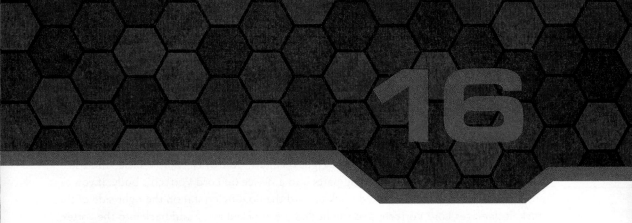

16

The Final Dimension

Story Summary

- Fight giant Vortech inside a vortex
- Arrive at the Citadel and start exploring
- Call upon allies to help destroy the Foundation element
- Finish the final battle against Lord Vortech

This chapter provides details on solving puzzles and defeating Lord Vortech in the Story Mode adventure.

Vortech's Descent

Lord Vortech brings the fight to the heroes before they can exit the newest vortex. Look at the top of the screen for the counter that shows three Location keystone icons (Figure 16.1). Keep an eye on Lord Vortech and move a character to intercept and grab the three Location keystones that come from his body.

FIGURE 16.1 You must catch several Location keystones.

Lord Vortech fights back. He'll trap you in a red portal, so move your character's minifig to different pads to escape. Avoid the lasers that shoot from his eyes if you can by using the LJ to fly around the screen, and wait for the heroes to land on Lord Vortech's giant body.

A vehicle lands, and enemies attack you. Fight them off, destroy the blue vehicle, and use Gandalf's Magic to turn the bouncing parts into a device on Lord Vortech's body. If you push this device over the checkered track toward the floating crystal on the right side of the track, it damages Lord Vortech, and the heroes are knocked away and back into the vortex.

Now the counter is showing five Location keystones. Move a character and grab five Location keystones as they fly from Lord Vortech's giant body. Avoid Lord Vortech's lasers again until the heroes land on the right side of Lord Vortech's chest. Destroy the flying black cube that attacks you, and use Wyldstyle's Relic Scanner to locate the bouncing parts needed to repair the checkered track on the left side of the screen (Figure 16.2).

FIGURE 16.2 Two objects must be pushed on checkered tracks.

Change to Gandalf, destroy the vehicle that lands, and fight off the enemies that come from it. Use those parts to build another object on the left side of the track and push it toward the crystal. Fight off enemies as they attack you.

Another flying black cube enemy appears near the right side of the screen. Use Batman's Grapple ability on the orange handle that is visible on the black cube. A glowing blue sphere is then visible inside the flying black cube. Hit the blue sphere three times with Batman's Batarang to destroy the cube, and then use the parts to build (B) a boost pad. Drive the Batmobile onto the pad to destroy the large vehicle behind it. Use the parts left over to build another device on the checkered track on the right side. Push this device toward the crystal, and Lord Vortech takes more damage. The heroes are again knocked off Lord Vortech and returned to the vortex.

This time, you need to collect seven Location keystones. Catch them as they fly from Lord Vortech's body. After you've got all seven, avoid four attacks from Lord Vortech's laser eyes. The heroes land on Lord Vortech's belt buckle.

Bane lands in a vehicle on the left and attacks the heroes. When you attack Bane, he grows larger. Move toward the machine on the far left when Bane is super-large, and Bane rushes at it and destroys it. Use its parts to build a device on the checkered track. Push it toward the crystal.

Wait until Bane is large again and move close to the second (middle) machine. Bane rams into the middle machine and destroys it. Use its parts to build a second machine on the checkered track and push it toward the crystal.

Move toward the third (last) machine and wait until giant Bane destroys it. Build a machine on the track with the remaining parts and push that machine toward the final crystal.

More damage is done to Lord Vortech, and the heroes are knocked off the belt buckle. When the heroes return to the vortex, The Doctor arrives in the TARDIS and gives Lord Vortech a solid hit that knocks him out of the vortex and back to his citadel. The giant Lord Vortech waits in his citadel for the heroes to arrive.

A Lord on Vorton

A Game Save tool is here in Lord Vortech's shattered citadel, so use it to save your progress if you like. Fight off any enemies that appear, and move to the right. A Shift keystone sits on a pedestal. If you activate it, three portals appear.

Change to Batman and move him through the blue portal. Use his Grapple ability (B) on the orange handle to tip the large box onto the track. Then push the box forward on the track until it rotates onto the next section of track. Change to Wyldstyle.

Move Wyldstyle through the magenta portal. Move her in front of the large box and use her Relic Scanner (B) to find parts to repair the track. Go behind the box and push it to the end of the track. The box falls and destroys the Shift keystone device. Use the parts to build an odd signaling device that frees the Defender spaceship and allows it to fly and fire at the Foundation element in the courtyard. Lord Vortech destroys part of the area of the citadel where the heroes were standing.

Move Batman to the end of the walkway that remains (to the right, where the Shift keystone device was located) and use his Grapple ability (B) to pull up to the floating platform that remains. Activate the Scale keystone on top of the platform.

TIP

A Hidden Minikit

Destroy the statue on the other piece of floating platform to find one of five secret LEGO minikits.

Move to the far-left front corner of the citadel and locate the tube puzzle. Move a minifig to green (to make it large) and have that character pick up the large clear box and place it in the orange missing section of the tube puzzle.

Move another minifig to the orange pad, and then move that shrunken character into the tube puzzle. Then shrink one other character's minifig (on the orange pad) and move his/her character onto the orange section of floor; then move that same character's minifig to the green pad and push up another missing section of the tube puzzle. Change to the shrunken character in the tube puzzle and move all the way to the far right, and push the button to reveal an Elemental keystone device.

Move back to the center of the citadel and change to Wyldstyle. Fight off any enemies that attack as you move her to the three locations (two on the left, one on the right) where she can use her Relic Scanner to locate the parts needed to build the three Chroma power pads.

Move to the rear-left corner of the citadel and fight any enemies that attack. Move Wyldstyle to the purple target and use her Master Builder ability on the three purple glowing parts to build a giant Ghostbusters Proton Pack (Figure 16.3) on the wall. Notice that the pack also has a Chroma puzzle solution on it!

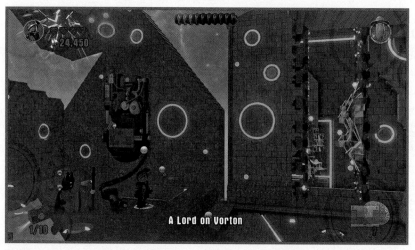

FIGURE 16.3 Build a giant Ghostbusters Proton Pack!

Cross over to the far-right rear corner of the citadel and move Wyldstyle onto the purple target. Jump up and grab the bar (A). Change to another character and move to the other handle to the right of Wyldstyle; then jump up and grab it (A).

You have opened up a dark area that can be lit only if you use Gandalf's Illuminate ability. Change to Gandalf and move into the dark area, and then move his minifig to the white pad. A device is running in the dark area. Destroy it and use the parts to build a power supply that activates a portal. GLaDOS appears and launches some missiles at the Foundation element in the citadel's courtyard. Lord Vortech is even angrier, and he destroys that section of his citadel.

Return to the Elemental keystone (at the front-left corner of the citadel) and activate it. Give a character the Fire element by moving that minifig to the red pad and then move to the back of the citadel and hit the ice covering the vertical wall (to the left of the throne—and look behind it and find a purple stud!) to melt it.

Change to Wyldstyle and climb up the vertical wall (LJ and A) until she is on top of the citadel's roof. Use her Acrobat ability to jump (LJ and A) to the opposite side of the roof, using the bars. Move Wyldstyle to the red pad to give her the Fire element and melt the ice covering the keystone device. When the device falls to the ground, jump down to it and activate the Chroma keystone.

If you solve the Chroma puzzle (using the Chroma puzzle solution on the Proton Pack on the rear-left wall), the Proton Pack activates and fires again at the Foundation element. Fight off any enemies that attack, and Lord Vortech destroys the rear-left section of the citadel.

Activate the Elemental keystone again and give a character the Fire element. Return to the entrance of the citadel. A flame device prevents you from exiting, but a hero with the Fire element can safely cross the entrance. Move out of the citadel and fight off any enemies that appear. Move the character's minifig to the green pad to give that character the Earth element, and hit the grow pad (Figure 16.4) with a blast of leaves (LJ and X). The Location keystone is revealed.

FIGURE 16.4 Hit the grow pad with a blast of leaves to reveal a keystone.

Activate the Location keystone by finding the white diamond at the citadel entrance, just behind the Game Save tool's original location.

Open the white diamond (by repeatedly pressing B), and a Dalek appears and fires on the Foundation element in the courtyard, destroying it. The citadel begins to collapse!

Final Face-off

In a video scene, the heroes will escape the collapsing citadel by grabbing a ride from the Defender spaceship, but Lord Vortech manages to knock them off, and they fall down to one remaining round section of the citadel courtyard (Figure 16.5). Fight off all the enemies that appear from the vortices.

FIGURE 16.5 It's the heroes versus giant Lord Vortech!

Run and jump to avoid Lord Vortech's laser eyes. When he attempts to drop a bunch of LEGO objects onto the heroes, use the debris left over to build a small device with an orange handle attached. Use Batman's Grapple ability (B) to pull on the handle. The device flips down, revealing a boost pad (Figure 16.6).

FIGURE 16.6 This boost pad gives you your first shot at Lord Vortech.

Get in the Batmobile and drive onto the boost pad to blast right at Lord Vortech's helmet and hurt him. When Lord Vortech tries to trap the heroes, move their minifigs to different pads to free them. If Lord Vortech tips the platform and tries to spill the heroes off, repeatedly press B to hold on tight until Lord Vortech releases the platform.

Fight off another wave of enemies and avoid the objects Lord Vortech drops onto the platform. Build a bunch of fireworks from the debris and use Gandalf's Magic on it to launch the fireworks at Lord Vortech. Hang on tight (by repeatedly pressing B) when Lord Vortech once again tips the platform (Figure 16.7), and then fight off another wave of enemies.

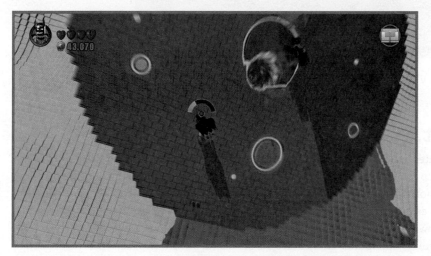

FIGURE 16.7 Hang on tight when Lord Vortech tips the platform.

When Lord Vortech dumps more debris onto the platform, change to Wyldstyle and use her Master Builder ability to build a large gun. Jump into the control seat (Y) and repeatedly press X to charge and fire the weapon at Lord Vortech.

Another short video begins, with a giant vortex appearing behind Lord Vortech. As he is pulled in, he screams "You cannot win!" The heroes are rescued by The Doctor. They jump in the TARDIS to follow Lord Vortech. The Doctor hands each of the three heroes a small object before releasing them out into the vortex.

Three vortices are open, and X-PO instructs the players to release their objects to create a prison for Lord Vortech. The heroes have won and defeated Lord Vortech—or have they (Figure 16.8)?

FIGURE 16.8   Who is that picking up this remaining block of Lord Vortech?

Up Next...

You've completed the Story mode, but you've still got so much fun stuff to do with LEGO Dimensions. Up next, you learn how to access more than a dozen LEGO worlds using the LEGO Dimensions minifigs. You learn how these worlds have plenty of areas that need repairs as well as how the worlds have many quests and secrets to be revealed. Once you understand how to enter a world, move around, and use the features found in each, you'll be ready for later chapters that go into deeper details for each world.

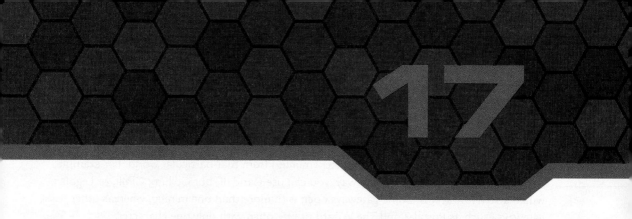

Adventure Worlds Overview

Worlds Summary

- Learn about the gateways and how to unlock them
- Get your bearings as you explore a world
- Learn how useful the map can really be
- Discover the Hire-a-Hero program
- Get all the answers about minikits, gold bricks, red bricks, and more

This chapter provides details on surviving, exploring, and solving the puzzles found in the adventure worlds.

The Gateways

You're not required to complete the Story mode before visiting any of the 14 worlds (but you do have to complete the actions covered in Chapter 2), so feel free to get on the elevator to the left of the gateway and head to the surface of Vorton. (Or change to a flying character and just fly up!)

On the surface of Vorton, you can find the various gateways spread out over two different levels. Starting on the lower level and moving left to right, look for the following gateways:

- Scooby-Doo
- DC Comics
- The LEGO Movie
- Midway Arcade (not covered in this book; available in March 2016)
- Back to the Future
- Jurassic World
- Mystery World (which you access with 24 gold bricks rather than with a particular minifig)

On the upper level, moving left to right, find these gateways:

- Chima
- The Simpsons
- The Lord of the Rings
- Ghostbusters
- Ninjago

- Portal 2
- The Wizard of Oz
- Doctor Who

To access a gateway, you need a character (minifig) from that particular world. For example, to access the Lord of the Rings gateway, you can use Gandalf, but Gollum, Gimli, or Legolas would also allow access. Some gateways open with more than one minifig, whereas other gateways—such as Portal 2 and The Wizard of Oz—open with only one character.

When you're standing near a gateway, if a minifig from that world is placed on one of the three pads, the gateway displays a spinning blue vortex in the background for a character to jump through. Use LJ to move your current character toward the open gateway and press A to jump in.

If you are standing near a gateway and one or more minifig faces appear in the center of the gateway (Figure 17.1), this means you have not placed a character from that world on the Toy Pad, and that gateway is currently not open.

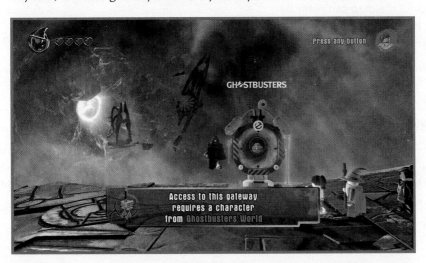

FIGURE 17.1   A gateway is not open if you see a minifig face on it.

Once you jump through a gateway, the character that unlocked that gateway is no longer required and may be removed from the Toy Pad. If you exit the world, however, you may not return to that world until a valid minifig is placed on the Toy Pad.

Getting Your Bearings

When you initially jump into a world, your character (and any other characters placed on the three pads) appear in front of the gateway. Turn around and take a look...the gateway is right behind you. If you get near it, it opens, and you can jump through and return to Vorton. (You can also press the Menu button and choose the Exit to Vorton option.)

There is no compass for the various worlds—no north, east, west, or south. However, when exiting the gateway, you are always facing away from it, so you can easily consider north to be the direction you are facing when you exit the gateway. South is behind you, west is to the left, and east is to the right.

TIP

Directions Are Based on a Gateway's Location

In upcoming chapters, I sometimes reference locations by saying "to the east of X" or "head north from Y" when giving directions. When I do this, I'm giving the direction with respect to the gateway.

As you travel around a world, the names of critical areas/locations appear at the bottom of the screen. For example, as you enter Munchkin Town, the words *Munchkin Town* appear (Figure 17.2) to let you know you've arrived in that area.

FIGURE 17.2 The names of important areas often appear when you arrive.

When you first enter a world, there is no correct direction or destination. Feel free to explore for a while. Head east or west or north. Just wander. Make note of any areas you enter (as the text briefly appears at the bottom of the screen) and just keep moving. If you get attacked, fight back! In the next couple sections, you'll learn how to spot special areas where you can receive quests (that is, missions to accept for rewards) or repair damaged areas (from Lord Vortech's attempted merging of the various LEGO worlds) or solve puzzles.

Many worlds have lakes and oceans. If you have a character with the Dive ability you can jump in, swim around, and see if there's anything interesting down there. (Hint: There always is.) (See Appendix A, "Character Skills," for a list of all the characters and their abilities.)

TIP

Don't Worry About Falling in the Water

When you're done swimming around, you might not always find a way to get out of the water. No problem! Press and hold Y and select and change to another character. As you continue your explorations, the character in the water just finds a way out and joins you shortly.

There are floating areas like the Temple in the Chima world (Figure 17.3), as well as areas beneath certain worlds that float in the clouds (such as Kansas in the Wizard of Oz world). These areas can often be reached only by a character who can fly. (Sometimes there are secret ways up or down, but they are rare.) Once you've got a flying character into these special areas, don't worry about your other characters; somehow, someway, they find their way there after a minute or so.

FIGURE 17.3 Some areas can be reached only by flying characters.

The Map

Once you've begun exploring a world, you'll probably want to start looking for things to do. Before you do that, you need to get familiar with that round circle in the lower-left corner of the screen. That's your map, and it can lead you to every secret a world holds.

The map is easy to use once you understand how it works. You always appear in the very center of it as a blue dot. (The second player appears as a green dot.) The direction you're facing is indicated by a small gray cone that projects out from the dot (Figure 17.4) and represents your field of view. As you turn in different directions, the cone moves, but the dot always remains in the center of the map.

FIGURE 17.4 The map shows the locations of gold bricks, quests, and more.

The map doesn't show you the buildings and various areas; instead, it indicates the locations of special features in the world, including these:

- **Gateways**—The gateway for the world is indicated on the map by an oversized blue circle.
- **Jukeboxes**—Each world has a jukebox that you can repair to change the background music in that world. Its icon is represented on the map by a musical note to help you find it when you want to change tunes.
- **Red bricks**—A single red brick is available in each world. The red brick icon appears randomly on the map at times until you obtain it. It's carried by the robot X-PO, but he's too fast to chase down. Once you've spotted him (or seen the red brick on the map), jump in a vehicle and follow him. When he spots you, a counter starts counting down, and when the timer runs out, X-PO disappears for a while. But if you manage to bump him before the counter stops, he drops the red brick. (Later in the chapter, you'll learn how to use that red brick.)
- **Races**—Scattered around each world are a number of race portals, which appear on the map as red rings with spikes (Figure 17.5). Some races are done on foot, while others require a vehicle; there are even some high in the air that require a flying character or vehicle. When you accomplish a race, you receive a gold brick or a large number of studs as a reward (depending on your speed). Some races do not become available until after you do a repair/upgrade on an area.

FIGURE 17.5 Participate in a race for some outstanding rewards.

- **Gold bricks**—A gold brick icon appears on the map to indicate the location of the brick itself. In some cases it's easy to find a gold brick (for example, in a chest that you must hit to open), but in other cases you must solve a puzzle (such as a Chroma puzzle). Sometimes, getting a gold brick requires a character's special ability (for example, Owen from Jurassic World can cut through vines). Each world has a large number of gold bricks to search for, so don't worry if you lack a certain character or can't reach a specific location; there are plenty of gold bricks scattered around that you will be able to find and access. (You also receive gold bricks for completing quests.)

- **Upgrade/repair locations**—Each world has a number of locales that can be repaired or upgraded. These locations are marked on the map with an icon of a crossed wrench and hammer. Move to the area where you see one of these icons and look for a character to speak to (by pressing B). Each repair or upgrade costs a certain number of studs, so be sure to keep an eye on your stud count and go hunting for studs when your count gets low. Press A to accept a repair/upgrade offer. When the repair or upgrade is complete, you often find a quest or a gold brick or another special surprise inside or nearby.

- **Quests**—On the map, a quest is represented by a small blue circle with a blue exclamation point (!) in the center (Figure 17.6). Move into such an area and look for a small white circle in front of a character. To accept the quest, speak to (B) that character. A quest remains active until it's solved or until you leave the world, but if you accept a second quest without having completed the first quest, the first quest is canceled, and you have to activate it again if you want to complete it. Some quests immediately award a gold brick when you finish them, while other quests require you to return to the character who offered the quest; if this happens, follow the blue arrow that appears on the screen to return to that character and get your reward. Some rewards require you to roam a world and collect objects; flashing red dots appear on the map to help you locate these objects. You can receive only one gold brick for each quest. However, some quests can be repeated if you leave and return to a world, but instead of getting a gold brick you receive a purple stud (worth 10,000 studs) when you complete the quest again. This is a great way to replenish your studs after making a lot of upgrades or repairs.

FIGURE 17.6 Quests are identified as small exclamation points on the map.

TIP

Pay Attention to the Up/Down Arrows

An arrow appearing over a gold brick, quest, or repair/upgrade icon indicates that the location specified is above or below you. If you're standing on top of a gold brick icon on the map, for example, and can't find the brick, look carefully at the gold brick icon. An arrow pointing up means its location is above you, while an arrow pointing down means the brick is beneath you. Arrows also appear over quest and repair/upgrade locations.

Hire-a-Hero

There are currently 44 characters that you can purchase and control in the LEGO Dimensions worlds. While it would be great to own them all, that's not required. If you encounter a puzzle or a quest or another task that requires a character you do not own, you frequently get the Hire-a-Hero option (Figure 17.7).

FIGURE 17.7 The Hire-a-Hero option can give you quick access to a character.

When the Hire-a-Hero option appears, you can spend a certain number of studs to temporarily gain access to the character displayed. The first time you use this feature, that character costs 50,000 studs for 30 seconds of use. The second time it is more expensive: 75,000 studs. A third use costs you 125,000 studs, and any further purchases of that particular character cost 250,000 studs. These purchases are not world specific: If you change worlds and need to use the Hire-a-Hero option for the same character but in a different world, the stud cost doesn't reset; for example, if you spend 50,000 in the Chima world to hire Owen and then change to The Wizard of Oz world and hire Owen again, it costs you 75,000 studs.

Despite the cost, the Hire-a-Hero option can really get you out of a bind when you don't want to purchase a character's minifig from the store.

CAUTION

The Hire-a-Hero Small Print

If a Hire-a-Hero option doesn't appear for a task, it most likely means that you already own a character or an upgraded vehicle that possesses the skill or ability needed to solve the puzzle. Check all your minifigs as well as the vehicles because you probably already have the means to solve the puzzle! Also, keep in mind that to solve some puzzles, you need multiple characters. In addition, Hire-a-Hero doesn't allow you to purchase vehicles and special items.

Studs, Gold Bricks, and Red Bricks

There are three things you need to collect as you play in the Story mode and explore the adventure worlds: studs, gold bricks, and red bricks:

- **Studs**—This is the currency of the LEGO Dimensions worlds. You need lots of studs to upgrade vehicles, make repairs and upgrades, and buy special abilities offered through red bricks. Plain gray studs on the screen are worth 10 studs each to your stud total (score), gold studs are worth 100 studs each, blue studs are worth 1,000 studs each, and the rare purple studs are worth 10,000 studs each! When you spot blue or purple studs, always grab them!

- **Gold bricks**—There are 480 gold bricks to collect in LEGO Dimensions, scattered all over the various adventure worlds as well as in the Story mode. Like studs, gold bricks can be used to upgrade vehicles and gadgets as well as pay for entry into the Mystery Dimension (see Chapter 35).

- **Red bricks**—There are more than a dozen red bricks to discover in LEGO Dimensions. X-PO holds them all, and he runs from you if you get too close to him. Chase him down with a vehicle and obtain a red brick from each of the various adventure worlds. A red brick unlocks a special ability, depending on where you found it. Press the Menu button, choose Extras, and search through the 14 red bricks (Figure 17.8) to see which special abilities you can purchase with studs. Table 17.1 lists the special abilities that you can unlock.

FIGURE 17.8 Purchase a red brick special ability from the Extras menu.

Table 17.1   Abilities You Can Unlock with Red Bricks

Ability	Stud Cost	Description
Dwarf's Bounty	1,000,000 studs	Doubles the value of each stud
Villain Disguises	500,000 studs	Gives every major level boss a disguise
All Hail King Homer	100,000 studs	Turns your character gold and allows you to detect gold bricks
The Way of the Brick	100,000 studs	Allows you to perform build-its faster
Master of CHI	500,000 studs	Lets you gain more CHI
DC Captions	500,000 studs	Gives characters comic book–style captions
Faulty Flux Drive	500,000 studs	Gives vehicles Back to the Future special effects
Rare Artefact Detector (R.A.D.)	200,000 studs	Detect minikits using onscreen arrows that point in the direction of kits
Aperture Enrichment Detector	200,000 studs	Locates quests
Pack Hunter	500,000 studs	Adds dino hats to enemies
Sound of the Doctor	500,000 studs	Replaces all music with Doctor Who theme tracks
We're Off to See the Wizard	500,000 studs	Plays Wizard of Oz music
Full Minifigure Apparition	500,000 studs	Makes a character into a semi-transparent ghost
8-Bit Music	500,000 studs	Plays an 8-bit music track

TIP

Redo Quests for Purple Studs

If you find yourself running low on studs at any time, revisit worlds and look for the purple studs on the maps. Go to them to redo quests and earn purple studs worth 10,000 studs each. You might also make a note where you find purple studs in different worlds (often hidden) so you can return with a flying character and zoom around and collect them quickly.

Have Fun

The adventure worlds are pure fun. Unlike with the Story mode levels, you can move back and forth between adventure worlds without needing to have finished one world or another.

Have fun exploring, and don't get frustrated if you can't locate a quest or solve a particular puzzle right away. Just move on to something else and come back later. Don't forget that the Hire-a-Hero option is available for most puzzles, and keep an eye on the map (and the up and down arrows) to locate quests, repairs/upgrades, and gold bricks.

Up Next...

It's time to learn about one of the 14 worlds! While you can visit worlds in any order you like (as long as you have a required minifig to unlock that world), this book covers them in left to right order starting with the lower level and then moving to the upper level. So that means it's time for the Scooby-Doo world, where you'll help Fred, Velma, Daphne, Shaggy, and Scooby-Doo investigate some spooky locations, solve some puzzles, uncover a trap or two, and ultimately save the day.

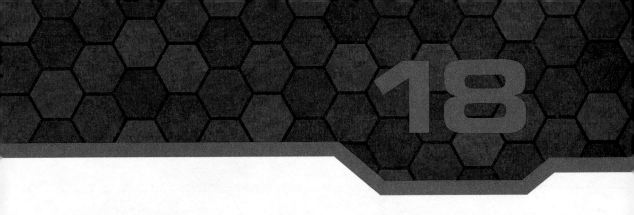

Scooby-Doo™ World

World Summary

- Gold bricks to discover: 27
- Locations to repair/upgrade: 5
- Red bricks to discover: 1
- Quests/mysteries to solve: 5
- Requires Scooby-Doo or Shaggy minifig to access

This chapter provides details on the Scooby-Doo world. This world's gateway is found on the lower-left level of Vorton.

Areas to Explore

When visitors arrive through the gateway, a number of areas can be used to help navigate (Figure 18.1). Look to the east of the gateway, and in the distance you see an abandoned lighthouse. There is a steep pathway you can follow all the way to the top. Beneath the lighthouse are some cave tunnels that are worth exploring.

FIGURE 18.1 There are a lot of places to explore on this spooky island.

Northeast of the lighthouse is the haunted mansion, and a curving path leads up to it. The path behind the lighthouse runs behind the house but does not give access to the mansion. To the right of the mansion is a small shed that you should not ignore.

TIP

The Valuable Returning Purple Studs

You can use Shaggy's flashlight (or Gandalf's Illuminate ability) to provide light inside the shed. Hidden in here is a purple stud worth 10,000 points. Even better, this purple stud reappears (in the shed) every time you leave and return to Scooby-Doo world. You'll find that purple studs in other worlds also reappear when you leave and return, so use this as a great way to increase your stud count.

Farther north of the mansion is the cemetery, and you can reach it by following the path to the right of the lighthouse that runs behind the mansion. There is another entrance to the cemetery from the front.

When you exit the gateway, directly ahead you see the fairgrounds—a great place to collect gold studs! In addition to finding a lot of gold studs, you can find some boost pads that can help you get a vehicle onto the rollercoaster track for some fun driving.

Locations to Repair/Upgrade

Be on the lookout for five floating ghosts. Each ghost offers (for a price) to upgrade or repair an area that then offers extras such as gold bricks. These are some of the repairs you can make by providing the ghosts with proper payment:

- **Restore the lighthouse**—Doing this adds a few surprises to the top of the lighthouse as well as a lot more studs to collect. The cost to restore the lighthouse is 70,000 studs.
- **Repair the haunted house**—If you make upgrades, you discover a few hidden gold bricks as well as add additional areas on the roof to explore and open up a few of the quests. The cost to repair the haunted house is 80,000 studs.
- **Restore the fairgrounds tent**—This upgrade makes available a locked area that contains a gold brick. The cost to restore the tent is 40,000 studs.
- **Restore the mausoleum**—This upgrade restores a special area in the cemetery that requires a character who can capture ghosts. The cost of this upgrade is 40,000 studs.
- **Unlock the jukebox** (Figure 18.2)—Doing this enables you to change the music playing in the background as you explore. Use X to change the music. The cost of the jukebox is 25,000 studs.

FIGURE 18.2 The jukebox lets you change the background music.

Available Quests

This world offers five quests. Three of them must be done in a specific order; the other two can be done at any time. These are the five quests:

- **Help Scooby-Doo's parents get to their hotel (1 of 3)**—After exiting the gateway, proceed straight ahead, toward the fairgrounds. Scooby's parents are on the left side, just as you enter the fair, and they want to get to the haunted mansion. Help them get there and fight off any skeletons or ghosts that attack. You can follow Scooby's parents by moving in the direction of the blue pointer arrow that appears onscreen (Figure 18.3). You are rewarded with a gold brick when they reach the mansion.

FIGURE 18.3 Escort Scooby-Doo's parents to the haunted mansion.

■ **Help Daphne locate Fred, Velma, and Scooby's parents (2 of 3)**—Once Scooby's parents have arrived at the mansion, Daphne asks for help in locating Fred, Velma, and Scooby's parents. There are a lot of hidden areas in and around the house, and you need to use Scooby's nose to look for clues (Figure 18.4) as well as Wyldstyle's Acrobat ability and Relic Scanner. Start by changing to Scooby-Doo. Press B and follow the clues into the house that lead to two different locations. One is upstairs and requires Wyldstyle's Relic Scanner (B) to locate a handle. Pull it and approach and release Velma (B). Downstairs, Scooby-Doo uncovers another handle that reveals his dad.

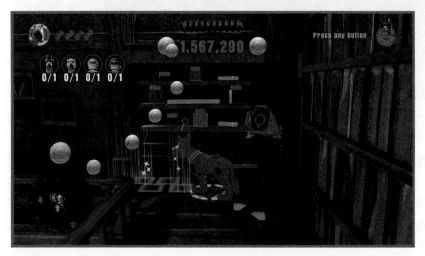

FIGURE 18.4 Scooby sniffs for clues to locate lost friends.

Now change to Wyldstyle and go outside the house. Move around the house until you find a vertical wall that Wyldstyle can climb. From there, use Wyldstyle's Acrobat ability to carefully jump and climb across various small platforms and metal beams. Press B when you're above Scooby-Doo's mom, and she returns to Daphne. Continue jumping and climbing until you spot another vertical wall. Beneath that vertical wall are a few small platforms. Drop down onto them and cross over two wooden planks to find Fred (Figure 18.5); press B to send him back to Daphne. Return to Daphne, and you are rewarded with a gold brick.

FIGURE 18.5 Fred is high up on the haunted mansion's roof.

- **Help Fred locate Old Man Robert's lost treasure (3 of 3)**—After you help Daphne locate her four lost friends, look for Fred on the stone path that runs between the lighthouse and the cemetery. Change to Scooby-Doo and use his nose (B) to follow a trail that leads back to the haunted mansion. Inside, Scooby locates a pressure plate on the upper floor. Stand on it to reveal a hidden handle on the first floor. Pull the handle, and Fred falls down a tunnel to a hidden area beneath the mansion. Jump down into the tunnel. Use Shaggy's flashlight to light up the inside of one of the ships; push the button inside the ship to release a number of ghosts. When you defeat the ghosts, bars lift on another ship and reveal a second button. Push the button to open a gate and give Fred access to the treasure (Figure 18.6). Your reward is another gold brick!

FIGURE 18.6 Help Fred find Old Man Robert's treasure.

Move Wyldstyle to the debris blocking the cave entrance and use her Relic Scanner. When an orange handle is revealed, have Batman use it to pull the debris down (B) using his Grapple ability and reveal the way out of the cave.

- **Help Velma find her glasses**—Inside the caverns beneath the lighthouse, Velma is looking for her glasses—not the pair she's wearing, but the 30 pairs she's lost over the years. Help her find all 30 pairs of glasses, and you gain another gold brick. These glasses are scattered all over the island, as well as under it. You have to look everywhere, including beneath the water, to find them all.

- **Help Velma explore the mausoleum**—After you restore the mausoleum in the cemetery, Velma asks for your help exploring the area. Unfortunately, the mausoleum is infested with ghosts and can be cleared only by a professional who has ghost-capturing experience. Of course, this requires a Ghostbuster minifig, and if you can manage to clear the mausoleum, you gain another gold brick.

Don't Miss

The Scooby-Doo world has lots of hidden areas and secrets to discover. The following are just a few to get you started:

- **The lost beach**—Somewhere on the island is a lost beach. There isn't a path or walkway to reach it, so you must swim to find it. Jump into the water and follow the shoreline around the island.... You'll know the lost beach when you see it. A couple keystone devices there help you solve a puzzle and recover a gold brick.

- **The sunken sub**—Beneath the waves are a number of structures you can explore. Keep an eye out for a sunken submarine, and when you find it, explore the area and collect a bunch of studs.

- **The cemetery**—If you enjoyed the keystone puzzles in the Story Mode, you'll find a fun Chroma puzzle to solve in the cemetery for a gold brick. Two of the color pads are easy to find, but the third will require Wyldstyle's Acrobat ability.

Up Next...

The DC Comics world's gateway is one of three worlds that's always available to you because you already own the Batman minifig that unlocks this world. Step through that gate and get ready to explore what happened after Lord Vortech tried to merge the various LEGO worlds. Superman's Metropolis and Batman's Gotham City have been joined, and there's a lot of work to do to repair the city. The citizens there can use your help.

DC Comics™ World

World Summary

- Gold bricks to discover: 28
- Locations to repair/upgrade: 9
- Red bricks to discover: 1
- Quests/mysteries to solve: 5
- Requires Batman, Superman, Wonder Woman, Aquaman, Joker, Bane, Harley Quinn, or Cyborg minifig to access

This chapter provides details on exploring the DC Comics world and finding quests to complete, special objects to collect, and characters to visit and fight alongside. This world's gateway is found on the lower-left level of Vorton (to the right of the Scooby-Doo gateway and to the left of the gateway for The LEGO Movie).

Areas to Explore

The destruction caused by Lord Vortech attempting to merge the various LEGO worlds appears to have merged parts of Gotham City with Metropolis. A lot of areas need repairs, so take a look around to see how you can help.

When you exit the gateway, to the far right is the Daily Planet. If you know anything about the Daily Planet, you probably know that it has a very large globe on the top of the building. That globe is now missing.

Look behind you, and you can see the futuristic shape of the LexCorp Building. Wayne Tower is almost directly ahead and to the left as you exit the gateway (it has glowing blue lights around its base), and the green toxic glow of Ace Chemicals is visible in the distance to the north. The dark streets of Gotham are not visible from the gateway, but you can find them west of Ace Chemical. Wayne Manor (Figure 19.1) sits between downtown Gotham and a nasty chemical spill at Ace Chemical, but you can probably find it easy enough due to the music and lights from the party that Bruce Wayne is throwing.

FIGURE 19.1 Looks like there may be a party at Wayne Manor!

Beneath Wayne Manor lies The Bat Cave (Figure 19.2). The manor is locked, so you need to find another way in. Jump down and examine the area around the waterfall behind and below Wayne Manor and look for a large door that only Batman can open. Inside the cave is a Chroma puzzle that is definitely worth solving if you can locate all three pads!

FIGURE 19.2 The Bat Cave can be found beneath Wayne Manor.

To the far west (and difficult to see from the gateway exit) is a red building known as Arkham Asylum. It's where Gotham puts its dangerous criminals, so be careful when you're in there. Pay a visit and look for a large maze you can solve by using an Elemental keystone device (Figure 19.3). Be careful to avoid the spike traps and look for handles to pull to open doors and get into closed areas.

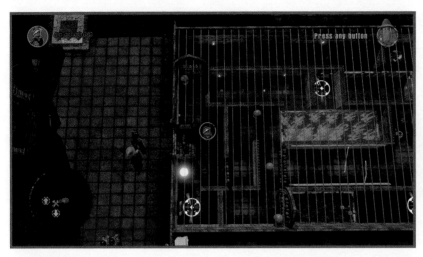

FIGURE 19.3   Arkham Asylum is one of the most dangerous places in the city.

TIP

Don't Ignore Vehicles

There are a lot of vehicles in this world. Destroy them to collect a lot of gold studs. Each destroyed car provides at least 3,000 studs.

Locations to Repair/Upgrade

Be on the lookout for nine areas that can be upgraded or repaired for a price. Following are the areas, which offer extras such as gold bricks or extra studs:

- **Restore the penguin hideout**—The hideout can be accessed only with a character who has the ability to melt ice. The cost to restore the hideout is 20,000 studs.
- **Restore the Superman statue**—The cost to repair the statue is 5,000 studs. There's no gold brick reward, but the statue looks great.
- **Restore the arctic world**—This upgrade makes available a locked area that has a gold brick inside. Wyldstyle can climb up and use her Relic Scanner to locate a cache of blue studs. The cost to restore this world is 90,000 studs.
- **Fund the Wayne Manor party**—This upgrade costs 60,000 studs, but it unlocks a few gold bricks you can discover by wandering around the mansion. For example, you can find one in the puzzle by pushing blocks on the checkered track (Figure 19.4).

FIGURE 19.4   You can find a gold brick if you solve this simple push puzzle.

- **Restore the Bat Signal**—For 90,000 studs, you can put the Bat Signal back in the sky. When the Bat Signal is fixed, Commissioner Gordon has a special quest for you, so look for him on top of a tall building in the center of Gotham.
- **Unlock the jukebox**—One of the inmates at Arkham Asylum can give you access to the jukebox. For 25,000 studs, you can unlock the jukebox and select the background music that plays by pressing X.
- **Restore the Daily Planet**—High up on the very top floor of the Daily Planet, you can pay 90,000 studs to repair the building. There's no reward, but Clark Kent is sure to appreciate the repair and mention it to Superman.
- **Restore the Atlantis building**—Deep under Gotham is the city of Atlantis. Find one of the divers and pay 90,000 studs to restore one of the larger buildings. With the right character, you might also gain entrance to the restored building and find a gold brick.
- **Fund the school of fish**—For 5,000 studs, you can make one more upgrade in Atlantis and provide a much-needed education for underwater fish.

Available Quests

Four quests are offered in this world:

- **Follow Lois Lane and Jimmy Olsen**—Speak to Lois Lane as she investigates the damage Lord Vortech has done to Gotham City. Follow her on a tour of the city and fight off any enemies that attack. Protect Lois Lane and Jimmy Olsen, and you're rewarded with a gold brick.

TIP

Quests Can Be Repeated

If you return to a world and assist with the same quest again, you're rewarded with a purple stud—worth 10,000 points! You can find repeatable quests by looking for purple studs on the map.

- **Help clean up the streets with The Flash**—The Flash needs help ridding Gotham of criminals (Figure 19.5). Try to keep up with him and fight off the bad guys to earn a gold brick.

FIGURE 19.5 Run with The Flash and help him capture escaped criminals.

- **Help Commissioner Gordon**—Apparently, an armored truck was destroyed, and the riches have been scattered all over Gotham. Accept this mission, and you need to hunt down a gold brick, a bag of jewels, and some cash. Find these three items and get a gold brick. Flashing red circles on the radar map help you find them.
- **Help Perry White's investigation**—Perry sent three reporters to investigate rumors about the city of Atlantis in the ocean. Hunt down all three reporters to get a reward. Don't look in the city but instead head underwater (Figure 19.6) and use the map to find the three flashing markers that help you locate the reporters.

FIGURE 19.6 Find the three lost reporters underwater in the city of Atlantis.

Don't Miss Out on These Areas

The DC Comics world has lots of hidden areas and secrets to discover. Following are just a few to get you started:

- **ACE Chemical**—Take a tour of the damage done from toxic waste at ACE Chemical. You need a character who can help clean up toxic waste for this nasty locale.
- **LexCorp**—This is the least-damaged building in Gotham City. With the right hero, you might be able to get inside and find a gold brick.
- **A Portal 2 Puzzle**—High above the streets of Gotham is a puzzle you can solve, but it does require a Companion Cube. Maybe GLaDOS will loan you one.

Up Next...

After your visit to the dark streets of Gotham City, it's time to lighten the mood with a visit to the LEGO Movie world! Everything is awesome in this world—bright, colorful, fun! Well, maybe not everything. There are still some bad guys to defeat, and plenty of repairs and upgrades are needed to get this world back to normal after Lord Vortech's damage. You already own the Wyldstyle minifig, so this world's gateway is open and ready for you to jump in!

The LEGO® Movie World

World Summary

- Gold bricks to discover: 28
- Locations to repair/upgrade: 5
- Red bricks to discover: 1
- Quests/mysteries to solve: 5
- Requires Wyldstyle, Emmet, Astronaut, Bad Cop or Rainbow Kitty minifig to access

This chapter provides details on The LEGO Movie open world. This world's gateway is found on the lower-left level of Vorton (to the right of the DC Comics gateway).

Areas to Explore

Welcome to Bricksburg and the surrounding areas (Figure 20.1)! Lord Vortech's attempt at merging the LEGO worlds has done some damage here, as it has in other worlds, so explore every corner to see what kind of assistance you can provide. As soon as you exit the gateway, look to the east, and you see The Wild West (but no explanation for why it's not to the west). To the far southwest is the Octan Tower, which reaches high into the sky.

FIGURE 20.1 The Wicked Witch's view of The LEGO Movie world from her broom.

To the northeast lies Middle Zealand and a huge castle that's fun to explore. Unikitty can be found high up in the clouds above the castle, but if you don't have a character or vehicle that can fly, you need to find another way to get up into the clouds.

To the northwest are skyscrapers as well as a number of buildings that are under construction or that need repair. Keep an eye out for various hazards, such as the lava lake in the middle of city. And definitely spend some time in the water if you have a character who can swim. There are some great areas to explore beneath the city.

Bricksburg has more studs to discover than you can imagine. They're everywhere, including just floating above the roads, resting on rooftops, and circling the entire city.

Also notice that there are a lot of statues dedicated to Lord Business. Feel free to demolish them if you have a character who can destroy gold structures (refer to Appendix A, "Character Abilities," for a complete list of characters and their abilities). Nobody will miss them.

Locations to Repair/Upgrade

There are five areas of the damaged city you should search for and upgrade or repair. Remember, some repairs and upgrades will provide additional quests while others provide puzzles to solve or bonus studs to collect:

- **Restore the saloon**—For 25,000 studs, you can have a construction worker bring the saloon back to life. This building is filled with blue studs (Figure 20.2). Use Wyldstyle to access the upper floor and keep collecting! There's a nice surprise on the roof, too.

FIGURE 20.2   The saloon is just one of many areas you can repair.

- **Restore the billboards**—This upgrade to the city costs 25,000 studs, but it adds tons of studs to the city for you to collect.
- **Restore the rainbow**—Who knew rainbows were so expensive? This upgrade, which costs 10,000 studs, provides a way up to the clouds, which you may need if you don't have a character that can fly.
- **Unlock the jukebox**—Once again, you can pay 25,000 studs to unlock the music machine and press X to change songs. You find the jukebox up in the clouds.
- **Restore the Octan Tower**—High up near the top of the tower, a worker offers to finish up the repairs for 25,000 studs.

TIP

Music Can Provide Hints

Cycle through the music playing on the jukebox, and you might find music that references an area you missed in a world you already explored. For example, cycling the music (X) in The LEGO Movie reveals a LEGO Movie World (Sewers) song…which tells you there must be some sewers in this city!

Available Quests

Five quests are offered in this world:

- **Help the other Batman defeat some bad guys**—Sulking on a rooftop in The Old West, find Batman (the *other* Batman) and help him defeat 30 attacking enemies. Your reward for beating them is a gold brick.

- **Help the other Batman defeat black boxes**—The flying black boxes are back. Help the other Batman defeat 10 of these flying machines to earn another gold brick.
- **Help Mrs. Scratchen-Post retrieve her cats**—Scour the city and find Mrs. Scratchen-Post's nine lost cats. These cats are hidden all over the place, and a few have even managed to get inside and out of easy view. Use the map to locate the general area, and then kick in doors and look everywhere. The cats are there, but some are hard to find. A gold brick is yours when you find them all.
- **Help Unikitty find all the lost instruction pages**—Unikitty has managed to lose 10 pages of instructions. Hunt them down and return them to her for a gold brick reward. These pages are not easy to find, but you can spot them because they sparkle.
- **Help the astronaut repair the sign**—The astronaut sends you on a strange repair quest: First, find the lost section of the Middle Zealand sign by looking for the large red dot. Once you've located the sign (with Wyldstyle's Relic Scanner), you need a flight vehicle to lift the sign (by pressing B when above it) high up into the air and place it (B) in the damaged section that floats above Middle Zealand (Figure 20.3). It can be a bit tricky to get the two pieces to join, so if you're having trouble, bump the two pieces together (the one you are carrying and the one floating in the sky) and see if they don't fit together.

FIGURE 20.3 Repairing the sign requires a flying vehicle.

Don't Miss Out on These Areas

There are a lot of fun areas that you don't want to miss, including these:

- **Bricksburg sewers**—Underneath the city streets are the sewer tunnels of Bricksburg. To get into the sewer, you need Gandalf to repair a launcher near the lava lake. Hunt around the tunnels for two giant stud containers. Also look for and chase down X-PO to get this world's red brick.

■ **Underwater cavern**—If you have a character who can swim (refer to Appendix A for character abilities), go beneath the city by jumping into the water, and then head down for a lot of studs and a surprise or two. Also be on the lookout for a tunnel (Figure 20.4) that cuts into the solid rock the city sits on. There are two entrances, and each takes you through and out the opposite side.

FIGURE 20.4 A secret entrance to a tunnel beneath the city.

■ **Weapons room**—Wyldstyle needs to use her Acrobat ability inside the castle to get up above the main entrance. Find a hidden handle and pull it (B) to open the armory gate and reveal a gold brick.

Up Next...

If you had a chance to travel to the past or future, which would you choose? Fortunately, with the Back to the Future world, you won't have to choose! With the help of the time-traveling DeLorean, you'll be able to travel to 1885 and 2015 (and then back to 1985) to solve some puzzles, find some gold bricks, and help repair the damage done by Lord Vortech to Hill Valley.

21

Back to the Future™ World

World Summary

- Gold bricks to discover: 28
- Locations to repair/upgrade: 10
- Red bricks to discover: 1
- Quests/mysteries to solve: 9
- Requires Marty McFly or Doc Brown minifig to access

This chapter provides details on the Back to the Future open world. This world's gateway is found on the lower-right level of Vorton.

Areas to Explore

When you arrive in Hill Valley 1985 (Figure 21.1), you find yourself high up on top of the MAXOM building, looking down onto the town's streets. (Note the ladders that allow you to return to the top of the building if you don't have a flying character.) In this town are two special accelerator switches you can use to travel back in time to 1885 or forward to 2015. Be aware that only the DeLorean or Doc Brown's time-traveling train engine can travel back or forward in time, so be sure to bring one of those vehicles along—you'll have to play through the Back to the Future Bonus Story Mode to access the build instructions for the DeLorean, so refer to Chapter 31 for that bonus level walkthrough.

Jump down to the town streets and look around. There's a small park in the middle of town, surrounded by various buildings you can explore. The town has a movie theater, a gas station, a barber shop, a candy shop, and much more.

As you explore the town, keep an eye open for areas that are in need of repair or upgrade. Check out the construction happening on a new major highway behind City Hall, as well as the back alleys.

When you're finished exploring Hill Valley 1985, get in the DeLorean or Doc Brown's train engine and drive onto the accelerator switch located in front of the MAXOM building (Figure 21.2) and hit 88mph to get launched into the future: Hill Valley 2015!

FIGURE 21.1 Hill Valley, circa 1985, is a pleasant little town to visit.

FIGURE 21.2 This accelerator switch is set for the year 2015.

Much has changed by 2015, so explore again—and be sure to hunt down areas that need repairs or upgrades. You'll definitely want to pay a visit to the movie theater for a fun holographic upgrade (Figure 21.3).

FIGURE 21.3 Holograms are popular in 2015, apparently.

The accelerator switch on the grass to the left of City Hall (Figure 21.4) can take you back to the past—to Hill Valley 1885.

FIGURE 21.4 This accelerator switch is set for the year 1885.

> **TIP**
>
> **Driving Versus Flying**
>
> Having a character who can fly will speed up your Hill Valley explorations a bit, but keep in mind that you can upgrade the DeLorean (as well as any other vehicles you might own) with some added speed that will help you cover ground much faster. With a well-timed jump, you can also hitch a ride on a flying car and get a tour of the city as it flies around. And you can also get a ride on the train in 1885.

Locations to Repair/Upgrade

You can repair or upgrade 10 areas in Hill Valley—but they're not all in the same time period:

- **Restore the present-day Hill Valley sign (1985)**—For 5,000 studs, you can rebuild the town sign. Behind the sign, find the glass box and have Marty break it open with his guitar (X) for some bonus blue studs. And be sure to give the new sign a few hits to find some hidden studs.
- **Fund the dig site (1985)**—An archaeology crew could sure use 35,000 studs to get their dig site prepared. Once it's restored, you can use a character (such as Scooby-Doo) to do some digging. There's a blue power pad that might be useful at some point.
- **Unlock the jukebox (1885, 1985, and 2015)**—The Jukebox is available in all three time periods for a cost of 25,000 studs. You can use it to change your background music (X).
- **Restore the cinema hologram (2015 world)**—For just 10,000 studs, you can fix the holographic sign for Bruce 19 on the movie theater.
- **Restore the future's Hill Valley sign (2015)**—This repair costs 5,000 studs.
- **Repair the clock (1885)**—This repair costs a lot of studs—70,000!—but it's worth it because the clock is needed in 1955 for Marty and Doc to be able to send Marty back to the future!
- **Build the past's Hill Valley sign (1885)**—The past is expensive! Repairing the town sign in 1885 costs 50,000 studs!
- **Restore the train station (1885)**—This is another expensive repair! Rebuilding the train station costs 70,000 studs.

Available Quests

Five quests are offered in this world—two in the past and three in the future:

- **Go shopping for Marlene McFly (2015)**—Marlene would rather spend time with her boyfriend than do grandma's shopping. Help her locate three items, and you get a gold brick.
- **Find the lost dog (2015)**—Doc Brown (Figure 21.5) has lost his dog, Einstein. Help find him for a gold brick.

FIGURE 21.5 Doc Brown is wearing some stylish sunglasses in the future.

- **Help Marty McFly Jr. (2015)**—Marty Jr. needs to be escorted back to his dad, so follow him and fight off any goons that attack. A gold brick is yours for your help.
- **Rid the town of Mad Dog and his men (1885)**—Mad Dog and his men are causing trouble in town. Go out and run all 15 of them out of town, and then defeat Mad Dog. Get a gold brick for your work.
- **Telescope repair (1885)**—Help Doc Brown hunt down the parts needed to repair a telescope for his wife, Clara. Finding all three parts gets you a gold brick.

Don't Miss

With three different time periods to visit, there are a lot of hidden secrets and fun locations to hunt down. These are just a few to be on the lookout for:

- **Hoverboard park (2015)**—In 2015, all the cool kids own hoverboards. Take Marty's hoverboard for a spin at the hoverboard park behind the MAXOM building. Using the boost pads, you can really get some speed (Figure 21.6).
- **Beneath the town (1885)**—Another great place to visit is below Hill Valley. With a vehicle, you can find a series of boost pads that allow you to get down beneath Hill Valley for some hidden studs and surprises.
- **The dig site (1885, 1985, and 2015)**—There's an interesting site to the left of City Hall that you should visit in all three time periods. (You need a character who can dig.) There's a Chroma puzzle to solve, too.

FIGURE 21.6   Try out your skills on the hoverboard out behind the MAXOM building.

Up Next...

The Jurassic World park is ready for you to explore once you jump through the Jurassic World portal. Here, you'll get to visit some of the most famous dinosaurs up close and personal. This island is full of surprises, so be sure to explore every nook and cranny, including the water and the areas outside the park.

22

Jurassic World™

World Summary

- Gold bricks to discover: 29
- Locations to repair/upgrade: 6
- Red bricks to discover: 1
- Quests/mysteries to solve: 3
- Requires Owen or ACU minifig to access

This chapter provides details on Jurassic World. This world's gateway is found on the far-right lower level of Vorton.

Areas to Explore

Jurassic Park is huge—and there are so many places to visit on the island! You start your visit by exiting the gateway just outside the main gate entrance (Figure 22.1).

FIGURE 22.1 The large gate to Jurassic Park is open. Come on in!

Inside the walls are a number of attractions. Stroll down Main Street and look for several park favorites, such as the T. Rex Kingdom and the Mosasaurus Feeding Area. The huge lake in the center of the park is home to one of the biggest dinosaurs you'll ever see, but before you can spot it, you need to figure out how to get his attention.

To the rear of the park is the volcano-shaped Innovation Centre. Inside it are work areas of the scientists responsible for bringing the dinosaurs back to life. John Hammond created Jurassic Park, and his legacy continues deep beneath the building, with some great areas to explore and quite a few surprises to discover.

Explore every nook and cranny because there are lots of secrets to discover inside the park. Although you probably want to spend most of your visit inside the park's tall walls, there's plenty to do outside as well.

Inside the High Security Area, Mosasaurus Lake hides a few secrets. If you're brave enough, you might also take a ride over to the Raptor Training area. If you hop in a Gyroscope vehicle and wander safely through the dinosaur preserve, you're sure to spot some big ones (Figure 22.2).

FIGURE 22.2   See if you can find this big fellow out in the wild.

Locations to Repair/Upgrade

Lord Vortech most certainly did some damage to Jurassic Park, and six areas need repairs or upgrades:

- **Restore the dinosaur battle statue**—At 60,000 studs, this is quite a pricey repair job—but it really is a nice statue!
- **Restore the John Hammond statue (Figure 22.3)**—Considering that Hammond created the park, don't you think 50,000 studs is a fair price to fix the man's statue?

FIGURE 22.3   Restore the statue, and then explore the Creation Lab behind it.

- **Unlock the jukebox**—If you'd like to be able to change the background music playing in this world, unlock the jukebox for 25,000 studs.
- **Restore the bait trap**—Dinosaurs have to eat, so chip in the 70,000 fee and get this device fixed so the Mosasaurus can eat. Pull the handle and see why it might not be a good idea to go swimming.
- **Restore the dinosaur skeleton**—For 30,000 studs, you can have a nice-looking skeleton added to the park. If you've got Scooby-Doo, check in the area for a special dig area that offers a container filled with blue studs.
- **Restore the Raptor cages**—If the park is going to be safe for visitors, the Raptor cages must be fixed. Spend 60,000 and make the place safe.

TIP

The Gyroscope Stud Machine

Do you like to collect as many studs as possible? If so, using the Gyroscope vehicle is one of the best ways to do this. It has a short turning radius, so when you roll over an object to destroy it, you can rotate quickly and grab the studs. With other vehicles, sometimes you overshoot the studs that scatter, but the Gyroscope will actually rotate in place with the RJ.

Available Quests

There are three quests for you in Jurassic World:

- **Help create a new dinosaur**—Lowery's deep in the Hammond Creation Lab, and if you find him, he can take you on for a great quest. He wants a tiny pet dinosaur created, but this quest does require a character (such as Cyborg) who has the ability to operate the tech equipment outside Lowery's office. You need to listen carefully to Lowery's description of what he wants and then choose three items to mix together. Get the right creature created, and you earn a gold brick.
- **Protect Masrani**—Masrani has crashed his helicopter, and 15 raptors have been attacking him while he's waited for help. Fight them off (Figure 22.4) and earn a gold brick.

FIGURE 22.4 Protect Masrani from the attacking raptors.

- **Save the turtles**—Next to a small lake, young Gray is asking for help finding and protecting three turtles. Locate all three by looking for the red flashing dots on the map, and then return to Gray for your gold brick reward.

Don't Miss

There are a lot of fun areas that you don't want to miss, including these:

- **T. Rex exhibit**—You'll need a Gyroscope vehicle to enter the exhibit: Drive it up on the gyroscope pad near the entrance, as shown in Figure 22.5. Once you're inside, Wyldstyle and Batman can work together to find a hidden gold brick.

FIGURE 22.5 You'll need the Gyroscope to open this exhibit.

- **The music store**—There's a Shift keystone here and a puzzle for you to solve. Take home another gold brick with the help of Batman, Gandalf, and Wyldstyle.
- **The Hammond Creation Lab**—Located behind John Hammond's statue, this lab is definitely a great place to visit for a few surprises.
- **The secret of Mosasaurus Lake**—Take a swim and try to find the secret at the very bottom of the lake—as well as a secret exit to the outside of the park.

Up Next...

The world of Chima is filled with magic and mystery, and you'll find plenty of areas that require a bit of Chi, the magical energy that helps both heroes and villains perform amazing feats. Look high and low for all the secrets in this world, and you too can become a legend.

23

Legends of Chima™ World

World Summary

- Gold bricks to discover: 28
- Locations to repair/upgrade: 9
- Red bricks to discover: 1
- Quests/mysteries to solve: 5
- Requires Cragger, Eris, or Laval minifig to access

This chapter provides details on the Legends of Chima world. This world's gateway is found on the upper-left platform of Vorton.

Areas to Explore

Arriving via the gateway, your heroes step into the Legends of Chima world and are surrounded by some amazing views! To the left is Gorilla Village. Hopefully you're not afraid of heights because the gorillas have some amazing surprises in store high up in the trees.

The gorillas have some interesting neighbors that you can meet in Crocodile Swamp. You know you've arrived when you see the big carved crocodile head (Figure 23.1). You find out really quickly that walking around the swamp is a bit slow, but don't let that keep you from looking around. There's a gold brick tucked away in a chest in this area; to release it, you need to have one of your Chima characters Chi Up (X). Look for a Chi charging station and press B to charge up your Chi character, and then press B to also fire Chi into a Chi altar to open the chest.

The swamp sits between Gorilla Village and Beaver Village, which has its own surprises above and below. Hunt around in Beaver Village until you find a darkened hut. Use Gandalf's Illuminate ability to find a box with an orange handle. Use Batman's Grapple ability on that handle, and then build a Shift relic device using the bouncing parts that are revealed. Send Gandalf through the magenta and blue portals (pads) to unlock a hidden gold brick.

When you return to the gateway, to the right are the Outlands. This snow-covered area has a few surprises to discover, so pay a visit before you head to the Lion Temple, the largest structure in this world (Figure 23.2).

FIGURE 23.1 Don't worry, it's safe to look inside this large set of teeth.

FIGURE 23.2 The Lion Temple is hard to miss in the Legends of Chima world.

There's a lot to explore inside and outside the Lion Temple, but be on the lookout for the treasure room inside, where you can find a series of puzzles that require Batman, Gandalf, and a Chima hero. Also, check out the roof of the Temple really well for five purple studs—worth 10,000 points each!

Finally, flying high in the sky above the Lion Temple is a large stone mountain, Mount Cavora, that can be reached only by a hero who can fly. Get up there if you can and discover its secrets, including a major repair that is the most expensive but also one of the most eye-catching.

Locations to Repair/Upgrade

It's hard to see the damage done by Lord Vortech in the Legends of Chima world, but many areas need repairs. Nine areas need major investments of your studs, so take a look and see where you can help:

- **Renovate Beaver Village**—For 80,000 studs, you can give Beaver Village a facelift.
- **Fund the market stall**—This world needs a place to sell stuff! Chip in 50,000 studs to get the market up and running (Figure 23.3).

FIGURE 23.3   The Market Stall area is needed for residents to buy and trade.

- **Unlock the jukebox**—If you'd like to be able to change the background music playing in this world, unlock the jukebox for 25,000 studs.
- **Unlock the bridge**—For 25,000 studs, you can unlock the jukebox that sits on the roof of the Lion Temple. Press X to change the background music that plays.
- **Excavate the Sunken Crocodile Ruins**—Restoring this ruin is rather expensive, but it's definitely worth the 60,000 studs. You need a character with the Dive ability to reach it.
- **Fund the training area**—The Chima heroes need a place to train, and building that costs 40,000 studs.
- **Restore the lion throne**—One of the most important restorations in the Legends of Chima world, this one costs 60,000 studs, but it provides a constant supply of Chi.
- **Restore the Phoenix Temple**—At 100,000 studs, this is the most expensive restoration in this world, but it unlocks a lot of hidden studs as well as a few surprises inside.
- **Restore the crocodile throne**—The crocodiles want someone to repair their king's throne, at a cost of 45,000 studs. Restoring the throne provides a nice giant stud if you have the right character to unlock it. And don't leave the hidden crocodile area until you solve the puzzle in a different room and find four blue studs plus a new puzzle.

TIP

Flying Versus Diving

You need at least one Chima minifig to access this world and use the various Chi orbs. All the characters are useful, but Eris has the Flying ability, which is very useful for moving around this world quickly. If you need a character with the Dive ability, check out Cragger, who is also a useful minifig for this world.

Available Quests

There are five quests for you in the Chima World:

- **Protect Gorzan's flower**—Protect the flower from attacking enemies. The flower can take only about five hits from enemies, so stay close to it and try to use ranged weapons (such as Batman's Batarang) to hit approaching enemies. You'll get a gold brick as a reward when Gorzan returns with a flower pot.

- **Help Plovar locate some teeth**—Follow Plovar and help him examine the crocodiles' mouths for gum disease (Figure 23.4). Attack one of the fleeing crocs to stun them and let Plovar do his examination. After three dental visits, you're awarded a gold brick.

FIGURE 23.4 Apparently crocodiles suffer from bad teeth in this world.

- **Reegull needs Chigull**—Help Reegull locate his remaining Chigull artificial Chi orbs. There are 15 of them scattered across this world. Use the map to locate the flashing red dots that indicate where Chigull can be found. Get all 15, and Reegull rewards you with a gold brick.

- **Protect the Chi**—Lagravis is concerned about citizens misusing the Chi that can be obtained from the throne. Defeat 20 unauthorized thieves who try to steal the Chi. Follow the blue arrow to find the best place to guard against the attacks, and receive a gold brick as your reward.
- **Free the beavers**—Bezar needs to locate three missing beavers (Figure 23.5). Help him find and free them from their cages, but be sure to rebuild the cages or they won't return to Bezar. If you help them return, you get a gold brick for your trouble. This quest requires a character with the Dive ability.

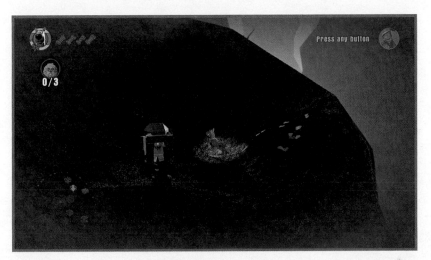

FIGURE 23.5 Free three beavers from their cages with a character with the Dive ability.

Don't Miss

There are a lot of fun areas that you don't want to miss, including these:

- **Sunken Lion Ruins**—You need a character with the Dive ability to reach these ruins, which are filled with a bunch of blue studs (worth 1,000 points each), so try to pay a visit.
- **Spiral Mountain**—Tucked behind Beaver Village is a spiral trail filled with gold studs and a gold brick on top. You need the right hero to unlock the puzzle.
- **The Gator's Mouth**—There's a huge secret hiding spot in the Gator's Mouth, but it requires a character who can dive. Be on the lookout for a ring of blue studs as well as a secret crocodile hideout.

Up Next...

It's the Simpsons! You're going to have a lot of fun in the town of Springfield. Lord Vortech's damage is visible here and there, so there will be plenty of chances for you to help rebuild and repair. But there are also plenty of secrets in Springfield to discover. Be sure to take a ride on a few of the Krustyland rides while you're visiting!

24

The Simpsons™ World

World Summary

- Gold bricks to discover: 29
- Locations to repair/upgrade: 7
- Red bricks to discover: 1
- Quests/mysteries to solve: 5
- Requires Homer, Bart, or Krusty minifig to access

This chapter provides details on The Simpsons world. This world's gateway is found on the upper-left platform of Vorton, to the right of the Chima gateway.

Areas to Explore

Welcome to Springfield (Figure 24.1)! If you watch the TV show *The Simpsons*, you're going to find a lot of familiar locations to visit, as well as dozens of familiar faces from the show. But even if you're not familiar with the television show, you'll have fun exploring this very colorful and very odd town.

FIGURE 24.1   The city of Springfield has a lot of fun areas to explore.

Springfield Elementary sits beneath the large Springfield sign (that is currently damaged...see if you can repair it). There are some open windows around the building that you can jump in to take a look. One of the rooms has a chalkboard with a funny joke for Gandalf to explore.

The Springfield Power Plant (Figure 24.2) is where Homer Simpson works, but be careful walking around the area as it appears that there has been a massive toxic waste spill. The two large cooling towers also have a few secrets down inside, but you need a character who can fly into them.

FIGURE 24.2   Take a look inside the nuclear power plant towers.

Mr. Burns's mansion is where the richest person in Springfield lives, and Krustyland is where the townsfolk go for fun rides. There are some very colorful houses around town, and you'll want to take a drive through the neighborhood and see if you can spot Homer's wife, Marge.

What else is there in this town? Well, Springfield Cemetery offers up a fun chase if you've got a character (such as Scooby) who has the Dig ability, and the KBBL Radio Tower and Buzz Cola Factory are definitely worth exploring if you like to collect studs.

Locations to Repair/Upgrade

Springfield didn't suffer as much damage from Lord Vortech as other worlds, but there are still a number of areas that need repairs, as well as some locales that Mayor Quimby has decided need to be upgraded:

- **Renovate Springfield Elementary**—For 60,000 studs, you can fix up the school and reveal the location of a gold brick on the second floor.
- **Restore the Jebediah Springfield statue**—This upgrade costs 40,000 studs, but this is for the town's founder!

- **Unlock the jukebox**—If you'd like to be able to change the background music playing in this world, unlock the jukebox for 50,000 studs.
- **Restore the Kwik-E-Mart**—Lord Vortech made sure this convenience store was destroyed during the Story Mode. Help Homer bring back the store by investing 35,000 studs (Figure 24.3).

FIGURE 24.3   The Kwik-E-Mart must be completely rebuilt.

- **Restore the Krustyland entrance**—This fun park needs an eye-catching entrance. Spend 35,000 studs on it if you agree.
- **Renovate Mr. Burns's garden**—You'd think Mr. Burns could afford to pay for this himself, but if you feel like chipping in the exorbitant 100,000-stud fee, he is sure to say thank you. Well, maybe.
- **Restore the Springfield sign**—High on the hill behind Springfield is the town sign, which you can help repair by chipping in 55,000 studs. There's a gold brick tucked away inside the sign, and you can get it if you have the right character to unlock it.

TIP

No Height Limits in Krustyland

Many of the rides in Krustyland can actually be ridden. As you approach a ride, press Y to get on it. You can even press B to get a different camera view of your ride. Don't forget to take a ride on the giant Krusty head vertical drop!

Available Quests

There are five quests for you in Springfield:

- **Help Find Mr. Burns's hounds**—Willy needs your help to find some lost dogs. Find all five, and Willy rewards you with a gold brick when you return to him. Look on the map for the glowing red dots for help finding the dogs.

- **Provide escort duty to Hans**—Hans Moleman needs to deliver some food to the elementary school, but he keeps getting attacked. Escort him to his final destination (Figure 24.4), fight off attackers, and get a gold brick as a reward. Follow the blue arrow on the screen to tag along with him—but watch out...Hans is a terrible driver. You can run this quest over and over, and you get a purple stud each time you help Hans.

FIGURE 24.4   Escort Hans as he drives around Springfield, delivering food.

- **Protect Grampa Simpson**—Help Grampa Simpson fight off hooligans. Defeat 25 enemies, and Grampa gives you a gold brick. It's a bit of a mystery why these nuclear power plant employees are after Grampa, but if you manage to find the secret beneath the power plant, the mystery might be solved.

- **Help Mayor Quimby clean up the town**—There's a nasty toxic waste spill that the Mayor needs you to clean up. A gold brick is your reward, but this quest does require a character that has a Hazard Cleaner.

- **Find the Donuts**—Hans Moleman has another job for you: Find the 30 lost donuts, and you get a gold brick. These donuts are scattered all over, and you need to follow the red dots on the mini map to find them all.

Don't Miss

Springfield has many secret locations and hard-to-spot locales, so spend some time in the town exploring every nook and cranny. While there, be on the lookout for these special sites:

- **The secrets beneath Springfield**—If you have a character who has the Dive ability, take a look underneath the city by diving into the water (Figure 24.5). You can find more than one surprise down there.

FIGURE 24.5   There's more to explore in the water beneath Springfield.

- **The town treasury**—If you have a character who can cut through gold walls, you might find where the mayor has been hiding all the town's money. Destroy everything inside town hall and see how many gold studs you find!
- **Underground power plant**—A secret entrance (that requires the Taunt-O-Vision) gets you beneath the power plant, where there are lots of secrets to uncover. Remember, you can pick up Homer's Taunt-O-Vision and place it near silver objects. When you drop the Taunt-O-Vision, it will explode and destroy the silver objects.

Up Next...

The Simpsons world couldn't be more different than the world described in the next chapter—the Lord of the Rings world. Here, you'll discover a world of elves and orcs, wizards and warriors, and good versus evil. Gandalf is a great character to play in this world (it's his home, of course), but you'll find fun challenges for almost any visiting LEGO character you place on the Toy Pad.

25

The Lord of the Rings™ World

World Summary

- Gold bricks to discover: 28
- Locations to repair/upgrade: 8
- Red bricks to discover: 1
- Quests/mysteries to solve: 5
- Requires Gandalf, Gollum, Legolas, or Gimli minifig to access

This chapter provides details on The Lord of the Rings world. This world's gateway is found on the upper-middle platform of Vorton.

Areas to Explore

Welcome to Middle Earth! Depending on where you're standing, you can see either sunlight or a sky filled with volcanic ash. Middle Earth has a lot happening right now, with the hobbits, elves, humans, and dwarves all defending against the evil Sauron. You need to explore this world carefully; there are many hidden areas and secrets to uncover.

When you exit the gateway, you find yourself in Hobbiton. It's a nice quiet place to explore. Not only can you find the jukebox somewhere around here, but one of the houses has the parts to build a Location keystone device. Activate it and find the white diamond to find a chest with a gold brick inside. There are a few other surprises for those who look carefully.

From the gateway, look to the right (east), and you see the towers of Minas Tirith (Figure 25.1). You'll definitely spend some time in this fortress, solving a few puzzles and collecting studs. Behind the fortress is a destroyed statue, the Argonath; help repair it, and you'll receive a nice reward.

Mordor is a very dangerous place. Plenty of enemies are nearby, and there's also deadly lava. Other dangers here are Saruman, a wizard who turned evil and now serves Sauron, and many, many orcs.

Thankfully, Mordor is surrounded on all sides by heroes, including the elves of Rivendell. Many secrets wait to be discovered in Rivendell, including a Scale keystone relic device and a tube puzzle that can get you another gold brick.

Explore every corner of Middle Earth, even beneath it. Many of the repairs and upgrades you do in this world open up other secrets, so collect studs wherever you can find them!

FIGURE 25.1 Minas Tirith is a huge fortress with many hidden secrets.

Locations to Repair/Upgrade

Middle Earth already suffered much damage before Lord Vortech arrived, with Sauron's army of orcs running rampant over the land. Many areas can use some repair work, and many of them offer up quests or hidden secrets. Look for all of these repair or upgrade opportunities:

- **Restore the water mill**—For 40,000 studs, you can help the hobbits by repairing the mill. After the upgrade, look inside for a giant brick that contains dozens of studs.
- **Invest in the crop field**—You can help the hobbits feed their families by fixing up the crop field for 35,000 studs. The reward is handsome: giant bricks that contain plenty of studs to collect (Figure 25.2).

FIGURE 25.2 Help the hobbits put some food on the tables.

- **Unlock the Jukebox**—For 25,000 studs, you can repair the jukebox and change the background music that plays.
- **Restore the Rivendell Council Chamber**—For 55,000 studs, you can help the elves in Rivendell fund repairs to the large chamber.
- **Restore the forge at Mordor**—This repair costs you 45,000 studs, but if you do it, you find some giant bricks filled with studs. (Also, be sure to look in the nearby cave for another giant brick filled with purple studs. Do not miss it!)
- **Restore Barad-Dur**—This is the most expensive repair in Middle Earth. This 100,000-stud restoration costs plenty, but Sauron will be appreciative when his tower rises high into the sky (Figure 25.3).

FIGURE 25.3 Restore Sauron's tower to show him that it pays to be nice.

- **Restore the Argonath statue**—Repairing this collapsed statue costs 60,000 studs, but inside the helmet is a gold brick you can nab if you have a character who can destroy silver objects.
- **Restore the courtyard at Minas Tirith**—The castle has taken some damage, and you can chip in 50,000 studs to repair it. A Shift keystone relic puzzle becomes available after this repair.

TIP

Boulders Are Filled with Valuable Studs

In Mordor, when you spot giant glowing boulders, hit them a few times. There are always blue studs tucked inside.

Available Quests

There are five quests to discover in Middle Earth:

- **Find three troublesome hobbits**—Sam needs your help in rounding up some bad seeds in Hobbiton. Find the three troublemakers, and you get a gold brick as a reward.
- **Protect Gollum from the orcs**—Gollum wants you to follow him and protect him from any orcs that might attack. If you protect him and let him complete his task, you are rewarded with a gold brick. You need Batman or a character who has Stealth ability to get Gollum through the gates of Mordor.
- **Go fight some bad guys with Saruman**—Saruman wants to demonstrate his loyalty to Sauron, and he's asking for some assistance. If you follow Saruman (Figure 25.4) and help him defeat a few orcs, he gives you a gold brick for your trouble.

FIGURE 25.4 Help Saruman punish some bad orcs.

- **Defeat an underwater beast**—Boromir needs you to investigate the lake to determine whether a large creature is still around. You need a character who can swim underneath the water. Defeat the beast if you find it, and Boromir gives you a gold brick. You can find the location of the creature by looking for the red dot on the map in the lower-left corner.
- **Find some sunken treasure**—If you have a character with the Dive ability, you can help the orc commander recover some treasure. Find all five gems and return to the commander for your reward. Look for mint-green boxes in the water where you dive.

Don't Miss

Middle Earth is filled with secrets—what would you expect from a place filled with elves and orcs and wizards? Keep your eyes open as you wander the land, and maybe you'll spot some of these special locales:

- **The tapestries**—Hanging from the walls in Minas Tirith are numerous striped tapestries. These tapestries hold a surprising number of gold studs, so give them a few hits each time you pay a visit to the fortress.
- **The waterfall**—If you have the right character, take a peek behind the waterfall in Rivendell for a surprise.
- **The Mines of Moria**—There's only one way into the mines (at first), so use Gandalf and Batman to clear the doors and then proceed in (Figure 25.5). You can find a *lot* of studs here, along with a number of puzzles and rewards.

FIGURE 25.5   The Mines of Moria hold secrets and lots of wealth!

Up Next...

The world of Ninjago is a mysterious one, with lots of unusual characters roaming the land, and not all of them friendly. Fortunately, Sensei Wu and his students are working to repair the world after the damage done by Lord Vortech. But they need more help, and you'll find plenty of quests and repairs to be made to this colorful and magical world.

Ninjago™ World

World Summary

- Gold bricks to discover: 27
- Locations to repair/upgrade: 8
- Red bricks to discover: 1
- Quests to solve: 5
- Requires one of seven minifigs to access

This chapter provides details on the Ninjago world. This world's gateway is found on the upper-middle platform of Vorton.

Areas to Explore

The world of Ninjago is filled with magic and mystery, and as you explore this world, you'll encounter a number of amazing characters and locales. Even after Lord Vortech's attack on the various LEGO dimensions, this world came through with less damage...or at least that appears to be the case. Many places still need help with repairs or upgrades or ridding the area of enemies. As you wander around the world of Ninjago, keep an eye open for these key locations:

- **Steep Wisdom Tea Shop**—Upon entering the world of Ninjago, if you immediately scan the area that includes the Steep Wisdom Tea Shop and have the right character, you might find a gold brick challenge. Don't be disappointed if you lack the right character because this world is filled with puzzles that are suitable for a single Ninjago hero to solve, as well as Batman, Gandalf, and Wyldstyle.

- **The arena**—To the west (right) is the arena. It needs some upgrades, but inside you can find a fun combat challenge that yields a gold brick if you win. If you leave and return to this world, you can win a purple stud every time you pay a visit to the arena and win the challenge.

- **The monastery**—Farther to the west is the monastery (Figure 26.1). It's quite a hike to get to the top, but if you have a flying character, it's even easier. Once inside, find the training area and a fun challenge.

FIGURE 26.1 Flying is a much faster way to get up to the monastery.

- **The volcano**—Heading north from the monastery, watch your step around the volcano. The volcano holds many secrets down inside its walls, so explore all over and keep your eyes open for surprises. While you're in the area, you might also consider helping out Ed and Edna by repairing a bridge that leads to their storefront.

TIP

Steam Vents Are Filled with Studs

In and around the volcano, keep an eye out for steam vents. Destroy them to get a large mix of standard and gold studs. This is a great way to collect studs.

- **The Valley of Despair**—If you head east, you can go to the Valley of Despair, where there's a fun keystone relic challenge and a quest from a powerful sensei.
- **The fishing village**—Continue east from the Valley of Despair to the fishing village and look for a way to raise up a sunken fishing boat for another keystone puzzle to solve.
- **The Ninjago Temple**—The front door of the Ninjago Temple is locked. You need a ninja's skills to get inside, but you already have those because you needed a ninja to enter this world (Figure 26.2).

Finally, scattered throughout the world are tall, thin buildings with plenty of secrets tucked inside each level. Make your way to the top of each one and look inside for studs and other surprises.

FIGURE 26.2   You have to go up if you wish to open the Ninjago Temple.

Locations to Repair/Upgrade

Although the world of Ninjago doesn't look as damaged as the DC Comics world, for example, there are still eight repairs and upgrades to be considered:

- **Restore the arena**—It's an expensive repair, but for 80,000 studs, you can get the Ninjago arena back into working shape (Figure 26.3). Restoring it gives you access to a quest.

FIGURE 26.3   Repair the arena and fight in a tournament.

- **Unlock the jukebox**—For 25,000 studs, repair the jukebox and change the background music that plays.
- **Restore the bridge**—For 70,000 studs, you can rebuild the bridge. Cross it and receive a quest from Sensei Garmadon.
- **Restore the noodle bar**—The citizens of Ninjago love their noodles. If you can spare 40,000 studs, repair the noodle bar, and a gold brick becomes available to any character that has the Stealth ability.
- **Restore the blacksmith shop**—For 40,000 studs, repair the blacksmith shop and become eligible for a race for a gold brick.
- **Recover the boat**—A boat has recently sunk. Restore it for 40,000 studs, and then go hunting on board for a gold brick.
- **Fund the training area**—For 80,000 studs, you can restore the training area. Destroy all 12 training dummies before the timer runs out, and then use a character who has the Acrobat ability to retrieve the gold brick that becomes available.
- **Repair the staircase**—While your ninja skills can get you most places, unless you have a character who can fly, you need to invest 30,000 studs to repair the stairs to reach Ed and Edna's Scrap N Junk building and make a valuable discovery by exploring it (see Figure 26.4).

FIGURE 26.4   A staircase is helpful for reaching this particular building.

Available Quests

There are five quests for you in the world of Ninjago, but they're important ones:

- **Fight in the Tournament of Elements**—If you agree to fight in the Tournament of Elements, Master Chen pits you against some formidable opponents. Defeat all three opponents, and a gold brick is yours...along with a year's supply of Mr. Chen's noodles.

- **Help P.I.X.A.L. locate components**—The robotic fighter P.I.X.A.L. needs help finding nine components for the creation of a new invention by her creator, Cyrus Borg. Track down the parts, and you get a gold brick as a reward.
- **Seek enlightenment**—Follow Grand Sensei Dareth (Figure 26.5) into the volcano on a quest for enlightenment. Fight off some bad guys, find enlightenment, and a gold brick is yours.

FIGURE 26.5 Follow Sensei Dareth on a dangerous journey to the volcano.

- **Learn the elemental powers**—Sensei Garmadon has a series of tasks for you to perform that will give you a deeper understanding of the various elemental powers. Complete the tasks and your reward will be another gold brick.
- **Send skeletons back to the underworld**—Sensei Garmadon has another quest for you. Locate six skeletons and lure them to a launcher that will send them through a vortex. A gold brick is your reward if you are successful.

Don't Miss

What else is going on in Ninjago? There are a number of hidden areas and many secrets to be found in this world. As you explore, make certain to pay visits to the following:

- **Beneath Ninjago**—If you have a character that has the Dive ability, use it to find the many secrets that lie beneath the water. Look around the sunken ship, and be sure to solve the Chroma puzzle that's down there, too.
- **The Fishing Boat**—The fishing boat offers some fun puzzles you can solve (Figure 26.6), and it also has a number of special rewards, so look around (and under!).

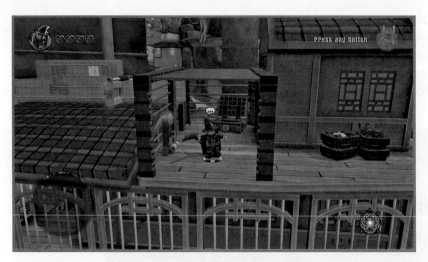

FIGURE 26.6 Puzzles can be found all over this fishing boat.

Up Next...

There's a very strange setting waiting for you to explore in the Portal 2 world. An AI (artificial intelligence) known as GLaDOS needs your help (although she's not always grateful for it) to repair Aperture Science, her home and a source of unusual puzzles and strange technology. Get ready for a mind-bending world where up is sometimes down and a tool called the Portal Gun is more handy than any weapon.

27

Portal™ 2 World

World Summary

- Gold bricks to discover: 27
- Locations to repair/upgrade: 6
- Red bricks to discover: 1
- Quests/mysteries to solve: 5
- Requires Chell minifig to access

This chapter provides details on the Portal 2 world. This world's gateway is found on the upper-right platform of Vorton.

Areas to Explore

Unlike many of the other worlds in LEGO Dimensions, the Portal 2 world consists of a single area called Aperture Science. Aperture Science is the home of GLaDOS, an artificial intelligence being with questionable motives. She and her assistant, Wheatley, monitor the activities that go on at Aperture Science. You'll find Wheatley much more helpful than GLaDOS, although he can be a bit wordy, and sometimes his help is anything but helpful.

Aperture Science (Figure 27.1) sustained some serious damage when Lord Vortech attempted to merge the LEGO worlds, and a number of areas don't work properly. Many of them you can repair or upgrade, but in order to reach others you must find alternative pathways. You can find many interesting areas as you wander around after exiting the gateway. Chell's Portal Gun is an absolute requirement for many of this world's puzzles, but having a character who can fly is also extremely useful.

GLaDOS's chamber (Figure 27.2), for example, greets you when you arrive. GLaDOS may be stuck here in the chamber, but she manages to keep an eye on your activities no matter where you go.

FIGURE 27.1 Welcome to (what remains of) Aperture Science.

FIGURE 27.2 GLaDOS is stuck here, but she has eyes everywhere.

A number of test chambers here require the Portal Gun, and many also require other characters and abilities that Chell does not possess. Test Chamber 02, for example, has a gold brick waiting for you, but you need the Unikitty minifig to get it.

Be sure to look for the waiting room and the Bring Your Daughter to Work Day projects area, where you can collect a lot of studs if you're feeling destructive.

Locations to Repair/Upgrade

Aperture Science can be a confusing world to explore. There are plenty of dead ends and walkways that go up and down and end abruptly. Be careful as you explore; a misstep can send you falling and losing studs. As you explore, be on the lookout for the following areas, which are in need of repair and upgrade:

- **Restore the relaxation chamber**—For 35,000 studs, you can repair the relaxation chamber (Figure 27.3) and jump across to find some blue studs. Be sure to relax.

FIGURE 27.3   The relaxation chamber is just what a hero needs in this world.

- **Unlock the jukebox**—For 25,000 studs, Wheatley gets you access to the jukebox so you can change the background music.
- **Restore the portrait room**—GLaDOS kindly requests that you pay 45,000 studs to repair the portrait room. Find a way to look behind the large portrait for a surprise.
- **Restore the science project stands**—It costs you only 50,000 studs to restore the Bring Your Daughter to Work Day projects (Figure 27.4).
- **Restore the turret control room**—The turret control room is an important facility. GLaDOS requests that you pay 30,000 studs to recover it.
- **Restore the choir room**—Why GLaDOS needs a choir room is unknown, but feel free to chip in 40,000 studs to return it to Aperture Science.

TIP

Computers Provide Lots of Studs

Computer equipment costs a lot of money, so be sure to destroy as much of it as you can. Anything that looks expensive in this world has a tendency to provide a lot of gold studs.

FIGURE 27.4 Aperture Science proudly supports Bring Your Daughter to Work Day.

Available Quests

There are only a few quests for you in the Portal 2 world, but they're important ones:

- **Bake a cake**—GLaDOS said there's no cake, but if you have the correct ingredients, Cake Core helps you bake one (Figure 27.5)!

FIGURE 27.5 GLaDOS lied about the cake, but it exists!

- **One job**—Wheatley's got a job for you. He needs three boxes placed in particular spots. He doesn't have hands and is prepared to reward you a gold brick if you can help him with this in Test Chamber 03.
- **Extinct species**—Cave Johnson wants to pit you against 30 Mantis Men. Fight them off and make a glorious contribution to science. Get a gold brick for doing it.
- **Collection services**—GLaDOS wants to send you on a scavenger hunt. Collect 10 spheres scattered all over Aperture Science; use the flashing red dots on the map for help in finding all of them. Then return to GLaDOS for a reward.
- **Two jobs**—Find three of Wheatley's little boxes (Figure 27.6), which are scattered all over Aperture Science and need to be found. A gold brick is your reward if you can locate all of them.

FIGURE 27.6 Help Wheatley by solving this fun but tricky little puzzle.

Don't Miss

What else is going on in Portal 2? There are a number of hidden areas and many secrets to be found in this world. As you explore, make certain to pay visits to the following:

- **(Back to the) Future Aperture Labs**—After exiting the gateway into the Portal 2 world, head left (clockwise) and enter the first doorway to find a special time machine accelerator switch that can be used only with Doc Brown's DeLorean. If you have the right characters, solve the tricky test chamber puzzle and get a reward.
- **The surface**—Whereas most of the other worlds have an ocean or lakes to explore, the Portal 2 world has a grassy surface up above to explore. A gold brick is yours for hitting all five scarecrows. Be sure to return to the barn when you're done so you can head back down (Figure 27.7).

FIGURE 27.7 Without a flying character, the barn is your way up and down.

- **Power cells**—On one of the outer areas of Aperture Science you can find three empty power cells. Using a flying vehicle, lift the three batteries that are located nearby and drop them in place for a gold brick.
- **Hacking Puzzle**—If you have the Doctor Who minifig, you can solve a special puzzle in the waiting room. Move The Doctor around and collect the five red discs while avoiding your enemies; you can press A to jump hard to make them change direction.

Up Next...

Next, you're off to see the wizard. The Wizard of Oz, that is. You'll find a unique world to explore—a land filled with color and danger above and the colorless Kansas (complete with tornado) below. Munchkin Town is a great place to start, so once you arrive... just follow the yellow brick road.

28

The Wizard of Oz™ World

World Summary

- Gold bricks to discover: 27
- Locations to repair/upgrade: 8
- Red bricks to discover: 1
- Quests/mysteries to solve: 5
- Requires Wicked Witch minifig to access

This chapter provides details on The Wizard of Oz world. This world's gateway is found on the upper-right platform of Vorton.

Areas to Explore

From high in the sky (Figure 28.1), the Wizard of Oz world might look a bit sparse in terms of locales to visit. Three obvious areas that stand out are Emerald City to the north (straight ahead), the witch's castle to the west (she's called the Wicked Witch of the West for a reason), and Munchkin Town to the east.

FIGURE 28.1 Three major areas are easy to spot in this world.

But there's a lot more here than meets the eye. Look for the Tin Woodsman's house...in the woods, of course. Scarecrow hangs out in the cornfield (and he has a quest for you), and the Cowardly Lion is in the nearby apple orchard, waiting with his own quest.

Situated between the Emerald City and the witch's castle is the haunted forest. This is definitely a place to be on your guard. Flying monkeys and the witch's guards are scattered all over this world, so be careful while exploring.

Emerald City is a safe place, as is Munchkin Town. Both of these areas offer a number of puzzles and secrets and repairs/upgrades. You can find a few quests here as well.

The witch's castle is hard to miss, and sooner or later you need to pay a visit. The drawbridge is closed, so you need to find another way into the castle. Fortunately, you have a Wicked Witch who can fly. Once inside, locate the handle you need to pull to lower the drawbridge. Solve the Chroma puzzle here (Figure 28.2) to get a gold brick.

FIGURE 28.2 There's a Chroma puzzle deep in the heart of the witch's castle.

When you're finished exploring the Land of Oz, hop on the Wicked Witch's broomstick and fly down beneath Oz for a nice surprise.

Locations to Repair/Upgrade

As you explore, be on the lookout for these areas that are in need of repair or upgrade:

- **Restore the bridge**—For only 50,000 studs, you can help the residents of Munchkin Town repair their bridge. A giant brick becomes available if you've got the right character to open the cage it's in.
- **Unlock the jukebox**—For 25,000 studs, the citizens of Munchkin Town can enjoy whatever song you select to play in the background.
- **Restore the talking tree**—The tree might be a little rude, but go ahead and spend the 35,000 studs to bring him back to the apple orchard.
- **Restore the witch's lair**—The Wicked Witch wants a place to lurk (Figure 28.3), and it costs you 50,000 studs to give it to her.

FIGURE 28.3   Do the witch a favor and repair her lair.

- **Restore the caravan**—For 40,000 studs, you can restore the traveling caravan. Find the locked-up giant stud behind the wagon.
- **Restore the barn**—This one's expensive: 60,000 studs to repair the destroyed barn. Inside are a Scale keystone and a puzzle you can solve to get a gold brick. You need a character with the Dig ability to restore the barn.
- **Restore the wizard's machine**—The wizard needs a machine repaired, at a cost of 40,000 studs. Activate the machine, and it spits out a lot of gold studs.
- **Restore the weather machine**—Back in Kansas, you can spend 40,000 studs to repair the weather machine (Figure 28.4). This repair requires a character (such as Emmett or Doctor Who) who can repair items with the Fix-It ability. Fix the machine, start it up, and it rains gold studs.

FIGURE 28.4 Fix the weather machine and start it up for a nice surprise.

Available Quests

These are some of the quests in the Wizard of Oz world that require your assistance; a gold brick is rewarded for each successful quest completed:

- **Missing gold bricks**—The Munchkin Mayor needs your help repairing the yellow brick road. Find 15 missing bricks, and the mayor rewards you with a gold brick. You might have to fight off some flying monkeys!

- **Scarecrow's puzzles**—Find Scarecrow in a cornfield and follow him to the first puzzle (Figure 28.5). From there, use clues to get to the end and receive a reward. This is a good quest to accept after you've found your way around this world and know its many locations.

FIGURE 28.5 Help Scarecrow with his puzzles.

- **Jump start a rusted heart**—The Tin Woodsman needs your help finding three items (Toto, Mrs. Woodsman, and a pig) to start his heart. Find all three items and return to the Tin Woodsman for a gold brick.
- **Be brave**—The Cowardly Lion needs your help defeating some of the Wicked Witch's guardsmen. Follow him and help protect him, and you get a gold brick when you reach the end of the road.
- **No place like home**—Auntie Em is lost. If you help her find her way back to the farm and protect her from attacking flying monkeys, she'll toss a gold brick to you.

Don't Miss

There are many fun areas and interesting activities going on in the Wizard of Oz world. Following you'll find a few that you should be on the lookout for, but the list is by no means complete; exploration is the key to finding them all:

- **Gyrosphere obstacle course**—Behind the witch's castle is a fun little test (Figure 28.6) of your driving skills—but you need the Gyrosphere (from the Jurassic World Level Pack).

FIGURE 28.6 The Gyrosphere obstacle course is challenging.

- **Dorothy's house**—Visit the house that started it all. Right in the middle of Munchkin Town, it has a secret for the right character to solve.
- **Haunted forest**—If you have a character who can trap ghosts, visit this spooky place just outside the witch's castle and earn a gold brick.

Up Next...

If you don't know The Doctor, you're about to get acquainted. As one of the most beloved British television shows in the world, Doctor Who has hundreds of episodes to draw on for heroes, villains, and locales, and your assistance is needed by The Doctor to help solve some puzzles, defeat some bad guys, and repair the world.

29

Doctor Who™ World

World Summary

- Gold bricks to discover: 27
- Locations to repair/upgrade: 7
- Red bricks to discover: 1
- Quests/mysteries to solve: 10
- Requires The Doctor or Cyberman minifig to access

This chapter provides details on the Doctor Who world. This world's gateway is found on the upper-right platform of Vorton.

Areas to Explore

When the heroes emerge from the gateway, they land in 21st-century London. But in the Doctor Who world, much as in the Back to the Future world, there are unseen fragments that you can visit if you have the right tool—in this case, the TARDIS. The Doctor needs to travel to the different fragments and destroy the Dimensional Discombobulators (Figure 29.1) to reunite the world, so find the TARDIS and start exploring!

FIGURE 29.1 Find the Discombobulators and destroy them to merge the world fragments.

TIP

Multiple Ways to Access World Fragments

If you don't currently have the TARDIS on the pad or would prefer to use seven heroes, you can press B on the Time Corridor device located near a TARDIS docking station to be randomly transported to one of the five other fragments. Using the TARDIS, however, enables you to select which fragment to visit.

After you enter the TARDIS and fly it onto a TARDIS docking station, press B to enter the TARDIS. Inside, The Doctor can access three controls (Figure 29.2) by standing on one of the three circles on the floor:

- The yellow circle lets you change to various incarnations of The Doctor, but you have to unlock them before you can use them. Each new Doctor incarnation is unlocked after you lose all your hearts. When the current Doctor incarnation dies, the Doctor returns to life as a different doctor. There are 12 in all, and you'll be able to switch between them using the yellow circle.
- The green circle lets you change the background music that plays inside the TARDIS.
- The blue circle lets you move between the six different locations: 19th-century London, 21st-century London, Mars, Skaro, Telos, and Trenzalore.

FIGURE 29.2 The Doctor can access three circles inside the TARDIS.

The following sections describe the six places you need to visit in the Doctor Who world to find the Discombobulators and destroy them.

19th-Century London

The Dimensional Discombobulator is fairly easy to find in this world. It's the large silver object you see as you exit the TARDIS. Destroy the object (try The Doctor's Sonic Screwdriver or K-9's missiles), and then build the Discombobulator from the bouncing pieces.

Next, use Wyldstyle's Relic Scanner to locate a terminal for The Doctor to access. Access the terminal by pressing B and you will be shown a puzzle (Figure 29.3) that requires you to rotate a red circle to allow electrical current to flow. Use the LJ to move the pointer to one of the three red circles and press X to rotate it. If you select the correct circle, the Discombobulator self-destructs, and 19th-century London merges with 21st-century London.

FIGURE 29.3 Solve this puzzle to destroy a Discombobulator.

Mars

When you land on Mars, look for the large silver rock near the TARDIS landing point. Using a character who can destroy silver objects (such as K-9), hit the silver rock with The Doctor's Sonic Screwdriver (press X) and rebuild the Discombobulator from the remaining parts.

Have Wyldstyle locate the terminal (behind the Discombobulator) with her Relic Scanner. Use The Doctor to activate the terminal (by pressing B) and solve a new puzzle (Figure 29.4) to destroy the Discombobulator. Mars then rejoins 21st-century London.

FIGURE 29.4   Solve another puzzle to destroy another Discombobulator.

Skaro

Find the large silver rock and destroy it to build the Discombobulator. Use Wyldstyle's Relic Scanner to locate the terminal. There's no game to play or puzzle to solve here; just have The Doctor access the terminal by repeatedly pressing X. The Discombobulator is destroyed, and Skaro joins with 21st-century London.

Telos

The Discombobulator on Telos is covered in ice. Use The Doctor's Sonic Screwdriver (press X) to shatter the ice and rebuild the device. Use Wyldstyle's Relic Scanner to locate a damaged accelerator switch; have The Doctor repair it and then drive a vehicle onto it to destroy the Discombobulator. Telos rejoins with 21st-century London.

Trenzalore

On Trenzalore, find and destroy the large silver rock (using K-9), and then rebuild the Discombobulator. Have Wyldstyle locate a terminal nearby with her Relic Scanner and have The Doctor repair the terminal (press B). Then press B again to turn on the terminal and repeatedly press X to destroy the Discombobulator. Trenzalore merges with 21st-century London.

When all six fragments of Doctor Who world have merged, it's time to go explore. All the various quests and locales that need upgrades or repairs should be visible on the map, so go look around!

Locations to Repair/Upgrade

Until the six fragments are reunited into a single world, you can't do much in the way of quests or repairs/upgrades. Once you've merged the fragments, however, it's time to go repair the damage done:

- **Restore the 3W facility**—Missy needs a good place to hold the Cybermen, so consider spending 40,000 studs to repair the facility for her.
- **Unlock the jukebox**—The jukebox is in the Silurian Lair, and you can pay 25,000 studs to restore it and change the background music.
- **Restore the mausoleum**—The Cybermen might be evil robots, but you can help them by paying 30,000 studs to restore the mausoleum. If you have a character who has the Drill ability, look for the gold brick inside.
- **Restore the Telos Base**—For a mere 50,000 studs, you can repair the Telos Base plus gain access to another gold brick if The Doctor can solve another puzzle.
- **Restore the Dalek head**—The Dalek drives a hard bargain: Pay 60,000 or be exterminated! Go ahead and pay it if you have a flying vehicle that can lift cargo because there's a gold brick waiting for you up there (Figure 29.5).

FIGURE 29.5 That is one large Dalek in need of repair!

- **Restore the winter playground**—A Cyberman wants 30,000 studs to fix the winter playground. You should probably pay it, or you'll be assimilated.
- **Restore the Mars space shuttle**—The shuttle needs to be fixed, and you can pay 40,000 studs to get it operational again.

Available Quests

There are a whopping 10 quests for you to attempt in the Doctor Who world:

- **Rescue the humans**—Help Madame Vastra rescue five humans being held underground by Silurians. You need a character who can break through the cracked earth (Cracked LEGO Walls is the ability) and reveal a dark pit inside the building. Drop down into the pit and explore the Silurian Lair to find the missing humans; get a gold brick as a reward.
- **Find the nonhumans**—Missy needs you to help locate some Zygons who are impersonating humans. Go find three of them (using the flashing red dots on the map), and Missy gives you a gold brick.
- **Pick a fight**—Strax requests that you help him find some parts that have been stolen by a group of clockwork droids. Follow him and help fight off 30 of these mechanical men for a gold brick reward.
- **Wish a happy birthday!**—Captain Jack Harkness would like to provide a birthday gift to the Face of Boe in the form of a song-and-dance routine. Go round up some of his Ood dancers and bring them back for a nice reward. Use the red dots on the map for assistance in locating the dancers.
- **Get out of the fire**—Missy has yet another quest for you: Help locate three ice warriors and rescue them from fire (Figure 29.6). You need a character who can put out fires to win this gold brick.

FIGURE 29.6 Three ice warriors need to be rescued from the fire.

- **Pick a fight 2**—Madame Vastra needs you to help defeat 30 Zygons, and she's willing to send Strax to help you! Defeat them and get your gold brick.

- **Repair the fixer-upper**—Strax needs your assistance cleaning up Madame Vastra's mansion. Make the five repairs inside the room and collect your gold brick from Strax. (Hint: The Doctor needs to fix the music box.)
- **Battle the plastic people**—Captain Jack Harkness needs your help again. Take on the Nestenes and 30 of their mannequins for a gold brick.
- **Defeat the metal rats**—Help Madame Vastra defeat 30 Cybermats to help prevent the larger Cybermen from waking up.
- **Help the friendly Dalek**—Rusty the Friendly Dalek would like you to tag along and help him defeat some Daleks. A gold brick is waiting for you if you can survive.

Don't Miss

There are many secrets to be discovered in the Doctor Who world. Keep your eyes open and the TARDIS close by, and maybe you'll spot one of these:

- **The giant TARDIS**—Over in Trenzalore, be sure to go inside the giant TARDIS and look under the platform (Figure 29.7) for a surprise. Don't get too close to the energy column!

FIGURE 29.7   Look under the floor in the giant TARDIS for a giant brick.

- **Keystone puzzle**—Over in Skaro, when coming in from 19th-century London, look in the large building to the left of the giant Dalek. A puzzle here (Figure 29.8) uses the Location and Shift keystone relics. Solve it to get a giant brick.

FIGURE 29.8 A special two-keystone puzzle is found in Skaro.

- **Visit the coffee shop**—Who knew 19th-century London had coffee shops? Stop in and bring along a Companion Cube (from the Portal 2 Level Pack) to find a nice surprise.
- **Survive on Mars**—For humans to survive on Mars, they must have—among other things—oxygen and food. Find the biodome, do some repairs, and see if you can get the Mars oxygen and food supply started up again.

Up Next...

When the city is filling up with spooks, specters, and ghosts, who you gonna call? That's right: Ghostbusters! With a proton pack and a ghost trap, get ready to help Dr. Venkman and the other heroes clean up the town and rid New York City of all the supernatural visitors.

30

Ghostbusters™ World

World Summary

- Gold bricks to discover: 27
- Locations to repair/upgrade: 7
- Red bricks to discover: 1
- Quests/mysteries to solve: 5
- Requires the Peter Venkman minifig to access

This chapter provides details on the Ghostbusters world. This world's gateway is found on the upper-right platform of Vorton.

Areas to Explore

New York City took some major damage during Lord Vortech's attack on the various dimension. Those attacks also freed up a ton of ghosts that had been stored in the Ghostbusters' containment facility, and they will attack if they spot you or if you get too close. As you wander around the city, you can see a lot of familiar locations that the Ghostbusters have visited or are involved in.

When you first arrive through the gateway, you're very close to the library, so pop your head in there and see what's waiting. Also nearby is the Metropolitan Museum of Art, where an enemy of the Ghostbusters is still stuck in a painting (Figure 30.1); he's got a quest you might want to try.

Eventually find your way back to Ghostbusters HQ. It needs some repairs, but Janine, the Ghostbusters secretary, also got a call from the mayor, who wants to put you to work.

What else should you be on the lookout for? Two of the largest sites to visit here are Liberty Island and a certain famous ship that arrived here more than 100 years after it struck an iceberg.

If you have a character who can fly, find the tallest building in this world and head up. Gozer is waiting on the roof (Figure 30.2), and you can investigate Dana's apartment while you're up there, too.

Pay a visit to Ray's Bookshop if you can. Also head over to WKRR and see if you can get Dr. Venkman's television show back on the air. Also be on the lookout for two keystone puzzles (Scale and Chroma) hidden around the perimeter of the world.

FIGURE 30.1 Vigo is stuck in a painting and has a quest for you.

FIGURE 30.2 Gozer greets a visitor who reaches the rooftop.

Locations to Repair/Upgrade

Seven repair and upgrade jobs in New York City require your hard-earned studs, so help out NYC and hunt down these areas that need fixing up:

- **Restore Ghostbusters HQ**—It's a bit pricey for a unique fixer-upper, but if you've got 55,000 studs, you can get some repairs done on the place and find a new quest.
- **Unlock the jukebox**—The jukebox is in Dana's apartment, and you can pay 25,000 if you'd like to restore the jukebox and change the background music.
- **Restore the TV studio**—Fixing up the TV studio costs 55,000 studs, but there's a puzzle to solve inside for a gold brick. Be sure to look behind the curtain (Figure 30.3).

FIGURE 30.3 There's something spooky going on at the TV studio.

- **Restore the park**—For a mere 45,000 studs, you can repair the park and find some gold statues to destroy for bonus studs.
- **Restore the Institute for Advanced Theoretical Research**—For 50,000 studs, you can fix up the institute. Step inside, pull the two levers, and get a rush of studs sprayed at you.
- **Restore the Statue of Liberty**—Lady Liberty has lost her head (Figure 30.4), and you can help repair her by paying 60,000 studs. If you have a character with the Mini Access ability, you can find a gold stud waiting inside.

FIGURE 30.4 The Statue of Liberty seems to be missing an important body part.

- **Restore Ray's Bookshop**—Ray Stantz could use 50,000 studs to make repairs on his bookshop. If you can afford it, go for it and find a new quest inside.

Available Quests

There are five quests for you to attempt in this world:

- **Assemble Vigo's army**—Vigo, the scourge of Carpathia, needs your help assembling his army because he's currently stuck in a painting. If you care to help him, follow the red dots on the map to locate the five haunted items he needs. You get a gold brick for your trouble.

- **Go bust some ghosts**—Janine is inside Ghostbusters HQ, and she's got a job for you! The mayor needs your help cleaning up the town. Visit the three red dots on the map and use the Proton Pack to catch all three ghost swarms in a Ghost Trap before returning to Janine for payment.

- **Find the missing books**—Janine is helping Ray in his bookstore when some ghosts appear and cause trouble. Some books are missing, and if you can find all 10 of them, using the flashing red dots on the map, Janine rewards you with a gold brick.

- **Bringing guests to Louis's party**—Help Louis Tully round up five friends for his party, celebrating his 26 years as the Ghostbusters accountant (Figure 30.5). He chips in a gold brick if you can convince them to come.

FIGURE 30.5 Louis is hosting a party and needs you to round up some guests.

- **Complete Slimer's quest**—Slimer wants to prove he can be a valuable member of the Ghostbusters team, so join him and capture four swarms of ghosts for a gold brick reward.

Don't Miss

The Ghostbusters encounter a lot of mysteries and secrets as they seek to protect New York City from the bad guys, but they're always busy so it's possible you might encounter some of these next surprises before the Ghostbusters get around to them:

- **Dana's apartment**—Be sure to check the fridge (Figure 30.6), and if you've got a character with the Tracking ability (such as Scooby-Doo), you can find some other interesting things in the apartment that lead to a gold brick.

FIGURE 30.6   There are strange noises coming from the fridge in Dana's apartment.

- ***The Titanic***—*The Titanic* has finally arrived in New York City, but it's got a nasty swarm of ghosts inside. Clean it up for a gold brick. When you're done, head up and explore its three decks.
- **A full-torso vaporous apparition**—Visit the library and see where it all started for the Ghostbusters. There's a puzzle to solve inside, too, and you can do it if you have a character with Mind Control ability (Figure 30.7). While you're there, destroy all the tables and shelves of books (the Proton Pack does massive damage) to find a fortune in studs!

FIGURE 30.7   Control the librarian's actions to solve a puzzle for a gold brick.

Up Next...

Between Chapters 1 and 30, you have the instructions to solve all the Story Mode levels and dive deep into the LEGO worlds. But LEGO Dimensions isn't finished with its surprises yet! Up next, you can read about bonus levels that are provided with certain special LEGO Dimensions packs.

31

Bonus Level: Back to the Future™

Story Summary

- Meet Marty McFly and find 1985 Doc Brown
- Rescue Doc and travel back in time in the DeLorean Time Machine
- Find 1955 Doc Brown for help in returning to the future
- Help Doc Brown prepare for the lightning strike

This chapter provides details on solving the Back to the Future bonus level that becomes available with the Back to the Future Level Pack containing Marty McFly, the DeLorean, and the hoverboard.

Gotta Get Back in Time

Marty and the heroes find themselves in Doc Brown's workshop, but there's no sign of Doc. Destroy the table to the right of the large speaker and use the bouncing parts to begin the repairs on the speaker system. When you're finished, start exploring the workshop.

> **TIP**
>
> **It's Okay to Jump On the Bed**
>
> Jump on Doc Brown's red bed three or four times to find some hidden blue studs.

There are some shelves and a jukebox on the left side of the workshop. They all have glass that can be broken by pressing X to play Marty's guitar *really loudly*! Use the LJ to direct the sound waves and use the bouncing blocks from the destroyed shelves to continue repairing the large speaker.

Change to Marty and stand to the left of the workshop (beneath the moose head) and press B to get the instructions to build the hoverboard. The hoverboard follows Marty, so climb to the top-left corner of the workshop and press Y to ride the hoverboard to the far-right corner (Figure 31.1).

FIGURE 31.1 The hoverboard is useful for crossing gaps between platforms.

Push the white box off the edge, and then jump down. Use the bouncing parts from the broken box to build a handle. Press B to pull it, and the robot opens the shades on the window before exploding. Use its parts to finish repairing the speaker.

Move Marty to the front of the speaker and press B to start playing his guitar. After knocking over some stacks, Doc Brown calls Marty and asks Marty to bring his camera and meet him at Twin Pines Mall.

Doc Brown arrives at the mall, and it's time to build Doc's time machine DeLorean! Follow the onscreen instructions to build the vehicle.

Once the time machine is built, the Libyans attack Doc Brown. He gets hit by a baseball, and it's up to Marty to go back in time and rescue Doc. Before heading back in time, use the Game Save tool to the left to save your progress.

Hit the phone booth and the two nearby boxes and other items near Doc's truck with a blast from Marty's guitar (X). Use the bouncing parts to build a handle that you can push to open the back of Doc's truck. Inside find another pane of glass. Hit it with Marty's guitar (X) and use the bouncing parts stored inside to build a boost pad.

TIP

Find the First Secret LEGO Item

There's an orange handle in the bushes that Batman can pull on with his Grapple ability (B) to reveal 1 of 10 secret LEGO parts for this level.

Jump in the DeLorean and drive onto the boost pad (Figure 31.2) to launch the vehicle into Doc Brown's equipment to create some bouncing pieces. You'll also need to destroy the shopping carts for more bouncing pieces; this requires a character who can destroy silver LEGO such as the Wicked Witch. The Libyans' van jumps over the bushes to attack, tossing explosive bananas.

FIGURE 31.2 Drive onto the Boost Pad to destroy some equipment to save Doc.

Change to Gandalf and use his Magic on the bouncing pieces to build an accelerator switch (Figure 31.3). Drive the DeLorean onto the switch, and Marty and the heroes travel back in time.

FIGURE 31.3 This accelerator switch sends you back to the past.

Marty and the heroes are stuck inside a barn and must find a way out. Destroy some crates against the back wall, and use the bouncing parts to build a ladder that allows Marty to climb up to a higher level.

TIP

Two Purple Studs

Look in the hay on the left side of the screen for two purple studs (worth 20,000 points each). Also explore the walkway until you find a Batarang target. Change to Batman and hit the target (B) to reveal another secret LEGO piece.

Have Gandalf jump on the hoverboard and move to the right (LJ), to another walkway. Move behind the brown box and push it on the track until it falls off the walkway to the ground below.

TIP

A Secret in the Barn

Use Gandalf's Magic on the hanging net to release the parts inside. Press B to use Gandalf's Magic to move those parts to repair the scarecrow and discover another secret LEGO piece.

Move Gandalf down to the ground and use his Magic on the bouncing parts to build a boost pad. Get in the DeLorean vehicle and drive onto the pad to burst out of the barn and head to Doc Brown's house.

Doc watches video footage of the events and figures out he needs the power from a lightning bolt to channel power to the DeLorean to send Marty back home...to the future.

On the streets of downtown Hill Valley, three cable plugs must be connected (Figure 31.4) to power the accelerator pad. There's also a Game Save tool here, so use it if you want to save your progress.

Push the first cable on the checkered track until it makes a connection. (This cable is located in front of the LOAN sign on the main street. The other two cables are up high on building roofs.)

Next, have Marty hit the glass behind Doc's red vehicle with a blast from his guitar (X). Use the parts left over to build a handle that must be pushed to open the red-striped awning (Figure 31.5).

FIGURE 31.4   Three cables must be connected to send Marty home.

FIGURE 31.5   This handle helps you get to the rooftops.

Change to any character and jump on top of Doc's red car. Bounce high and jump onto the red-striped awning. Use LJ and A to jump up onto the roof. Hit the ladder to the left, and the other heroes can climb up. Destroy some boxes near the track and use those parts to repair the checkered track, and then push the second power plug into place.

Don't jump down from the roof. Instead, move to the right and look for some blue handles on the wall. Change to Marty and use the hoverboard to cross the space (from right to left) between the two raised platforms, and then jump up to the next level of roof to make the final plug connection.

Destroy the various objects on the roof to reveal more bouncing pieces that can be used to repair (B) the track. Have Marty use his guitar (X) to blast out the glass door on the rear corner of the roof. Use the parts to build the final plug (Figure 31.6) and push it into place.

FIGURE 31.6 You need Marty's guitar for the final cable.

A lightning bolt hits the clock tower, and the electricity finds its way down to the accelerator switch. Jump down to the streets, get in the DeLorean, and hit 88mph on the accelerator switch.

Marty and the heroes return to Hill Valley, but are they too late to save Doc? Apparently Doc Brown got Marty's warning about the future and brought a glove to catch that dangerous baseball!

Up Next...

If you own the Simpsons Level Pack, not only do you get three minifigs (Homer Simpson, Homer's car, and Taunt-O-Vision) but you also get a bonus level (in addition to the level covered in Chapter 4). The next chapter provides the instructions for completing a very strange level that involves Homer and an odd dream he has after eating some bad chili.

32

Bonus Level: The Simpsons™

Story Summary

- Help Homer get to the chili cook-off at Krustyland
- Overcome some obstacles so Homer can reach Krustyland
- Taste three chili dishes and help Homer pick a winner
- Dream a strange little dream with Homer
- Find Homer's true love

This chapter provides details on solving The Simpsons Bonus Level that becomes available with The Simpsons Level Pack, containing Homer Simpson, his car, and the Taunt-O-Vision.

The Mysterious Voyage of Homer

Marge is doing her best to keep some news from Homer; she doesn't want him to know about the annual chili cook-off at Krustyland. But of course he finds out anyway. This level starts off with the heroes joining Homer on his front lawn. Break up the three boxes sitting in front of the garage door, and then change to Homer and use his Sonic Burp (press X) ability to break the glass on the lower two windows. Then use the leftover bouncing parts to build a ladder (Figure 32.1).

FIGURE 32.1 You need a ladder to get to the roof.

Climb up the ladder (as any character) and destroy the mess on top of the garage. When more debris falls to the ground, jump down and use the bouncing parts to build a jack. Then jump up and pull down on the jack three times to open the garage. Move Homer to the flashing spot, and press B to receive directions to build Homer's car.

After Homer's car is built, proceed down the road to the green toxic waste spill and drive the car up onto the boost pad to blast through the spill to the other side of the road.

TIP

Plenty of Hidden Blue Studs to Be Found

Use Gandalf's Magic on the garage door on the right to find some more blue studs. Have Batman use his Batarang on the target hanging on the garage door across the street to get blue studs, too.

At the end of the road, turn right and hit the phone booth with a blast of Homer's Sonic Burp (X) ability to destroy it. Use the bouncing parts to place three blue handles on the large truck that blocks the road. Hop in Homer's vehicle and drive to the truck. Press B when you're near it to use the car's Tow Bar ability to pull the truck. You now see a cracked panel that requires Homer's Rage ability.

Homer has a rage bar: It's the red circle that surrounds his picture in the upper-left corner of the screen. When it's full, press B, and Homer grows to Super Size Homer and can punch (X) the truck and remove it from the road (Figure 32.2).

FIGURE 32.2   Homer can use his rage bar to punch the large truck off the road.

The road is now clear, and Homer can head to Krustyland.

NOTE

The Rage Bar Doesn't Last Forever

Homer's rage bar fills up over time, and when it is full, it flashes. After using it, you see the rage bar start to deplete. When it reaches O, Homer returns to normal size. At any time while Homer is super-sized, you can press and hold B to return to normal size and save any remaining rage energy.

Get in Homer's car and stay on the road. When you reach the boost pad at the end of the road, drive onto it to get over the toxic waste spill.

TIP

A Hidden Arcade Game

Destroy the objects on the playground and use the bouncing parts to build a Midway Arcade stand. If you have the Midway Arcade minifig, you can place it here and play a game.

Near the entrance to Krustyland is a phone booth. Hit it and the two nearby bushes. Use the bouncing parts to add three blue handles to the large doors. Then use Homer's vehicle and Tow Bar ability (B) to pry open the doors (Figure 32.3).

FIGURE 32.3 Pull open the doors to enter Krustyland.

Inside the doors are three parked cars and a Game Save tool. Change to Homer, stand on the small flashing circle, and press B to get the instructions to build the Taunt-O-Vision.

You can destroy the silver car in the middle only by placing the Taunt-O-Vision near it and then removing the Taunt-O-Vision's minifig from the game pad. This causes the Taunt-O-Vision to explode and destroy the silver car. Grab the blue studs and also press B to place the remaining three blue handles on the right wall. Again use Homer's vehicle and its Tow Bar ability to pry open the next set of doors.

Inside is the Springfield chili cook-off. You need to locate three individuals—Ned Flanders, Mr. Burns, and Chief Wiggum—and try out their chili. (You can see their faces in the top middle of the screen.) Find the large tree and destroy the objects near it. Use the bouncing parts to build a firetruck (Figure 32.4) to put out the fire at the booth behind it. Press Y to jump on the truck and use LJ and X to aim a stream of water at the fire.

FIGURE 32.4 Put out the fire to reach Ned Flanders's chili cook-off entry.

When the fire is out, change to Homer and move him to the small flashing circle in front of Firehouse Ned's Five Alarm Chili to taste (B) Ned's contest entry. Homer's not too impressed.

Up next is Mr. Burns's booth, but a bunch of fireworks have accidentally ignited. You need to find a way over the fireworks. Use Homer's Sonic Burp (X) to destroy the water bottle near the fireworks, and then use the bouncing parts to build a boost pad. Get in Homer's car and drive onto the boost pad to jump over the fireworks.

Stand on the flashing circle in front of Mr. Burns's booth to try his chili (B). Homer actually likes it! But he still has one more chili to test. At the end of the event, find Chief Wiggum surrounded by rats. You have to distract the rats, so place the Taunt-O-Vision minifig back on a pad. Then pick up the Taunt-O-Vision and place it far from the rats. In this case, you don't want to remove the minifig to create an explosion. Instead, the rats are attracted to the television show playing and allow Homer to move onto the flashing circle in front of Chief Wiggum. Press B to test the chief's chili.

Homer's not a fan of Chief Wiggums's chili, but then it hits him, and he passes out, eventually waking up in a very strange place.

Move to the left to make the floating fish disappear and the water freeze. Move Homer onto the top of the large rock and use his Sonic Burp to shatter the ice. A large snake appears and runs away. Use the bouncing parts to build a boost pad that can launch Homer's vehicle to the top of the ledge to the right (Figure 32.5).

FIGURE 32.5 Homer's car can reach the high ledge to the right.

On top of the stone ledge, use the bouncing parts to build a ladder for the heroes to climb up. As Homer's strange dream continues, use his car to pull on the three blue handles and reveal a giant butterfly that drops some bouncing parts on the ground. Build a push handle and push on it until the sun falls from the sky. Use the bouncing parts to build a large bridge that falls and allows the heroes to move to the opposite side.

TIP

A Special TARDIS Platform

Before crossing the bridge, if you move to the far left, you find a large red double-decker bus. Destroy it and use the parts to build a very unusual platform. If you have the Doctor Who minifig and his TARDIS, you can place the TARDIS on this stand to visit another secret location.

Cross the bridge and destroy the two large glowing stones. Use the bouncing parts to begin building something (B). Change to Homer and use his rage bar to grow big and destroy the third stone object with the cracked walls (Figure 32.6). Use the parts to finish spelling out HELP on the ground. Then follow the very slow tortoise.

FIGURE 32.6 Homer can use his rage bar to break through this wall.

The heroes (and Homer) discover a very large pyramid. Large objects keep getting tossed over the edges, and you have to avoid them as you climb to keep from losing hearts.

Climb up a few levels and push the large brown block on the right side of the pyramid down the track (Figure 32.7). This reveals an accelerator switch in a hidden area. Drive Homer's car onto this switch to open up a staircase that lets the heroes move higher.

FIGURE 32.7 Push this large block to reveal a hidden accelerator switch.

On the next level up is another brown block on the left that you must push away to reveal a glass wall that Homer can shatter with his Sonic Burp (X). Inside, drive Homer's car onto another accelerator switch to open up another set of stairs.

On the next level up, to the far right are some silver LEGO objects (Figure 32.8) that Homer must break up using the Taunt-O-Vision. Place the Taunt-O-Vision near the silver objects, and then remove its minifig. Use the parts left over to repair the track and push away the final brown box. Use Homer's Sonic Burp (X) to shatter the glass, and then drive his car onto the accelerator pad inside the hidden space to open up the stairs.

FIGURE 32.8 Use the Taunt-O-Vision to destroy these objects and repair the track.

Climb the stairs and go to the right until you find a bundle of vines. Destroy it and use the bouncing parts to build a statue on the upper-right side of the pyramid. Move to the left side and destroy another bundle of vines. Use the bouncing parts to build a second statue on the left side of the pyramid. (The two statues are Itchy and Scratchy, two very popular cartoon characters that Homer and his family enjoy watching.)

When the second statue is completed, the pyramid starts to shake. Move Homer to the top of the pyramid and have a discussion with a very wise coyote (with the voice of Johnny Cash!). In the distance, a flying train approaches and collides with Homer...who wakes up on the docks with a lighthouse in the distance.

Jump in the back of the fishing boat and destroy the two boxes. Use the bouncing parts to repair the controls on the ship and use it (Y and LJ) to move a crate over to the docks with the crane (Figure 32.9). Destroy the two glowing life preserver poles. Use the bouncing parts to build a pole on the side of the roof. Change to Homer and use that pole to jump up to the roof (LJ and A). Up top, use Homer's Sonic Burp (X) to shatter the glass and reveal a way down into the building.

FIGURE 32.9 Use the crane to move this crate out of the water and onto the dock.

Jump down into the room and break open the doors. Destroy the other objects (but avoid the green toxic waste) and use the bouncing parts to build a crank handle. Press B and rotate LJ to turn the handle to have the toxic waste sucked away. Destroy the remaining shining objects and build a boost pad. Drive Homer's car onto the pad to blast over to another stretch of wooden dock.

Follow the dock to its end until you find another boost pad. Jump onto it with Homer's car to jump to the rocky base of the lighthouse. Climb the ladder and find the canisters of toxic waste behind the bars. Use the Taunt-O-Vision to destroy the bars, and then use the bouncing bars to repair the ladder. Climb the ladder and use Homer's rage bar (hold B) to destroy the large cracked wall on the right side of the lighthouse (Figure 32.10). Enter the lighthouse and enjoy the reunion of Homer and Marge!

FIGURE 32.10 Homer's dream is almost over after he breaks this wall.

Up Next...

The Portal 2 universe is all about solving puzzles in a mysterious location called Aperture Science, and the evil computer in control named GLaDOS does her best to ruin your chances at success. In the next Bonus Level, you'll once again find yourself back in the Aperture Science facility with some new challenges for Chell and her Portal Gun to solve.

33

Bonus Level: Portal™ 2

Story Summary

- Arrive at Test Chamber 89 and begin testing
- Solve more puzzles in Test Chamber 90
- Avoid some sentry turrets in Test Chamber 91
- Escape into the maintenance area
- Battle GLaDOS in Test Chamber 93

This chapter provides details on solving the Portal 2 Bonus Level that becomes available with the Portal 2 Pack, containing Chell, a Companion Cube, and a Sentry Turret.

Test Chamber 89

The heroes arrive at Test Chamber 89, and they need to team up with Chell and her Portal Gun if they wish to escape GLaDOS. Chell's Portal Gun can open two portals: an orange portal and a blue portal. Move through one portal, and you exit the other portal. Movement can occur in both directions, so moving in and out of any portal returns you through the opposing portal.

You use Chell's Portal Gun by moving the LJ to aim and pressing and holding X (blue portal) or B (orange portal) to fire. Fire (LJ and B) to open an orange portal on the nearest white pad to the right of Test Chamber 89. Fire again (LJ and X) on a second white pad hanging on the wall higher up on the right to open the blue portal (Figure 33.1).

In various test chambers, Chell sometimes has to place a Companion Cube (CC) on a large pink button. The button's effect remains only if the button is continuously pressed, so you typically need to leave the CC on the button and go perform a task. By placing a Companion Cube onto the button, you can open doors, drop other objects, and get other effects. An elevator door remains open in Test Chamber 89 as long as the Companion Cube is left on the button (Figure 33.2). Enter the elevator to move forward in the Aperture Science Testing Facility.

FIGURE 33.1 Open two portals (orange and blue), one below and one up high.

FIGURE 33.2 Place a Companion Cube on a button to hold it down.

Test Chamber 90

Test Chamber 90 further tests the heroes' problem-solving abilities. (There's a Game Save tool here, so look for it if you want to save your progress.)

Walk up the stairs and move Chell onto the small circle (that shows her image) and build the sentry turret. The sentry turret can fire at a sentry target on the wall (Figure 33.3), lighting up a yellow line that activates one of the flat portal walls where Chell can fire the Portal Gun. Open up a blue portal on the flat portal wall, and then open up an orange portal on the flat portal wall on the opposite side of the room. (You can easily open an orange portal first and a blue portal second; the choice of color doesn't matter.)

FIGURE 33.3   A sentry turret is needed to fire on sentry targets.

Move Chell to the small platform and press the red button using B to open a platform on the rear wall where you can see the exit elevator. You need to open a portal above the door to the elevator; choose the color that's not already open on the far right side (where the button was pressed). Move through the portal until you land on the platform near the exit. Enter the elevator to proceed to Test Chamber 91.

Test Chamber 91

Once you're in Test Chamber 91, move to the right until you see six sentry turrets that you must avoid. There's a Game Save tool to the far left if you wish to save your progress. Open an entry portal on the flat white panel beneath Wheatley, and then open an exit portal on the opposite side of the room. Enter the portal to safely avoid the sentry turrets or they'll reduce your character to zero hearts and you'll have to start over. Press Y and select your sentry turret to make it appear. Press B to hop on and ride it and place it in front of the sentry target.

On the platform above the sentry target is another blank portal wall. Open up a new exit portal on this wall, and then reenter the portal to the left of your sentry target to move to that higher platform.

Press Y and select your Companion Cube. Place the CC on the pink button to activate the excursion funnel (Figure 33.4). Press A to jump into the excursion funnel, and it moves you across the room to the opposite side. Move up the staircase and place a CC on the pink button to open the exit. Enter the elevator.

FIGURE 33.4 Excursion funnels slowly move you from point A to point B.

TIP

Some Hidden Purple Studs

To the far right is a small platform that raises and lowers. Move Gandalf onto that platform, ride it down, and use his Illuminate ability to light up a small dark recess. Inside are two purple studs.

Chell and the heroes find themselves in the maintenance areas of Aperture Science. If you follow the walkway, you come to a leak of blue repulsion gel falling from the ceiling. There's also a Game Save tool here to save your progress. Walk into the drip and press A to jump very high and land on the topmost platform.

Press Y and select your sentry turret. Place it so it fires at the sentry target. This stops the dangerous pounder machine so you can cross to the right and jump down to the lower platform.

Open an entry portal on the flat target platform and an exit portal on the angled target wall hanging up high on the far right (Figure 33.5). Jump through the entry portal and move through the blue energy wall.

Place a CC on the square red button, and a drip of repulsion gel drops from the ceiling. Open an entry portal beneath the drip and an exit portal on the angled wall on the far right. Move down the stairs and jump (A) while standing in the exit portal's drip of repulsion gel. Use this high jump ability to get up to the far right platform. Move through the blue energy wall and into another elevator.

FIGURE 33.5 Use two portals to move to the upper platform and through the blue energy wall.

TIP

Some Hidden Blue Studs

Move to the left and use Wyldstyle's Relic Scanner to locate a ladder. Climb up and grab a bunch of blue studs plus a secret LEGO piece.

In the next area, find the Game Save tool if you want to save your progress. Move the heroes down the staircases until you find a red square trigger. Place a CC on it to activate a drip of repulsion gel that fires against an angled wall to the right. Return to the location of the Game Save tool and press the red button to cause a leak of propulsion gel to cover the floor. You need to time your run to start when the first pounder machine moves up. Run through the propulsion gel, and then jump when you reach the drip of repulsion gel. If you time it right, you can jump up and through the blue energy wall to the far right.

TIP

Sometimes It Helps to Fly

Sometimes it can be quite difficult to get to a platform or higher position in the Portal 2 challenges. If you have a character who can fly, you can always use that character to take the shortcut. It's not cheating—it's using a valuable asset!

On the next platform, move down the stairs and locate (and press) the red button. Some repulsion gel spills out on the floor above. Move back to the previous platform, change to any character other than Chell, and use the gel to jump up to the higher platform to trigger a red square button. A portal wall shifts position.

Change to Chell and go back down one flight of stairs. Open up an exit portal inside the cage on the far right (Figure 33.6). Go through an entry portal and press the red button to spill out some propulsion gel on the floor above. Move Chell through the portal to return her to the platform above.

FIGURE 33.6   There's a red button in that cage that needs to be pushed.

Open an entry portal on the flat wall in front of the orange propulsion gel and open an exit portal on the angled wall connected to the left-side platform. Get a running start as you enter the entry portal and, if you time your jump (A) correctly, you end up on the top of the right-side platform, where you can place your sentry turret (Y) to fire at the sentry target and open a closed area above and behind the two raised platforms.

Open an exit portal on the angled wall inside that new area. Jump down, move through the entry portal, and make your way to a new elevator that returns you to Test Chamber 92.

Test Chamber 92

In Test Chamber 92, find the Game Save tool if you want to save your progress. Wheatley fixed this chamber so that it's very easy to exit. Place a CC on the pink button on the floor and head for the exit. Before you can reach it, however, GLaDOS does some sabotaging to the room so the puzzle is a little more difficult to solve.

Move to the far right and press the red button (B) to release a glowing orange sphere of energy that bounces back and forth across the room. Next, move to the rear of the room and place your sentry turret so it fires at the sentry target and adjusts the angle of a platform to the left.

Now, open an entry portal on the blank wall where the orange sphere will bounce and place an exit portal on the blank wall above the angled section at the rear of the room (Figure 33.7). You'll have to time the placement of the portals with the movement of the orange sphere.

FIGURE 33.7   An energy sphere will move through one portal and out another.

The orange energy sphere enters the portal, exits the other portal, bounces off the angled platform, and enters the odd machine in the far back-right corner of the room, disabling the sentry turrets on the higher platform.

Have Chell pick up the Companion Cube (B), and then move her onto the launch pad to the right of the entry portal you created to launch her up to the higher platform. Have Chell place the CC in the excursion funnel so it floats up and presses on the pink button. Stairs appear, and the door to the exit elevator opens. Enter the elevator.

Test Chamber 93

Test Chamber 93 has a Game Save tool, so look for it if you want to save your progress. Move to the right of the Game Save tool and press the red button to activate an excursion funnel.

Place your sentry turret so it fires on the sentry target (to the left of the test chamber entry door). Fire until you move some sections of the left wall and reveal a launch pad. Change to Chell and step on the launch pad on the floor to launch her to the left. The angled launch pad then shoots her across the room to a higher platform (Figure 33.8).

FIGURE 33.8   Get to the top of the platform and look for the excursion funnel.

Press Y and select the Companion Cube. Have Chell move the CC to the left and drop the CC into the excursion funnel so it floats up and presses the pink button. This activates a glowing orange energy sphere. Move back to the right and get on the moving square platforms to collect some studs. While moving to the right, open an exit portal on the flat wall to the rear of the room. Return to the lower platform and open an entry platform on the flat wall where the energy sphere is bouncing. Allow the energy sphere to move through the exit portal and into the odd machine that activates a flat wall in a new area.

Return to the higher platform and use one of the moving squares to cross the gap and move through the blue energy wall into the new area. Place an entry portal on the first flat wall and an exit portal on the angled flat wall. Move down the blue steps and place a CC on the pink button. The exit portal moves up to an area above the entry portal. Step through the entry portal and move into the elevator.

Now it's time for (another) showdown with GLaDOS. She's released a neurotoxin poison into the air, so you're going to have to work fast.

Place entry and exit portals on the two flat walls behind GLaDOS. Next, place a Companion Cube on the pink button on the floor to the left of GLaDOS and fire an energy sphere through the portals so it hits GLaDOS.

Move to the right and climb up the debris to a small platform. Place your sentry turret so it fires at the sentry target; you might have to experiment with where the sentry turret is placed to get the device to keep firing at the sentry target. Move Chell to the launch pad, and she flies across the gap where an excursion tunnel is visible. Jump down into the excursion tunnel and float up. Jump out of the excursion tunnel and press the red button to open another flat wall behind GLaDOS.

Jump down, open entry and exit portals behind GLaDOS, and place the CC on the pink button again to hit GLaDOS with a second energy sphere. The room takes more damage.

Move to the left and use the repulsion gel on the floor to jump up to a higher platform. Move forward on the platform and press the red button to place another flat wall behind GLaDOS. Move back to the center of the room, place two portals on the flat walls behind GLaDOS, and use the CC on the pink button (Figure 33.9) to launch a third energy sphere at GLaDOS.

FIGURE 33.9 Place the Companion Cube on the button to fire one final energy sphere.

GLaDOS is defeated, and Wheatley leads Chell through a back room to a gateway. The heroes can return to Vorton!

Up Next...

It's time to help The Doctor defeat one of his most nefarious enemies in the Doctor Who Bonus Level that's covered next. It's probably one of the most complex levels in the Dimensions game, so prepare yourself for a major challenge!

34

Bonus Level: Doctor Who™

Story Summary

- Fight off the Daleks and build the TARDIS
- Travel to London 2015 in the TARDIS
- Visit snowy Victorian London... more than once
- Destroy three Power Sources to reveal The Doctor's true enemy
- Defeat Davros and the Dalek army on Skaro

This chapter provides details on solving the Doctor Who Bonus Level, which becomes available with the Doctor Who Level Pack and contains The Doctor, the TARDIS, and K-9.

The Dalek Extermination of Earth

The heroes arrive with The Doctor in a future London that is under attack by the Daleks. Quickly use The Doctor's Sonic Screwdriver to repair (B) the mechanism on the left (Figure 34.1). The gate unlocks, letting the group move up to the city street. Move to the right until you spot a Dalek Energy Shield. You will need to find and destroy three Power Sources to take it down. Keep moving to the right until you spot the first Power Source; then move The Doctor near it, press B to open it up, and then press X to destroy it.

A group of Daleks attack. Destroy them, move to the left, and look for a larger Dalek near the three flying Daleks. Hit this large Dalek, and then press Y to jump on it and use LJ and X to fire the large Dalek's laser at the flying Daleks. Fight off all remaining Daleks, and then move The Doctor to the circle with The Doctor's image beneath the flying Daleks and use the bouncing parts to build a TARDIS dock station. Follow the onscreen instructions to build the TARDIS.

When the TARDIS is built, you will need to press and hold Y to enter the TARDIS. Inside, The Doctor and the heroes are safe...for now. Move The Doctor to the circle on the floor with his image on it (Figure 34.2) to build K-9. Use K-9's ability to destroy silver LEGO objects to clear away the boxes in front of the TARDIS control console. Press B while standing on the circle with the TARDIS image on it to use the TARDIS to travel through time.

FIGURE 34.1 The Doctor's Sonic Screwdriver comes in handy on this level.

FIGURE 34.2 The TARDIS provides a safe haven and is where you find K-9.

Travel Back to London 2015

Of the 14 different locations possible with the TARDIS, only central London 2015 is currently unlocked. Use the LJ to move and select that location, and press A to accept. The TARDIS leaves future London and travels back to 2015. You are on the hunt for the second Dalek Power Source to destroy, and now you need to move to the right. Be aware that if you get too close to the store windows, you'll be attacked by Autons, mannequins who are being controlled by an alien intelligence (called the Nestene Consciousness).

In the center of the road are a number of glowing objects. Destroy them and use the bouncing parts to repair the techno panels on the side of the truck. Have The Doctor activate one of these panels (press B), and then repeatedly press B to control the crane and plant a tree. After the tree is planted, Daleks appear and attack, along with three more Autons. Fight them off, and then enter the TARDIS and fly it back to the TARDIS dock station and press B to leave London 2015.

Exit the TARDIS and move to the right. The tree you planted back in 2015 has now grown. Change to Wyldstyle and move to the tree. Use her Acrobat ability to climb the tree (by pressing A twice), and then jump onto the top of the double-decker bus to cross the large gap in the road. Then use K-9 to destroy the silver cars in front of the building.

TIP

Remember: The TARDIS Can Fly

You can also enter the TARDIS and fly it over the gap and to the right of the bus.

Use the bouncing parts to build a special platform. Change to The Doctor, climb onto the platform, and stand on the button to raise the platform to the second floor. Jump off the button and enter the small balcony on the left side of the building. Go inside and press X to have The Doctor use his Sonic Screwdriver on the machine inside. When the Daleks attack again, enter the TARDIS (Y) and fly it to the dock at the far-right end of the road. Press B to leave future London.

Welcome to Victorian London

The heroes arrive in a snowy Victorian London. Move to the left after exiting the TARDIS and destroy the wagon beneath the frozen scaffolding. Use the bouncing parts to build an oven. Jump on the end of the oven a few times (Figure 34.3) to get the fire going and melt the ice.

Climb up and turn the dial at the top of the scaffolding to move the balcony to the outlined area (press B and then rotate LJ clockwise; do this twice). Up in the top-left corner of the building is a purple stud. Grab it, return to the TARDIS (Y), fly back to the docking pad, and press B.

Back in future London, you find that moving the balcony to the upper-right corner has now given The Doctor a way to enter the building. Climb onto the platform, step on the button to raise it, and then have The Doctor jump and grab the blue bars just beneath the open balcony. Climb up into the room and repeatedly press X to use The Doctor's Sonic Screwdriver on the machine inside. When you do this, you disable the shield over the Power Supply. Enter the TARDIS (Y), fly it back to the dock, and press B.

FIGURE 34.3   Jump up and down to get the fire started to melt the ice.

When you return to Victorian London, climb up the scaffolding again and press B and rotate LJ clockwise to move the balcony back to the upper-left corner (Figure 34.4). (Do this three times.) Reenter the TARDIS (Y), fly back to the dock, and press B.

FIGURE 34.4   Move the balcony to the upper-left corner.

Back in future London, notice that there are blue bars on the upper-left balcony of the building. Move The Doctor onto the platform and step on the button to raise it. Jump onto the balcony, enter the room, and then move left and out of the room (there's a hole in the left wall), toward the Power Supply. Press X to destroy the second Power Supply. One more Power Supply to go!

Destroy any attacking Daleks. One group of Daleks that bursts through a wall to the right of the building can only be destroyed by K-9's missiles. Change to Batman and use his Stealth ability (B) to go through the destroyed wall and into the alley and approach the handle. Press B to pull the handle and lower the energy shield.

Avoid the Daleks by jumping and running. Move down the alley and destroy the shiny objects. Use the parts to build a round device that must be pushed onto the checkered track. Note that the track isn't completed; two sections are missing. Enter the TARDIS and fly it to the dock (which is outlined in white) and press B to leave future London.

TIP

Remember: The TARDIS Can Also Turn Invisible

While flying around in the TARDIS, you can tap B to make the TARDIS invisible.

When you arrive in London 2015, use K-9 to destroy the silver box to the left of the locked gate. Use the bouncing parts to build a push handle. Push it until the chain breaks and the gate opens. Enter the new area and destroy the object in the rear-left corner; use its parts to repair one of the checkered track sections. Change to The Doctor and move to the machine on the right. Press B to repair the machine; it dumps out the remaining parts needed to repair (B) the missing track section. Get back in the TARDIS, dock, and press B to return to future London.

Reenter the alley and push the round device along the track (Figure 34.5) until it is next to the odd machine. Change to The Doctor and repeatedly press X while standing in front of the machine. The round device moves up and down. Have The Doctor jump on top of this device and then over the rear wall. Approach the window and press X to use The Doctor's Sonic Screwdriver to shatter it and reveal the final Power Supply.

FIGURE 34.5 Push the round object on the track toward the terminal.

Use K-9 to destroy the shiny silver machine and reveal a terminal inside. Move The Doctor to the terminal and press B to use his Hacking ability. A game opens up, and you must solve it (Figure 34.6).

TIP

Playing the Game

Move The Doctor around on the square steps by using LJ. You can move The Doctor to a colored pad (on the Toy Pad) that matches a missing section of the game to restore that section so you can move on to it. You need to collect four red tokens that are surrounded by moving enemies. When you step on a red token, repeatedly press X to capture it. When all four tokens are captured, you've successfully hacked the terminal. If an enemy approaches you, Press A to jump, and the enemy changes direction.

FIGURE 34.6 The Doctor must retrieve tokens on this bouncing game board.

Move The Doctor to the left and press X to use the Sonic Screwdriver to destroy the final Power Supply.

The energy shield collapses, allowing the heroes to move down the road. The Doctor teleports himself to the Dalek ship and sabotages its controls. Davros reveals himself to The Doctor, and The Doctor now knows when and where to travel in the TARDIS.

Dark and Dangerous Trenzalore

When you arrive at Trenzalore, destroy the three silver objects surrounding the large metal machine. There's a Game Save tool here that you should use to save your progress before continuing. Use the bouncing parts to build a control panel on the side of the machine. Press B, and then repeatedly press X to fire a blast from the machine. Use the parts to build bars that allow you to jump up to the surface.

Move up the hill and destroy the shiny objects behind the checkered track. Use the parts to build a control panel at the end of the track, and then push the statue on the track until it is in front of the control panel.

Turn the crank near the statue until a flaming sword appears on the statue. Push the statue back toward the gate covered in spiders. The spider web catches fire, and the spiders flee. The gate opens. Continue up the stairs. Move to the right until you spot a large vine and spider web blocking the way. Move back to the graveyard to the left, and you are attacked by 10 Silents. Defeat them, and the vine and spider web disappears, allowing you to move all the way to the top of the stairs. Jump onto K-9 (Y) and fire at the large obstruction to destroy it.

Use Gandalf's Magic to move the bouncing parts to make a rail that runs along the giant TARDIS (Figure 34.7). Jump on the rail and then move into the giant TARDIS.

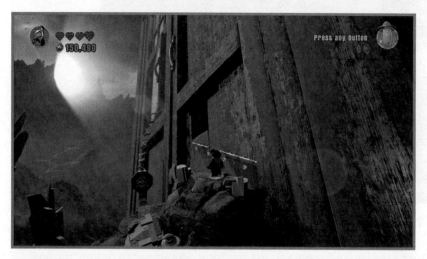

FIGURE 34.7 You need to build a rail to get inside the giant TARDIS.

Use the bouncing parts to start building a TARDIS dock. Change to Gandalf and continue to move around the platform, using the various bouncing parts to continue to repair the TARDIS dock. Once the dock is complete, a white outline of the TARDIS appears (Figure 34.8). Enter the TARDIS (Y), fly it onto the dock, and press B.

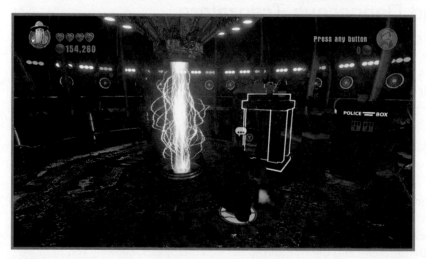

FIGURE 34.8 Use the TARDIS to travel to Skaro and confront the Daleks.

The Final Battle at Skaro

You find yourself at Skaro, the home of the Daleks. Inside the glowing room, change to The Doctor, move to the machine next to the TARDIS, and press B to repair it. (There's another Game Save tool at the back of the room if you wish to save your progress.) Next, move to the far left and press and hold X on the glowing machine there. Destroy it and the nearby objects and use the parts to repair the machine on the left side of the room. Enter the elevator (between the two arms). When you exit the elevator, you're attacked by some Daleks, so fight them off. Carefully jump onto the platforms and don't fall into the green toxic waste. Move to the right and again fight off any Daleks that appear.

After crossing the toxic waste, you need two characters to jump on the small steps to close two lids and stop the toxic waste that is spraying up. Have one character jump on a step, and then press Y to change to the other character and jump that hero up on a step. Once both sprays are stopped, a large barrel explodes. Use the bouncing parts to create a terminal for The Doctor to hack.

A puzzle appears above The Doctor's head (Figure 34.9). Use LJ to select one of the shapes and press A to rotate it. You need to create a path from the left green icon to the right-side green icon. The path turns green as it is completed. When the path is finished, the green slime stops flowing.

FIGURE 34.9 Rotate the shapes on the screen to create a green path.

Change to Batman and press B to use his Stealth ability. Jump over to the right and move through the room. You must jump quickly from room to room when the blue energy shields temporarily disappear—watch the shields and you'll notice a pattern in how they flicker on and off. When you reach the last room, press Y and select The Doctor, who can use the terminal. Play the game that appears and collect eight tokens.

When you have the eight tokens, the shield drops around the elevator. Fight off any Daleks that appear and enter the elevator, which takes you to Davros (Figure 34.10). When waves of Daleks attack, use K-9 to destroy the silver ones. After each attack, one of three mini power stations becomes unshielded. Destroy each unshielded power station and use the bouncing parts left over after the battle to build a control panel. There are two puzzles you'll now have to solve. Use The Doctor's Sonic Screwdriver on the panel and solve the first puzzle that is presented; pay careful attention to the order in which the various boxes briefly light up. Next, use LJ and A to select the boxes in the same order in which they were highlighted on the previously mentioned panel. The parts flip over, turning a smiling Davros into a frowning Davros.

FIGURE 34.10   The Doctor must confront the Dalek's creator, Davros.

The Doctor is successful in overriding the Dalek controls and has them attack Davros. Davros flies away, angry and plotting his revenge on The Doctor.

Up Next...

"Have you or your family ever seen a spook, spectre or ghost?"

"If the answer is 'yes,' then don't wait another minute. Pick up the phone and call the professionals..." GHOSTBUSTERS! Up next is a very fun Bonus Level that will have you assisting the Ghostbusters in cleaning up New York City and ridding it of the supernatural enemies. Strap on a Proton Pack and get ready to bust some heads...in a spiritual sense, of course.

Bonus Level: Ghostbusters™

Story Summary

- Repair Ghostbusters HQ and get Ecto-1 ready to roll
- Bust some ghosts at the Sedgwick Hotel
- Race through the streets of NY to capture more ghosts
- Face Gozer in a battle royale at the top of a skyscraper

This chapter provides details on the Ghostbusters Bonus Level that comes with the Ghostbusters level pack, with Peter Venkman, the Ecto-1 vehicle, and a Ghost Trap.

Firehouse

This level starts with the heroes tagging along with the Ghostbusters. They need to help with some repairs at Ghostbusters HQ, so jump on top of the cart of supplies with Wyldstyle or use Peter Venkman's Proton Pack and hit the gold object with a Proton Beam (X and LJ) to create a ramp. Move up to the higher platform and find the box of parts that needs to be pushed off the checkered track (Figure 35.1).

FIGURE 35.1 Push this box of parts off the shelf.

When you push the box off the track, a bunch of parts spill out. Use them to repair Dr. Ray Stantz's locker so he can suit up with his Proton Pack.

Next, destroy the blue and white ladder lying in front of some scaffolding. Use the parts to build some blue rails. Change to Peter Venkman and have him jump up to the middle level of the scaffolding. Destroy a glowing box of parts and use the parts to add more blue rails. Finally, climb along the rails to the end of the scaffolding and then up the ladder until you see a gold power box. Press X to fire a stream of energy from the Proton Pack. When a button is revealed (Figure 35.2), press B to push it.

FIGURE 35.2 Hit this power box with a Proton Pack blast.

The power is turned off, and Peter Venkman can jump over and grab the cable that hangs from the ceiling. Hold on to it for a few seconds to pull down a bunch of parts. Use these parts to repair Egon's locker.

After the three Ghostbusters are suited up, the face of Peter Venkman appears on the ground in a circle, and a bunch of parts fall from Stantz's locker. Move Peter Venkman to the circle and press B. When the build instructions for Ecto-1 appear, follow the steps to build the vehicle.

After you build the vehicle, Dr. Stantz's Proton Pack gets a little out of control, and more damage is done to the HQ. Use the bouncing parts to build an accelerator switch and drive Ecto-1 onto the switch to bust open the doors.

Foyer Throw-down

The Ghostbusters next head to the Sedgewick Hotel for some ghost bustin'. Ghosts have blocked the doors with furniture and other debris, and you need to clear it. Look for the Game Save tool here if you need it.

NOTE

Multiple Puzzles in the Sedgewick Hotel Lobby

To the far left of the doors you can use Wyldstyle's Relic Scanner on the wall to reveal a puzzle that requires a character with the Drone Access ability. Check the stairs heading up to the far right of the main doors for a purple stud worth 10,000 points.

To the far right of the doors is a checkered track puzzle. You need to rearrange the three luggage rollers so that each one rests on its respective color—blue on blue, red on red, and yellow on yellow. Solve this puzzle, and 1 of 10 special Proton Pack pieces is revealed. Look for the remaining 9 pieces hidden in this level.

Head back to the main doors and use Peter Venkman's Proton Beam (X) to pull the ghosts together. When the small meter is filled, the ghosts are all captured. Move Venkman onto the circle that contains his face and follow the instructions to build the Ghost Trap.

The Ghost Trap pulls all the wrangled ghosts down inside, rewarding you with some studs and giving you access to the door. You can move the Ghost Trap by pressing B and then walking it near the ghost swarm, or you can try to use LJ to direct the captured ghost swarm to the Ghost Trap. (It's typically easier to pick up the trap and place it near a swarm.) The door has a gold outline, and you can use the Proton Pack to trace a beam around the outline (Figure 35.3) and reveal a doorway. Head through the opening and into the ballroom.

FIGURE 35.3 Use the Proton Pack to cut the outline around the door.

Ballroom Blitz

The ballroom is covered in ectoplasmic slime, but that's not the worst part. Slimer is flying around near the ceiling, and you need to catch him fast before he does more damage. You also need to clear the room of all that slime. (Look for the Game Save tool on the far-right wall.)

NOTE

Secrets Behind the Paintings

In the ballroom you can hit five special paintings to collect five special objects that assemble to make a special Proton Pack piece. Some of the paintings are visible and some are not. Change to Wyldstyle and move to the left wall. Use her Relic Scanner to reveal one of these paintings. Locating the rest is up to you.

Use Peter Venkman's Proton Pack and try to aim for Slimer. The first time you hit him, he seeks shelter in a chandelier. Hit the chandelier with a Proton Beam until it's destroyed, and Slimer runs away.

Hit Slimer again with a Proton Beam, and he heads to another chandelier. Hit the chandelier with the Proton Beam until it's destroyed, and Slimer hides in a third chandelier. Destroy the piano and use the bouncing parts that are left over to build an accelerator switch. Hop in Ecto-1 and drive onto the accelerator switch until the chandelier drops and reveals Slimer. This chandelier is also filled with ghosts (Figure 35.4), so use the Proton Pack to pull them together, and then place a Ghost Trap (B) close to the swarm to capture them.

FIGURE 35.4 Use Ecto-1 to reveal some hidden ghosts.

Destroy the chandelier and use the bouncing parts to build a boost pad. You can destroy the large green obstacle by getting in Ecto-1 and jumping through it. You now see more of the ballroom, as well as that pesky Slimer, who tosses ectoplasm at you. Avoid the ectoplasm!

NOTE

Use a Proton Pack for Lots of Studs

Destroy everything possible in the ballroom. There are lots of studs available as you clear the room of obstacles so the Ghostbusters can do their job. The Proton Pack makes fast work of this. As Dr. Venkman would say, "We can do more damage that way."

Destroy two large tables near Slimer and use the bouncing parts to build a giant cake to distract him. Hit him with a Proton Beam to knock him to the rear of the ballroom. Slimer hides in one of the three cake covers, so pay attention as they shift and try to discover his hiding place. When another swarm of ghosts attack, hit them with the Proton Beam (X) to wrangle them together, and then place the Ghost Trap (X) nearby the captured swarm to pull them into the trap.

After you find Slimer's hiding place, hit the other two cake covers to reveal a purple stud and blue stud. Slimer runs and hides again, this time behind the bar. Hit the gold rectangle on the front of the bar and use the bouncing parts to build a crank. Hit Slimer with a Proton Beam and use the bouncing parts that appear to build a blender on top of the bar. Press B and rotate LJ clockwise to turn on the blender. Slimer gets tired. Hit him with a Proton Beam, and he hides in a large painting on the rear wall. Wrangle the ghosts that appear and use the Ghost Trap to capture them.

While Slimer is hiding in the large painting, trace the outline of the painting with a Proton Beam. The painting falls from the wall, revealing Slimer. Hit him with a Proton Beam, and he flees to a nearby table. Hit the table with a Proton Beam and then move Peter Venkman onto the circle that contains his face. Tap B repeatedly (Figure 36.5), and the entire team targets Slimer with their Proton Packs.

Slimer is tucked away in a Ghost Trap, and the team can leave the hotel.

FIGURE 35.5 The Ghostbusters tackle Slimer together.

Speeding to the Sedgewick

Outside the hotel, the streets are dark and deserted. There is a Game Save tool to the far right, so go ahead and save your progress before moving to the left and encountering the sleeping worker on a bulldozer. Be careful and avoid stepping on the steaming hot grates.

In front of the grates is an unattended bulldozer. Jump up and grab its shovel; the shovel falls, revealing some bouncing parts. Use them to repair part of the checkered track. Push the blue portable toilet off the tracks. When it falls onto the grate, it gives you something to jump on to avoid landing on the hot grates (Figure 35.6).

FIGURE 35.6 Safely jump over the hot grates to the bulldozer.

Jump from the track to the portable toilet and wake up the dozing worker with a Batarang or a blast of the Proton Pack. The worker raises the shovel and reveals some blue bars you can jump over and hold on to. This way, you can safely jump down to the street and continue moving left.

When you reach the end of the street, head south and keep following the street until you reach the scene of a wreck involving two buses. Destroy the nearby yellow canisters and the bus platform and use the bouncing parts to build a boost pad. Hop in Ecto-1 and jump over the buses. (A purple stud sits between the two buses, so head back and grab it.)

Follow the street until you arrive back at Ghostbusters HQ. (Check across the street for a purple stud.) Head into the HQ front door.

Something Big on the Horizon

Back in the basement of Ghostbusters HQ, Egon is doing some research. Steer clear of the purple toxic waste to the far left unless you have a character with the Hazard Cleaner ability. A Game Save tool is near the toxic waste; be careful if you wish to save your progress.

There are a lot of glowing objects in the basement. First destroy the desk on the raised platform (Figure 35.7). Use the bouncing parts to build a large red button.

FIGURE 35.7 Destroy this desk to find the parts to repair the Ghost Storage device.

Next, destroy the work table on the left wall. Use those bouncing parts to build a pressure plate. Have a character push the big red button *first*, and then go stand on the pressure plate *second* to reveal a gold box. Quickly change to Peter Venkman and destroy the gold box with a Proton Beam to reveal a lever. Pull it (B) to power up the Ghost Storage device.

Pick up the Ghost Trap (B) and place it in the Ghost Storage device by standing on the small target that appears on the ground in front of the Ghost Storage device. Don't get comfortable, however, because the Environmental Protection Agency (EPA) shows up and shuts down the storage device, releasing all the ghosts!

Cleanin' Up the Town

Back on the streets of New York, you can find a Game Save tool right outside Ghostbusters HQ. Save your progress and then get moving down the street to the left. When you run into the pesky ghosts who have blocked your way with a large floating sign, hit them with a Proton Beam. Then gather them together and trap them in a Ghost Trap. The sign drops, allowing you to proceed down the street.

Watch out for ghostly arms that pop up from the manhole covers, and capture any ghost swarms you can with Proton Beams and Ghost Traps. You eventually reach a large crack in the road that you can jump over only in a vehicle, so get in Ecto-1 and hit the boost pad.

Continue moving down the streets and clearing the ghost swarms. When you encounter another break in the road, build a boost pad by destroying the bus stop shelter to the right. Keep moving until you come across two large train cars blocking the road (Figure 35.8). Capture the ghosts here and release the train cars. Use the bouncing parts to build a boost pad, and then use it to jump over the trains.

FIGURE 35.8 Clear the trains of ghosts to build a boost pad.

Ahead you can see a crowd of people gathered outside a large tower. Hit the door on the rear of the ambulance with a Proton Beam. Use the bouncing parts to repair the Ghost Storage device near the entrance to the hotel. Insert a Ghost Trap into it (B) and walk through the door when it opens.

Ghost Central

The Ghostbusters are inside the hotel and must make their way to the roof. Capture any ghost swarms along the way and fight off the scary-looking dogs that exit the elevators.

After you move past the elevators, three ghosts appear. Your Proton Beam is useless against their metal shields (trash can lids), so hit the two gold lights and the gold box and use the parts that appear to build a magnet (Figure 35.9). After the magnet pulls away the shields, capture the ghosts and head to the roof.

FIGURE 35.9   Use the magnet to grab the ghosts' shields.

The Traveler

Gozer appears and hits the Ghostbusters and heroes with a powerful red energy beam. Move the minifigs to different pads to break away.

Start by destroying the two gold statues to the left and right of the stairs with a Proton Beam. Use the bouncing parts that are left over to build push handles on the spotlights, and then push against them to rotate the spotlights until they face the staircase. Inside each spotlight is a power coil. Stand behind a coil and draw Gozer's electric beam to power a spotlight (Figure 35.10). While she's blinded, hit her with a Proton Beam. She escapes by destroying the spotlight and sends five dogs after you. Fight them off until Gozer jumps back near the stairs.

FIGURE 35.10 Gozer can power up the spotlights if you hide behind them.

Move to the second spotlight and get Gozer to power it up with her electric beam. While she's blinded, hit her again with a Proton Beam. She'll destroy this second spotlight after you hit her with a Proton Beam.

Now it's time for full stream! Hit Gozer with a Proton Beam, and the other Ghostbusters do the same. She disappears but be careful! Red circles appear on the ground, and you need to avoid them to keep from getting injured by falling debris.

Gozer sends The Traveler, also known as the Stay Puft Marshmallow Man, to climb the tower and attack the Ghostbusters. The larger version sends mini-marshmallow man versions to attack. Fight them off and hit the gold object that appears in The Traveler's hand when you see it. Continue to fight off mini-marshmallow men and destroy any gold objects that appear in The Traveler's hand. When The Traveler is completely on fire, he sucks in the air around the heroes, so repeatedly press B to hold on!

When The Traveler is finally dazed (Figure 35.11), you need to build a boost pad near the edge of the building. Drive Ecto-1 onto it and knock down The Traveler.

FIGURE 35.11 While The Traveler is dazed, hit him with Ecto-1.

Once he's knocked down, move Peter Venkman to the target on the stairs and press B repeatedly to fire a Proton Beam at the large door to Gozer's world. The doorway explodes, destroying The Traveler. The Ghostbusters have saved New York City!

Up Next...

That's all the Bonus Levels! All that's left is to tackle the Mystery Dimension that requires 24 gold bricks. But if you've played through all the levels and the various worlds, you'll have more than enough gold bricks to open the gateway and jump through for one final challenge.

Bonus Level: Mystery Dimension

This chapter provides details on the Mystery Dimension Bonus Level that becomes available on the lower-right level of Vorton after you obtain 24 gold bricks.

Mystery Dimension

When the heroes exit the gateway, they find themselves in a very mysterious world indeed (Figure 36.1)! A flat brown surface has large, odd objects to the left and the right. Before the heroes can explore, however, a series of attacks begin.

FIGURE 36.1 Welcome to the real world.

There are 14 gold bricks to obtain in this world. You get one gold brick as a reward for defeating three waves of enemies in each world. In each case, Wave 1 consists of a small number of attackers but Wave 2 and Wave 3 get progressively more difficult.

In these waves, enemies from the various worlds you have unlocked attack, including the following:

- The Lord of the Rings
- DC Universe

- The LEGO Movie
- The Wizard of Oz
- Ninjago
- Doctor Who
- Scooby-Doo
- Jurassic World
- The Simpsons
- Portal 2
- Chima
- Back to the Future
- Ghostbusters
- Midway Arcade

After you defeat three waves for each of the unlocked worlds, sit back and enjoy a humorous video (Figure 36.2), in which Batman, Wyldstyle, and Gandalf meet a living, breathing human! (That's Joel McHale, who also provides the voice for X-PO.)

FIGURE 36.2 A fun little video is available after you defeat all the waves.

Up Next

Congratulations! If you've read (and played) through all the previous chapters, you've visited all the Dimensions worlds (with the exception of Midway Arcade that wasn't yet released, but should be by the time this book is in your hands), helped defeat Lord Vortech, and discovered many secrets and hidden locales and gold bricks and... well, the list goes on and on.

LEGO Dimensions is one of those games that can be played over and over again. With 44 characters to pick from, there's an amazingly large combination of heroes you can use to play through the levels and visit the various worlds. Trade characters with your friends and try out some new powers. Better yet, combine characters you own and team up to fight off baddies in the Mystery Dimension or just pick a world and go explore. Make sure to hunt down every gold brick (480 of them in all!) and every minikit, and then go play the bonus quests that become available in each world after you've discovered all of a world's minikits.

Of course, there are secrets on top of secrets; your author is still finding them today. And one of the biggest secrets is the fate of Lord Vortech. Is he gone for good? Probably not. Which means there could very well be a LEGO Dimensions 2 in the future, with plenty of new characters and worlds to visit and secrets to uncover.

Have fun with LEGO Dimensions!

James Floyd Kelly

Atlanta, GA

March 2016

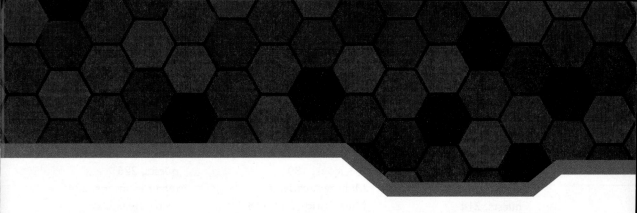

Index

REGISTER THIS PRODUCT
SAVE 35%*
ON YOUR NEXT PURCHASE!

How to Register Your Product

- Go to quepublishing.com/register
- Sign in or create an account
- Enter the 10- or 13-digit ISBN that appears on the back cover of your book or on the copyright page of your eBook

Benefits of Registering

- Ability to download product updates
- Access to bonus chapters and workshop files
- A 35% coupon to be used on your next purchase – valid for 30 days
   To obtain your coupon, click on "Manage Codes" in the right column of your Account page
- Receive special offers on new editions and related Que products

Please note that the benefits for registering may vary by product. Benefits will be listed on your Account page under Registered Products.

We value and respect your privacy. Your email address will not be sold to any third party company.

* 35% discount code presented after product registration is valid on most print books, eBooks, and full-course videos sold on QuePublishing.com. Discount may not be combined with any other offer and is not redeemable for cash. Discount code expires after 30 days from the time of product registration. Offer subject to change.

quepublishing.com